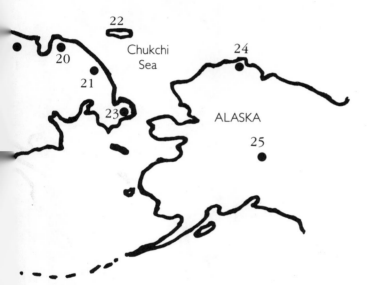

80th Parallel

• 16

22

Chukchi
Sea

24

• 20

21

23 •

ALASKA

25

**Key**

| | | | | | |
|---|---|---|---|---|---|
| 1 | Kunsan | | | | |
| 2 | Shenyang | 10 | Olenek | 18 | Srednekolymsk |
| 3 | Chi'ich'ihaerh | 11 | Kazack'ye | 19 | Nizhniye Kresty |
| 4 | Skovorodino | 12 | Tiksi | 20 | Pevek |
| 5 | Aldan | 13 | Buolkalakh | 21 | My Schmidt |
| 6 | Marka | 14 | Zemlya Bunge | 22 | Wrangle Island |
| 7 | Yakutsk | 15 | New Siberian Islands | 23 | Uelen |
| 8 | Zhigansk | 16 | De Long Island | 24 | Point Barrow |
| 9 | Batagay | 17 | Refueling Point | 25 | Eielson AFB |

# Stealth Strike

**Frank J. O'Brien**

*AERO*
An imprint of TAB BOOKS
Blue Ridge Summit, PA

FIRST EDITION
FIRST PRINTING

© 1990 by **Frank J. O'Brien**
Published by TAB BOOKS
TAB BOOKS is a division of McGraw-Hill, Inc.

**Library of Congress Cataloging-in-Publication Data**

O'Brien, Frank J.
   Stealth strike / by Frank J. O'Brien
     p.   cm.
   ISBN 0-8306-3472-X
   I. Title.
   PS3565.B6687S74  1990
   813'.54—dc20                  90-396
                                 CIP

TAB BOOKS offers software for sale. For information and a catalog, please contact
TAB Software Department, Blue Ridge Summit, PA 17294-0850.

Questions regarding the content of this book should be addressed to:

   **Reader Inquiry Branch**
   **TAB BOOKS**
   **Blue Ridge Summit, PA 17294-0214**

Acquisitions Editor: Jeff Worsinger
Fiction Editor: Gail Greene
Copyeditor: Suzanne L. Cheatle
Production: Katherine Brown
Cover Design: Lori E. Schlosser
Cover Illustration: Larry Selman, Waynesboro, PA

# Acknowledgments

*I* would like to extend my heartfelt thanks to a bunch of old fighter pilots who helped with certain aspects of this book. Their generous response proves once again that they are not cut from common cloth, and the years have failed to diminish the camaraderie cemented by countless hours of flying each other's wing. Helping to burnish the memories of better times, when we "slipped the surly bonds of earth" together, are: John O'Neill, Deputy Director, Mission Operations Directorate, Johnson Space Center, NASA; Jim Egbert, Col. USAF (Ret.); Morgan Sanborn, Col. USAF (Ret.); and Bruce Gordon, Maj. USAF (Ret.).

A tiger of more recent vintage, whose expertise on tactics was greatly appreciated, was Maj. Terry McKenna, Training Officer, 141st Tactical Fighter Squadron, New Jersey Air National Guard.

Many thanks to all.

*To Marge,*
*whose encouragement and understanding*
*lend wings to the mind and the heart.*

# Chapter 1

The midsummer of 1995 was turning out to be a real scorcher. The record-breaking heat had been so persistent that Colonel Jim Crawford was beginning to worry that his engine might suffer from the constant use of maximum air conditioning. Driving toward the Pentagon on a July day at three in the afternoon Crawford was contemplating going through this daily grind for another three years.

Twelve months ago, his assignment to the newly formed Strategic Command had come as a major promotion and was viewed as a stepping stone to bigger and better things. STRATCOM was hailed as "the keen edge of the cutting blade." It had been created specifically to manage the Strategic Defense Initiative, which had become operational only six months earlier, when the last unit had been positioned in orbit and had completed its checkout. However, the glamour and excitement of the new job soon turned into a tedious routine of monitoring, punctuated by occasionally scheduled exercises and simulations.

Star Wars had been designed to be totally automatic. It was even able to correct some of its own malfunctions. Crawford's job as shift supervisor, which had sounded so exciting in the beginning, had boiled down to little more than watching banks of status lights and glancing through reams of computer printouts for any anomalies being reported on any system.

In Crawford's eyes, the only significant function performed by STRATCOM facility was throwing the "cleared to fire" switch, and that would occur only if the balloon went up for real. After that, Star

Wars would be on its own, selecting and destroying Soviet missiles aimed at the United States as they rose from the atmosphere.

The security procedures at checkpoints from the main gate to the control room were painfully meticulous. He realized all too well the need for the repeated verifications of his identity, the close scrutiny by each guard, and the numerous electronic challenges. Still, it was an increasing aggravation to be treated like a total stranger by people he saw at the same time every day.

As he entered the dimly lit control room, however, he had to admit that he never failed to get a slight tingle of awe and excitement upon entering his bailiwick. For the next eight hours, he would be in charge of a system representing one of the greatest technological achievements of the twentieth century—comparable in complexity to the conquest of the moon.

The nerve center of STRATCOM was made up of three main sections: Threat Analysis, Communications, and System Status. The first consisted of large panels of frosted glass, reaching 40 feet from the floor to the acoustic ceiling. To the left of the Threat Board was the Communications section, made up of six large consoles replete with handsets, CRT screens, and illuminated push buttons. The displays for the System Status component occupied less than half of the wall facing the control dais, where Crawford sat. The information on these status boards would occupy most of his attention throughout the evening, since it enabled him to keep his fingers on the pulse of his Star Wars charges orbiting out in space.

Even though there were as many as twenty people at the various workstations on and around the dais, the room was surprisingly quiet. Barely audible conversations through boom mikes and headsets, plus the occasional muffled clatter of a data printer, combined to produce only a low background noise. Crawford was taking over the shift from Joe Shukay, who, because of his impressive credentials in the field of astrophysics, had played a key role in developing the theoretical concepts that made SDI a reality. It was widely recognized that his present assignment was only a short "grooming" period before moving up to flag rank.

"Anything cooking that I should know about?" Crawford asked as he sat down.

"No, Shukay replied." All systems are normal and everything is running smoothly. There are a couple of new items in the Read file that have to be signed off. Nothing earth shattering. My wife and I have a dinner party scheduled for tonight, and I've got to pick up some booze and snacks on the way home. Unless you need some additional briefing, I think I'll take off.''

"No. Everything looks okay. I've got it!''

When Shukay left, Crawford went through the Read file and studied the documents that had been added since his last shift. Even though they didn't seem like the stuff international intrigue was made of, the scope and critical nature of STRATCOM's operations made all these intelligence reports potentially valuable. This had definitely been the case for the past two years, during which the final vestiges of Gorbachev's era of Glasnost had slowly disappeared. The chill in East-West relations deepened steadily as the new regime of hard-liners consolidated their power, which in turn prompted them to take bolder approaches to dealing with those they perceived as enemies. Monitoring the vagaries of Soviet moves and countermoves made every scrap of information important. And, for the last three or four months, political tensions throughout the world had increased significantly.

The Soviets had objected strongly to Star Wars when it had first been deployed and had initiated numerous probings and saber-rattling moves to gain some concessions on the U.S.'s use of the system. They claimed that the balance of power had shifted completely to the American side, and had threatened to do whatever was necessary to rid themselves of this Sword of Damocles.

The balance had indeed shifted because, from all the tests run on Star Wars, it was an amazingly effective system. The Soviets had nothing to match it and justifiably felt like they were under an American nuclear thumb. They steadfastly refused to believe that the U.S. was not preparing for an immediate all-out attack.

Leaders in the Kremlin played adroitly on this "war hysteria," and were soon able to use it as a justification for their increasing aggression around the globe. Terrorism, border incidents, and the threats of direct action were all used to up the ante in this international poker game. This reaction by the Soviets had been anticipated, and the President of the United States, with the full support of congressional leaders, steadfastly refused to compromise the system by agreeing to constraints on its use.

This position however, had not been welcomed with open arms by some of the NATO members and other countries throughout the free world. France, Spain, and the Benelux countries all voiced strong opposition to the President's hard line, fearing that once again they would become the superpowers' battlefield. It had taken quite a bit of diplomacy by the Secretary of State to reassure these allies and to prevent a serious break in the free world's defenses. Fortunately, these efforts were aided considerably by the staunch support of the prime ministers of Britain and Japan.

After switching off the reading light and allowing his eyes to adjust to the half darkness, Crawford glanced at the Threat board to assess any subtle changes. Painted on the front of this wall of glass was a Lambert Conformal map of the world, as seen from the North Pole, with Russia on the top and North America below. Behind the glass was a large bank of multicolored lights and lens systems used to project active launch sites, missile trajectories, and predicted impact points on the map, as well as major target areas in the United States. Also shown was the position of the five Boost Surveillance and Tracking System units of the Star Wars system, which were the most crucial components in the entire project. Their job was initially detecting enemy ICBMs and supplying trajectory data to the designated killer satellites.

The Communications section was no less complex. The technicians working there had a mind-boggling selection of circuits and frequencies at their fingertips, enabling STRATCOM to talk to, or exchange data with, major military units throughout the free world. Satellite communication nets, hard-wired land lines, commercial networks, and microwave arrays were all available, as well as specialized systems peculiar to the various services and government agencies. Should problems develop with any primary means of communication, multiple backups were instantly available for each.

Crawford mechanically noted the ok status of all Star Wars units and checked off the appropriate blocks in his log. Each satellite had its own monitor board, laid out in the form of a generalized schematic, showing major systems and their relation to other components. Red, yellow, and green lights indicated the overall condition of each element, and just below these displays were banks of meters, dials, and gauges that presented more specific information on the various subsystems. Beside each satellite's technician was an interface station connected to the computers used to control and coordinate all the activities of STRATCOM. A permanent record of the data flowing to and from each Star Wars satellite intermittently chugged out of a high-speed printer at the technician's elbow. Should a problem become apparent with any part of the system, the tech could activate backup or alternate components with the push of a few buttons.

However, despite all the dials and readouts at each position that had to be monitored, the tech's job was made easy by the sophisticated level of automation designed into the entire Strategic Defense

Initiative. The computers diagnosed and corrected most problems on their own, leaving only the more complex to be solved by human intervention.

His shift was a little more than half over, and Crawford was drinking a second cup of coffee when suddenly the harsh sound of a warning buzzer brought him bolt upright in his chair with a massive shot of adrenalin. The yellow MALFUNCTION light was blinking on the board for the number three BSTS unit. While the technician worked frantically to bring the backup circuits on the line, the yellow light went out, and the red INOPERATIVE light flashed ominously.

"Kill that buzzer!" he directed a nearby sergeant, and, as the distracting noise was silenced, the gravity of what had happened sunk in. The loss of any BSTS satellite left a hole in the net that adjacent units would not be able to cover adequately in the event of an all-out attack. The technician at the third console sat back in his chair and looked up at the duty officer with a shrug. Crawford got him on the phone immediately, and the man was able to answer all his questions, except what had caused the problem.

"Colonel, it appears that we've had a serious failure in the satellite, and it's affecting all the circuits. I've tried to bring both the backup and the emergency systems on line, but I've gotten no response. Something must have happened inside the main structure, since as far as we can determine, the solar panels are still deployed and are working properly. According to our printouts, current output readings were right on the money up 'til the failure. We're going over the other data now to see if we can find anything out of the ordinary. I'll call you back when we're finished."

Even with so little information to go on, Crawford knew he had to notify the commanding general of STRATCOM, and knowing the Old Man's insistence on details, he expected a rough time.

General Cox didn't disappoint him. He instructed Crawford to gather up all available information and keep everyone involved close by until he could get there for a "complete" briefing. As Crawford hung up, the line from the tech's position started blinking.

"Colonel, we've gone over all the telemetry for the past four hours, and everything was normal right up to the time of the failure, with one exception. The last routine transmission was received almost a minute before the failure, and the internal temperature of the satellite was indicating extremely high at that point. Prior readouts were all normal. Do you think there could have been an explosion?"

"I don't know," Crawford answered, "but I think we'd better check out that possibility before General Cox gets here."

Using a secure phone reserved for priority calls, he directed the operator to connect him to the duty officer at the Space Detection and Tracking System, known as SPADATS, in Colorado Springs. A Major Nelson came on the line almost immediately, apparently surprised at getting a call on the scrambler. Crawford was hesitant to mention the reason for his call, even on a secure line, but still needed to impress Nelson with the urgency of his request.

"Major, we've been getting some oddball readouts on the orientation of one of our satellites. I'm sure it's just a glitch in the computer, but would you check that Star Wars Three is still tracking in its proper orbit?"

"Should be no problem, Colonel," Nelson replied. "Uh, let's see—an update on your bird should be coming in just about now. I'll have to go down to the printer to compare the data. Do you want to hold, or should I call you back?"

"I'll hold," Crawford answered quickly, hoping the eagerness of his reply didn't betray how badly he needed the information. Glancing at the clock, he figured that the general should just be pulling into the parking lot, and would be demanding some hard, detailed facts in approximately five minutes. After what seemed like an hour, Nelson came back on the phone and reported that, as of five minutes ago, the orbit and position of Star Wars Three were exactly as programmed. He added that the tracking data indicated nothing out of the ordinary. As Crawford hung up, a flashing light on the line from the technician's console caught his eye.

"Colonel, we've gone over all the printouts twice more, and still come up with the same answer. The only thing that doesn't make sense is the abnormally high temperature just before the failure. Is there anything else you want us to check?"

"No. Get somebody to keep an eye on your console and join me up here so we can brief General Cox on what little we know."

Although the general entered the control room in a sport shirt and slacks, the expression on his face made it clear that casualness was not the order of the day. General David Cox was a man whose reputation, as well as his force of personality, made respect automatic. A top graduate of the Air Force Academy, his career bordered on the spectacular, with below-the-zone promotions to nearly every rank. Because of a strong background in missile technology, just about all of his assignments had been in the Strategic Missile Wings of SAC. He expected his subordinates to work the same impossible hours he set for himself, which caused occasional grumbling in the ranks. When STRATCOM was formed, his background and performance made him a shoo-in for the command slot.

Crawford and the technician stood up and saluted, but were quickly motioned to their chairs as Cox sat down to look over the status board. The computer printouts were spread on the table so the general could see the normalcy of every reading, except for the mysterious jump in the temperature before the satellite went off the air. He scanned these carefully, as the technician pointed out exactly where the anomaly began. General Cox then sat back with a puzzled look and proceeded to quiz the technician on other possible causes of the failure. The technician's conclusion was that only something from outside the satellite could cause such a complete and sudden failure.

"How does that explanation sound to you, Crawford?" queried the general.

"Sir, until we have some indication to the contrary, it's the only logical scenario to follow. The first thing that comes to mind is a meteor strike, but the usual particles encountered by satellites are normally too small to cause the damage we've apparently had. If the meteor was of any size, it would have destroyed the satellite completely. Although the odds are against it, the meteor could have been just large enough to wreck the interior, without wiping out the entire unit. Let me call the observatory over at the university to see if they can shed any light on the situation."

"Good idea," agreed Cox. "Get right on it while I call the Joint Chiefs to let them know what's happened thus far."

Crawford was thankful that astronomers were night people, and easily got through to a professor working on a project. He asked if there had been any evidence of a meteor shower over the equator during the preceding twenty-four hours, and got the answer he more or less expected. The scientist replied that the Delta Aquarid shower was not due for another three days, but one of his students had been observing the southern sky the past few nights, and he would check with him to see if there had been anything out of the ordinary. A few moments later, he reported that the student had seen nothing unusual—only the normal, random meteor trails for this time of year. Crawford thanked the professor and relayed the information to General Cox. A grim look came over Cox's face, as the evidence almost ruled out a meteor strike, or reduced such an event to very long odds.

The three men looked at each other, silently groping for answers, when Cox dropped the bombshell.

"A couple of minutes ago, when I informed the Chairman of the Joint Chiefs what had happened, his first question was: 'Do we suspect enemy action?' I told him there was no way we could determine that with the facts available, but would certainly investigate the possibility. What do you think, Colonel? Could the Soviets have knocked that satellite down?"

Crawford was stunned at the implications of Cox's question. The idea was so frightening, he had not even allowed himself to think of it.

"I suppose it's a possibility, General, but how could they have done it? We don't have any reports indicating that they've had a breakthrough in their antisatellite missile program. Besides, the short-range scanning system on Star Wars would have picked up such a missile and destroyed it. We know that some of their satellites are equipped with offensive weapons . . . . Could they have maneuvered one into position to get a shot at Star Wars?"

"I don't know," Cox answered, "but maybe you'd better call SPADATS again and see if they've noticed a change in the orbits of any Soviet satellites. Since we know that Number Three is still up there, I think we can rule out an antisatellite missile attack, at least for the time being."

Crawford immediately got on the horn, and after a few minutes of checking the data, Major Nelson assured him that the only variations in the orbits of the opposition's satellites were due to normal decay. The general's expression took on an even darker cast at hearing this bit of news, and he said, "I hate to even think about it, but everything we've learned 'til now points to some type of ground-based weapon—a laser or particle beam of some sort. The fact that the satellite is in one piece pretty well eliminates anything that destroys by blast or destructive impact. I'm going over to see the Chairman of the Joint Chiefs and fill him in on what we know. At this time of night, he's probably at his quarters at Fort Meyer. Colonel, call the National Photographic Interpretation Center and talk to the people who analyze the photographs from our reconnaissance satellites. Tell them I want every picture taken over the Soviet Union for the past three hours, all telemetry printouts for the same period, and a photo analyst standing by. I'm going over there to take a look at what they've got before I brief General Woods. If they give you any static about this, use my name.

"I'm not too sure what we're dealing with, but if Number Three was put out of commission by enemy action, we've got a real touchy situation on our hands. Colonel, brief the entire crew before they go off duty. Everything they've seen or heard during this shift is top secret and must not be discussed with anyone, even those with the proper security clearance. Until further notice, I will personally handle all information releases dealing with this problem. And, most important of all, whatever we discussed concerning the possibility of the Soviets being behind this will remain *strictly* between us. Not even a hint of this option being considered will be given to anyone. When you brief your relief crew, just tell them we've had an equipment failure of unknown origin, and we are working on the problem. Is that understood?"

Both Crawford and the technician answered with a quick "Yes, sir!" as Cox gathered up the printouts and started to leave.

"I don't know what plans either of you have, but depending on who has to be briefed, and in what detail, I want you on call around the clock. Until we get a lot more information, I want to be prepared for anything. Call General Woods and let him know I'm on my way over."

*National Photographic Interpretation Center*

It was almost midnight when Cox arrived at First and M streets in southeast Washington. The nondescript warehouse with bricked-in windows looked abandoned, but it housed the very sensitive operation of analyzing the information and photographs received from the Big Bird and KH-11 spy satellites. Cox had to pass through the careful scrutiny of multiple guard stations before being taken to the photo analysis section. A gaunt man with thinning hair was waiting next to a large table covered with photos. The guide introduced him as Bob Phillips, the photo interpreter who had worked on the pictures Cox had requested. They shook hands, and Phillips explained what they would be looking at.

"These photographs were received from a low-orbit reconnaissance satellite, and represent information gathered from various parts of the Soviet Union over the last four to five hours. I've arranged them to allow a comparison of pictures taken of the same location on previous passes. As you can see, they are fairly detailed, considering the distance from which they were taken, and we normally look for any changes from one picture to another that might indicate something significant. Is there any area you're particularly interested in?"

"We're not sure just yet," Cox answered, "but for openers, let's start with northeast Russia. What I'm looking for is any unusual occurrence that might have taken place around nine o'clock this evening."

A slight smile crossed Phillips's face as he continued. "You'll notice that every item of interest is circled on each picture so that we can detect any movement from one pass to the next. These pictures in the middle of the table show northcentral Siberia before, during, and after the time period you are interested in. Everything on the pictures taken a little before eight is almost the same as those taken at nine and ten, with one exception. Look closely at these shots from the nine o'clock pass. Inside this circle you'll notice that we've picked up something exceedingly bright. It doesn't register on the before and after shots, so it must have been an event of a transient nature. It's marked on this picture only because it's something different, and from the photo, we can't really determine what it is."

"In your experience, Mr. Phillips, what kind of event would register like that on your photographs?"

The analyst gazed thoughtfully at the ceiling before answering. "I really couldn't say, General. Certainly, it would have to be something very bright to produce that much contrast with the surrounding area. Possibly an explosion, or the sun flashing off a large mirror."

"What about the sun reflecting off a lake or a wide river? Would that produce the same effect?"

"I doubt it, General. It's been our experience that such reflections are not that intense, and produce duller images on satellite photos."

"Has anything similar been observed in this area before?"

"No, I'm quite sure it hasn't. Frankly, I've never seen anything that looks like this in the ten years I've been working here."

"Is it possible to enhance this photograph in order to estimate where this bright spot originated, and the exact time that it occurred?"

"Yes, we can do that easily, and it should only take a few moments once I get the data entered into the computer. The time each picture was taken is printed on the lower right margin. The one with the spot was taken at zero three ten Zulu, or ten after nine local time tonight."

Phillips busied himself at the keyboard. A few seconds later, the printer clattered briefly, and Phillips tore off a short printout.

"Here are the coordinates of the center of the bright spot. It will take a couple of minutes to process the enlarged picture, but we can check the wall map to see where this point is located." Half talking to himself, Phillips read the numbers aloud as his finger followed the lines of longitude and latitude until he had the location pinpointed.

"The bright spot came from this area," he commented while holding his forefinger against the map, "close to the Lena River in the vicinity of Uolba, Zhigansk, Kuonara, and Kystatyam. They're the only towns in that locality of any size, but at least it gives you a ballpark estimate to work with."

"Yes, I'm sure that will be close enough. One other question. Do your satellites carry any gear that could tell us about the source of the bright spot, such as the temperature, wavelength, or color? Data like that might give us a better clue as to whether this spot is significant, or just an exploding gas line or a test of some new incendiary material."

"Each satellite does carry a spectrograph that is automatically triggered by any marked change of background contrast. I'm sure it would have recorded something as bright as what's on that picture. The computer should be able to give us the answer in a few minutes."

Once again he queried the data bank while using the light pen to identify the area in question on the screen of his monitor. About thirty seconds later, the printout had the answer. Phillips tore it off the machine and, after glancing at it, whistled softly in surprise.

"Never expected this. The spectrographic analysis of that light says it's monochromatic, with a wavelength of 5,700 angstroms. That puts it near the middle of the visible spectrum, but the single frequency is really odd. Normally, that kind of light is only emitted by lasers. Could be that the Soviets are conducting some kind of astronomy experiment, since laser techniques provide an accurate means of measuring very long distances. Our satellite must have been grazed by the beam during the aiming process."

Cox was pretty sure he had the answer. If not the complete picture, at least it was good enough to report back to Woods.

"Mr. Phillips, you've been a great help. Would it be possible to get copies of the before, during, and after pictures, and the enlargement? I'm sure I'll need them for some briefings I'll have to give in the next twelve hours."

"No problem, General. Take these with you."

As he signed the receipt and put the pictures in a manila envelope, Cox said, "Once my briefing is over, these will be kept at STRATCOM headquarters. Once again, thanks for the information, and I appreciate your cooperation."

*Fort Meyer*

Driving back to Fort Meyer, he hoped the police were busy in other parts of the city, since he wasn't strictly abiding by the local speed laws. After passing the main gate to the post, the road to the senior officers' quarters wound through areas of increasingly larger duplexes, befitting the higher ranks of their occupants. The street where the Joint Chiefs lived was on a hill overlooking Washington. Large, gracious brick homes on ample lots with manicured lawns and shrubbery lined the avenue, but no street names or house numbers were in evidence. This was just one of the post's security precautions surrounding the Joint Chiefs and their families. The dormered houses had been built around the turn of the century, when military budgets were less stringent, and tall trees of nearly the same vintage intertwined their branches over the middle of the street, intensifying the darkness that was only relieved by an occasional streetlight. As he drove along, Cox could now and then spot one of the patrolling armed guards.

When he pulled up in front of Woods's home, the general himself met him at the door. "What did you find out? Have we got anything to go on?"

"I think so, General," Cox replied as he spread the pictures and the computer printouts on the kitchen table while Woods poured them both a cup of coffee. "These are satellite photos taken on three successive passes over northcentral Siberia, at approximately eight, nine, and ten o'clock this evening. Notice that the early and late shots are identical, but the one taken at nine shows a bright spot here that doesn't appear on the others. The time of that picture coincides very closely with the time that Star Wars Three went off the air. I don't know how we deserved so much luck, but I'd be willing to bet that we've got a picture of whatever it was that took the satellite out. The photo analyst didn't know exactly what to make of it, but based on the spectrograph report, he seemed pretty sure that it was a laser.

"However, that's the puzzler," he continued. "There's been no word about the Soviets having a laser weapon this powerful. We know they've been working on it like everyone else, but if they had perfected a system that could reach that far into space, I can't believe we wouldn't have heard about it."

"I agree," Woods said glumly. "Just where in Siberia did this laser flash originate?"

"The analyst says it came from somewhere in the vicinity of these four towns," Cox replied, handing Woods the paper on which he had jotted down the names of the Russian cities. "None of them ring a bell with me."

Woods stared at the paper for a moment and said, "Nor with me, Dave. It's obvious that the Secretary of Defense and the President must be briefed on this whole thing immediately, but I'm a little leery of taking it to that level, with the sketchy information we have available.

"Nevertheless, I'm going to call Walt Martin on the scrambler now and have him meet me at the White House right away. While I'm gone, I want you to notify the Joint Chiefs that we're holding an emergency meeting as soon as I get back. I also want the Director of the CIA and the head of the Scientific Advisory Committee there. Perhaps they can add something to bolster our case, or disprove it. You will conduct the briefing, using the photos and anything else you think we'll need. Before the briefing, check the code name assignment list and see what we'll call this project. After that, everything dealing with this matter will be classified top secret, on an absolute need-to-know basis. Until we can determine what the Soviets are up to, the fewer people who know about it, the better."

Then, glancing at the clock over the stove, he added, "I'd better get rolling. You go down to my office and set things up. I'll be there as soon as I can."

*The White House*

Woods was pacing nervously in the White House anteroom, waiting for Secretary of Defense Walt Martin to arrive. Five more anxious minutes went by before Martin and the President came in at almost the same time. The Secretary of Defense appeared quite alarmed at being summoned at such an unaccustomed hour. He was a tall, slender man in his mid-sixties, with a distracted air that often mislead people into thinking he was mild-mannered and somewhat timid. But Woods knew that during his many years as the senior senator from Virginia, the Secretary of Defense had acquired a reputation for hawkishness and had been a close friend of the man now occupying the Oval Office.

The usual pleasantries were foreshortened by the urgency used to call the meeting. Woods got straight to the point. "Mr. Secretary, this evening at a little after nine, Boost Surveillance and Tracking System Satellite Number Three in Star Wars was knocked out of operation. I say 'knocked out' because, from all the evidence we could gather, I believe it was accomplished by some type of Soviet weapon." Woods paused as the President and Martin sat stunned. He continued, "There is a gap in our defenses, although units two and four should provide some coverage of that area. The bottom line is that Star Wars is now operating at a reduced capability. General Cox, the commander of STRATCOM, has gathered up what we know of this matter, and with your permission, I'll run down the sequence of events from the time we knew of the problem until now."

Martin glanced at the President and then motioned to Woods to continue. The entire scenario was covered in detail, and the photos and printouts passed around.

Then Woods spoke again. "Mr. President, this appears to be a deliberate and blatant act of aggression committed by one nation against another. Unfortunately the information available in situations such as this is never as complete or as conclusive as we'd like. But the risks of not taking immediate action would be disastrous. The security of this country is, in large measure, dependent on Star Wars, and any reduction in its capability places some targeted areas in serious jeopardy. I have already taken the precaution of putting our forces on increased states of alert, and it would be my recommendation to move them up even higher. If the Soviets decide to use this weapon against another of our satellites, the United States would be totally exposed and helpless. Therefore, Mr. President, I suggest we consider the destruction of Star Wars Three as an act of war, and I strongly suggest that appropriate countermeasures be initiated at once."

A flurry of questions followed, but with so little information available, not many answers were forthcoming. After a few thoughtful moments, the President spoke, "I agree that what you've shown us does seem to indicate that the Soviets are responsible for the destruction of the satellite. But there is still an element of doubt. And, I am sure the Soviets are aware of the difficulty we would have in producing conclusive proof.

"Our position is just a little too weak for me to call General Secretary Petrov on the hot line and accuse him outright. I've dealt with Petrov at two summit meetings, and he's a tough person to reason with. I think he'd take a particularly hard line in this matter since he has so much at stake. Based on his past performances, I'd expect him to nail us right to the wall at the outset and then enjoy watching us squirm.

"If it comes to a showdown, I doubt that we can count on too much solid support from Europe, with the exception of the British. Even though Star Wars is almost as much of a shield for them as it is for us, I don't feel comfortable with letting NATO in on this just yet. The situation over there has been tense of late. Perhaps when we have more of a handle on things, we could send a special envoy to Downing Street to brief the Prime Minister. One thing I definitely don't want to do is take this to the U.N., at least not yet. I agree with General Woods that the situation calls for some kind of action, but I think more options would be available to us if we decide what must be done, do it, and then bring it up in the Security Council. I don't want to be hamstrung by a lot of debate if we have to act, and act fast. What we need is something more definitive, regardless of how much posturing Petrov may resort to.

"Is it possible to get a look at that satellite, to see exactly what was damaged, and how? If we had some photos, it would be a lot easier to bargain with the Soviets when the confrontation occurs, assuming they are behind all this. I can almost visualize Petrov sitting by the hot line, waiting for me to call."

Actually taking a look at Star Wars Three to access the damage had not occurred to anyone up to this point. The satellite could not be brought down, since it had neither the proper engines nor a reentry heat shield. And the Space Shuttle was unable to reach the altitude of Star Wars to let astronauts look over the damage.

Finally, Walt Martin posed a question to everyone. "Would it be possible to see the satellite through a large telescope at some observatory, and if so, what details would be visible? How about the Hubble Space Telescope we've got in orbit? When the scientists were pressing us for Shuttle cargo space a few years ago to get that thing up there, they were telling us it could do everything but talk. I think now's the time to prove it."

Woods fielded the Secretary's question, "I don't know much about telescopes, but the one out at Mt. Palomar should certainly be able to see something that close. As far as the Hubble scope is concerned, I'm not sure. When I was briefed on that system before it went up, there was something mentioned about the difficulty of taking pictures of satellites in geosynchronous orbit. It could be tricky, since the Hubble satellite is moving with respect to Star Wars, and is in another orbit. Carmen DiAngelo should be able to give us a reading on this. I'll give him a call."

The President and Martin agreed, and while they brainstormed other options, Woods got on the scrambler. After a prolonged series of rings, the president of the Scientific Advisory Council answered, his sleepy voice not disguising his irritation at being roused at this early hour.

Woods replied, "Carmen, this is Chuck Woods. I'm with the boss and I have a question we need your help on right away. Would the telescope at Palomar or the Hubble telescope be able to see a satellite in geosynchronous orbit in sufficient detail to take a photo? Also, are there any other telescopes that could give us a look at such a satellite?"

"There are some numbers I'll have to look up on Palomar before I can give you a firm answer. I'm quite sure the Hubble won't suit your purposes, but there is one other system I know of that might be just what you're looking for. I'll go down to the office now and dig up the stuff you need."

Woods went back to the others and reported on the conversation with DiAngelo. "He will have all the details for my meeting with the Joint Chiefs as soon as I leave here."

The President settled matters, saying, "I would feel better with something more concrete to go on than what we have now. If you think the idea of using a telescope of some kind will give us the information we need, then work out the details at your meeting. When you have a plan developed, give me a call on the scrambler and we'll get together right away to discuss it."

*The Pentagon*

Cox was starting to feel the effects of his long night as he entered the plush offices of the Chairman of the Joint Chiefs of Staff. He went into the conference room to a bank of red phones and started calling the top military brass. After the word had been passed to all the participants, he leaned back in the chair for a gaping yawn and a prolonged stretch.

He noted casually that Woods's office suite was quite a bit more upscale than his. The conference room, known as the "tank," was fairly standard, with a massive polished table surrounded by large, overstuffed leather swivel chairs. Woods's office, however, was dominated by a large, stand-up desk with an angled top. The oak-paneled walls were nearly covered by plaques and citations from foreign governments, photos of the units and people Woods had served with, and other mementos of his long, illustrious career. Cox also noted that the Chairman's desk was meticulously neat, with none of the ordered confusion that so often typified his own desk.

It wasn't too long before the conferees started arriving, unshaven and a little rumpled as a result of the urgency of the Chairman's call. Cox knew them all, and went through the amenities of greeting General Cunningham of the Air Force, Army Chief of Staff General Fredericks, Chief of Naval Operations Admiral Sullivan, General Morrison of the Marine Corps, and Dr. DiAngelo of the Scientific Advisory Committee. Woods, also looking a little rough around the edges, had just arrived from the White House and motioned Cox to a chair while announcing to the group, "John Egbert of the CIA is on his way down by helicopter and should be here any minute. Help yourselves to the coffee."

Cox was jotting down some other particulars he wanted to cover, when the director of the CIA arrived. As soon as Egbert had poured his coffee and was seated, Woods opened the meeting.

"Gentlemen, I apologize for the urgency in calling this meeting, but an event occurred last evening that demands our immediate attention. I also hope that we can produce some additional inputs to the situation that will enhance the information I have already given the President and the Secretary of Defense. I have to be in the Oval Office at seven o'clock, so we have very little time to consider the matter at hand and come up with a consensus. When I meet with the President, I want to offer him some viable options. At this point, I'll turn the meeting over to Dave Cox, who will brief you on what little information we have, concerning what I perceive as an extremely dangerous situation. The code name assigned to this operation is PROJECT MONGOOSE."

Cox covered in precise detail every event that had taken place since nine o'clock the previous evening. The photos were passed around, along with the computer printouts and the spectrograph analysis. Although the military people scanned these documents with interest, none exhibited any signs of familiarity with the information. However, both Egbert and DiAngelo seemed to spend a significantly longer time perusing each document than any of the others. When Cox mentioned the names of the four towns in the vicinity of the laser flash, he noticed an expression of surprise cross Egbert's face for just a moment.

As Cox finished his talk with a summary of the opinions he and General Woods had formed, the buzz of conversation filled the room. General Woods finally called for order, and asked if anyone had even a scrap of information that would shed some light on the problem at hand. The military brass looked quizzically at each other, but Cox kept his eyes on the two civilians. Both DiAngelo and Egbert seemed deep in thought and were saying nothing to the others. Finally, Egbert spoke up.

"Gentlemen, I believe I do have something to add. For quite some time, the CIA has been getting reports from a usually reliable source that the Soviets have developed a high-energy physics research facility at Zhigansk. This town fits the data we've just looked at almost too well—it's right on the Lena River, and if I remember my reports correctly, those other towns were a source of laborers when the expansion program began a year ago. The construction phase is now over, and the scientific staff arrived a few months ago with trainloads of crated research equipment. We've gotten nothing lately on the type of work being done, but that laser flash is just too coincidental. It's my guess that the Soviets have used the research facility to build some kind of laser weapon, and last night was the opening play in a brand new ball game."

General Woods asked the question for everybody, but was looking straight at DiAngelo as he spoke.

"Dave Cox and I arrived at the same conclusion last night. What bothered us most was that we haven't heard of any weapon, even in the research stage, that had the power to project a laser beam that far. Our trip over to Sary Shagan back in 1989 certainly proved that the Soviets were nowhere near producing a weapon of such capabilities. Does anyone know of such a device, even one that's still on the drawing board?"

Dr. DiAngelo decided it was time to let the others in on a theory that had been forming in his head since Cox's briefing.

"General Woods, I am fairly certain the Soviets are capable of building just the type of weapon you describe. I am also convinced that what our people saw at Sary Shagan six years ago was nothing more than a skillfully contrived red herring, while the real laser research was being conducted at Zhigansk. For years, they have concentrated their research in the area of chemical lasers, which would certainly be able to reach into space if some difficult technical problems were solved. The main thrust of their effort has been lasers using oxygen-iodine or deuterium-fluorine as a lasing substance. The spectrograph data would fit either of these approaches. Based on this morning's briefing, I would conclude that the Soviets found the solutions to these problems and now have a workable laser weapon."

The announcements of the two civilians hit the group like a thunderclap. After a few seconds of silence, General Woods said grimly,

"Gentlemen, before I see the President I need a consensus on the primary question: Was Star Wars Three knocked out by enemy action? I'd like to know what each of you think."

Woods paused, and then looked at each man in turn for his answer. Any question posed to this group always generated considerable discussion and a variety of opinions. However, when the count was in, all had agreed that the Soviets were responsible. Despite the gravity of this decision, Woods was relieved by the absence of controversy. At least he could present their position to the President and the Secretary of Defense on a solid basis.

"I think we should reconvene at nine o'clock to consider whatever comes out of my meeting with the President. In addition, since we're going to be engaged in a serious confrontation with the Soviets, I think we should review our contingency plans, and be ready with a list of appropriate actions when we meet later this morning.

"One last reminder. All of you are aware of the problems that would be generated if what we discussed here this morning leaked out. What I will be telling the President is that we might very well be standing on the brink of another world war; therefore, we will undoubtedly have to brief some people on what's happened. But until things are finalized, I want this matter kept strictly between those of us here. In addition, as a precautionary measure, I have moved all our forces up to DEFCON 4, and put SAC and Space Command one notch higher. Does anyone have any questions?"

No one spoke up, and as they prepared to leave, Woods told Cox to remain for a moment.

"Dave, I want you at this next meeting in case some technical questions arise. Leave your notes so I can prepare a briefing similar to yours. Be at the White House at quarter to seven, and between now and then, swing by your shop and the photo analysis lab to check on any new developments."

\* \* \*

Although the meeting Woods convened at the Pentagon later that morning now had an objective, there were still plenty of questions on how to achieve it. He started by telling them what the President had wanted, and why. Then he outlined the task at hand.

"Gentlemen, our first job is to get pictures of that satellite, and it appears that some sort of large telescope is the answer. Since the mechanics of the problem are in Dr. DiAngelo's bailiwick, I'll ask him to kick things off. As soon as we come up with a plan of action, I'm due back at the White House to brief the President and the Secretary on how we're going to go about it."

DiAngelo began without bothering to stand up, "First of all, taking pictures of something that small so far away, will require a fairly large and sophisticated telescope. And, after looking at some figures, I don't think Palomar will do the job. It's designed for deep, deep space and is just too large for our purposes. If we magnified the image it would produce to the size we need, the resolution would be so poor that the details would be lost and we would learn very little about the condition of the satellite.

"After checking some technical data on the Hubble Space Telescope, I find that this, too, will not solve our problem. Once again we are dealing with a system designed for deep space, and another major problem is that the Hubble is too sensitive to light to record details on an object as bright as Star Wars Three. The satellite itself emits no light, but to provide the sharp detail needed, it must be photographed in direct sunlight. However, this would so overload the Hubble's optical system that the pictures would be worthless. We could compensate for this somewhat by introducing maximum attenuation into the optical scanners, but the results would be 'iffy.'

"The other drawback with the Space Telescope arises because it is in a lower orbit than Star Wars, and thus is moving with respect to anything in geosynchronous orbit. This means we could only get pictures of the satellite when the Hubble was in a position to see it. There is a mechanism on the telescope to keep it looking at an object while its platform moves in space; however, the system is limited to a tracking speed of four degrees per minute. My people say this is not fast enough to keep it locked onto Star Wars as the Hubble passes underneath. Even if we bypass the limiting circuits on the tracking system, I don't think we'd get the kind of pictures we need. Therefore, I'd recommend we consider the Space Telescope only as an emergency alternative.

"There is one telescope system, however, that I believe is exactly suited for our job: the Ground-based Electro-Optical Deep Space Surveillance system currently being operated by the North American Air Defense Command. These telescopes are part of a worldwide network that also includes radar, cameras, and radio receivers that keep tabs on everything in orbit. One of the primary functions of GEODSS is to locate new objects in space and to provide accurate data on their tracks. They also are used to inspect foreign satellites we know are in orbit, but whose purpose is not clear. The system is made up of two forty-inch telescopes fitted with 35mm cameras. Viewing through the combination of the camera and the telescope is equivalent to looking through a telephoto lens one hundred twenty-nine feet long. Connected to these telescopes through a computer are two five-inch spotting scopes that scan large areas of the sky. Once they locate an object, the larger scopes are slaved into position for a close-up look.

"GEODSS was specifically designed to be effective at ranges from three thousand to about twenty-five thousand miles. This latter figure corresponds almost perfectly with the altitude of something in geosynchronous orbit, such as Star Wars. TRW, who built the system, claims that by using charge-coupled device arrays, it can produce real time images of a basketball-sized object in synchronous orbit. Given these factors, I don't think we'll find anything more tailor-made for our purposes.

"Another favorable thing about GEODSS is its accessibility. One of the three sites in the network is located in the United States, at the White Sands Missile Test Range, and has the added convenience of an Air Force base located within the complex.

"We will only need three people to operate the equipment: one at the telescope, one at the computer, and one to run the camera and process the pictures. The people with these skills are already at the GEODSS facility, and it's just a matter of selecting the best one in each area. All their personnel usually work with sensitive information, so security-wise, this should be a plus."

Woods turned to the Air Force Chief of Staff, saying, "George, get in touch with the commander at GEODSS and have him pick three of his sharpest troops for MONGOOSE, and have them standing by when our man gets there later today. Also, notify the Special Operations section at Andrews that we'll need an aircraft ready to leave for Holloman within two hours."

Then to Cox he said, "Dave, pick a senior officer to head this team. To minimize the number of people knowledgeable about MONGOOSE, I'd suggest using the shift chief when Number Three went off the air. Tell him to get over to Andrews just as soon as he can get a bag packed. His flight will be leaving in two hours. Have him use a military police escort so traffic holdups will be minimal."

"Crawford's a good man," Cox replied. "I'm sure he can handle this properly."

"Good! Unless you hear otherwise, plan on being here at noon, to go over what comes out of my meeting with the President."

*The White House*

After adjourning, Woods had his secretary call for an appointment with the chief executive. Word came back quickly that Woods and the Secretary of Defense were to be at the Oval Office at ten. When Walt Martin learned of this, he asked Woods to come over to his office to go over the presentation before boarding the helicopter for the trip across town. The President was waiting when they arrived, and listened intently as Martin went over what had been discussed at the Joint Chiefs meeting concerning PROJECT MONGOOSE. His only question was, "How soon can things get underway?"

The Secretary of Defense answered, "Colonel Crawford will be on his way to Holloman within the hour and should be out there around one o'clock their time."

The President thought for a moment, and then said, "Under the circumstances, it sounds as if you've got all the bases covered. Have you decided who the team will report to, and the security aspects of the project?"

Martin answered quickly, "No one will be given any details about MONGOOSE, unless such information is essential to the mission. Anyone whose services are needed in a support role will be told nothing, or only given the information needed to perform their task. Our team at White Sands will report directly to the Joint Chiefs, as will any other group we may have to form. Colonel Crawford will be issued orders signed by General Woods, giving him broad authority to requisition anything needed to accomplish the job. With your permission, Mr. President, I'd suggest that the three people from GEODSS be briefed in general terms on the project. It's not so much of a 'need-to-know' situation, but being aware of the gravity of what they're working on will convince them of the need for absolute secrecy."

The President nodded his approval, then added: "Give me a report in the morning on how things are progressing. I want everyone to stay on top of this very closely, and if anything else unexpected happens, let me know immediately."

# Chapter 2

## The Pentagon

The MONGOOSE team chief left Holloman at three in the afternoon, and used the first hour of the flight to put together some briefing notes on what had been accomplished at GEODSS. They would be on the ground at Andrews about 8:30 P.M. Eastern Time, and the pilot had notified the Communications Center at the Pentagon of their ETA. As the airplane started its letdown into the Washington area, Crawford realized that it wouldn't be long before he would be facing the Chief of Staff. To ensure against any hitches in the briefing, he again checked that the photos and logs were in chronological order and his notes arranged properly.

At five o'clock, General Cox was trying to finish up some of the more pressing items on his desk so that he could go home with at least a partially clear conscience. A call from the Comm Center notifying him that Crawford was inbound canceled any hopes for dinner with his family. Instead, he went to the Pentagon cafeteria, but found after sitting down with his tray that his appetite was gone. In its place was a gnawing worry about what Crawford would be bringing back from Holloman. If the pictures confirmed that Star Wars Three had indeed been taken out by a laser weapon, the worldwide consequences would be staggering. The entire Star Wars system, along with U.S. communication and navigation satellites, could be reduced to just so much space junk in an instant. U.S. spy satellites, which provided the National Command Authority with critical intelligence, could be picked off one by one as they came over the horizon. Without communications, current intelligence, and a viable defense against incoming missiles, the entire country would be virtually paralyzed and completely vulnerable. With America so neatly checkmated, the Soviets could easily gain control of the West and bring the straying Soviet Bloc members back in line.

Cox had only been picking at his food as these troubling thoughts raced through his mind. Now he gave up entirely and finished his coffee with a gulp. Glancing at the clock, he saw that Crawford should be landing shortly, so he headed up to George Cunningham's office to wait out the last few anxious minutes.

When the airplane stopped in front of Base Operations, a nearby parked helicopter started its engines. Crawford barely had time to thank the crew before he was rushed to the chopper and it lifted off for the Pentagon. General Cunningham's aide was at the helipad and quickly ushered him to the Chief of Staff's office. General Cox was there, and both he and Cunningham were eager for details on the trip to White Sands. Crawford gave a quick summary of some problems they had in locating the satellite, and went on to explain the sequence of the photos as they looked at each set. Both officers were grim after seeing the evidence and photos.

Crawford volunteered the idea about laser beams that had come to mind while photographing the satellite at GEODSS, adding that the multiple hits on the solar panels, and particularly the scorch marks, ruled out a meteor strike. Cox and Cunningham agreed that the laser weapon theory was the best explanation for what they saw in the photographs. But the lack of intelligence information on a weapon of this magnitude kept them from being totally convinced.

Cunningham glanced at his watch, saying, "I think we've done all we can tonight. I'll go over to General Woods's quarters now, since he'll undoubtedly want these for tomorrow morning's meeting." Then, as Cox and Crawford got up to leave, he added, "Colonel Crawford, I'd like to extend my thanks for a job well done at White Sands. All of us appreciate your efforts."

* * *

The Joint Chief's conference room was crowded the next morning. The service commanders were there, along with Dave Cox, John Egbert, Dr. DiAngelo, White House Chief of Staff Tom Whitney, and Walt Martin. Because of the urgency of the situation, General Woods wasted no time in gaveling the meeting to order. He introduced General Cunningham, who gave a quick rundown of what had taken place at White Sands. As he passed out the photos in the sequence in which they had been taken, he mentioned that they should particularly note the pattern of the damage and the burn marks around the edges of the holes. When everyone had seen the photos, he tossed out the laser weapon theory, and added that the computer printouts refining the photographic information were also available. Once the group had reviewed the pictures thoroughly, nearly all were convinced that the satellite had been destroyed by the Soviets, but the Secretary of Defense and the White House Chief of Staff were not completely sold on the idea.

Martin spoke first. "In spite of what I've seen here and the other evidence we went over before the trip to White Sands, I still cannot believe that a weapon this powerful could be developed without the intelligence communities knowing about it. We're also discarding the theory that a meteorite could have caused such damage to the satellite. Could a small cluster of meteorites be the cause? Dr. DiAngelo, I'd like to hear your thoughts, now that you've seen these pictures."

"Walter, as I said previously, the construction of such a weapon is certainly possible if the Russians have found the solutions to some basic problems. Whether they've achieved this or not, I can't say. However, after looking at these latest photographs, I'm positive that we can rule out meteorites. The burn marks around the edges of the holes are characteristic of laser strikes. The heat generated by a meteor impact would be maximized internally. I'd say we've got pretty conclusive evidence of an overt hostile act by the Soviets. The only question that remains is how they did it."

Before Tom Whitney could voice his doubts, the Director of the CIA interjected some startling news. "I'd like to add something to Carmen's remarks. Since MONGOOSE first broke, I've had my people around the world looking for any information about particle-beam weapons, lasers, or any other device that could destroy an object in space. Yesterday we got a report from a fairly reliable agent in the Soviet Union that the main project at a high-energy physics facility is in its final test phases. This agent is located in the general area of Siberia we are interested in, and his messages take a fair amount of time to reach a secure pickup point. The location and the date of his message points the finger right at Zhigansk."

A murmur went around the table at this news, and heads were nodding in agreement. Whatever objection Whitney had, he didn't pursue it. His only comment was that the President must be informed immediately and should see the photos for himself. Also, Woods and Cunningham should go to the White House with Whitney to brief the chief executive.

## The White House

When informed that Whitney had arrived, the President excused himself from a budget meeting, and once back in the Oval Office, buzzed his secretary to send in the group that was waiting.

As they went through the photos, with Cunningham pointing out the significant highlights, the President looked increasingly grim. When the formal briefing was finished, Whitney filled him in on the new information from the CIA and DiAngelo's opinion.

The Chief Executive sat quietly for a few moments, staring at one of the photos, before saying, "This evidence is certainly conclusive, and coupled with what we saw after the satellite went down, I feel we are facing a definite threat to national security. This could have grave implications; however, without ironclad proof of Russia's involvement, we don't have a clear-cut case on which to take overt action. To even consider a nuclear strike, we would have to catch them with a smoking gun in their hand. Another question I have is, why didn't they knock down all five satellites, once they had the capability?"

No one had an immediate answer, so Whitney finally broke the silence. "This is just a guess, but maybe they felt such a move would be too provocative. Possibly, the weapon is not capable of sustained operation at this phase of its development, or perhaps this was just its initial test."

"You're probably right, Tom," the President replied. "Any of those reasons could apply, but in any event, the time has come for some type of diplomatic action." He saw a surprised look come over Martin's face at the mention of diplomacy. "I know what you're thinking, Walt, but I think we ought to avoid military action at this point for the following reasons: First, we should keep things at a talking level until we have concrete proof, and it's entirely possible that such proof may never be found. Second, the Soviets should know that we know what happened, and that they are the prime suspects. Third, they must be advised that we view this action as extremely grave, and a direct threat to our national security. Last, establishing a dialogue will give us a chance to feel them out to a greater extent, while allowing us to formulate a counterplan."

Martin reluctantly agreed. He also suggested that the Secretary of State be notified so that a meeting with the Russian ambassador could be arranged.

"Absolutely!" the President answered. "Tom, give State a call, and ask Ray Butler to come over here right away."

Fifteen minutes later, the Secretary of State arrived, obviously out of breath and quite puzzled over the urgency of Whitney's call. The President gave him a quick rundown on the MONGOOSE situation, and showed him the photographic evidence. After Whitney and Martin filled in some backup information, the President asked for Butler's thoughts.

Butler, clearly shaken by what he had just seen and heard, didn't answer immediately. His mind was racing with the myriad problems he saw ahead, and the potential danger in each. "Our first move, Mr. President, is to have the Soviet ambassador here tomorrow morning and to confront him with the accusation. I suggest we show him none of the evidence, and just play the situation by ear, once he is made aware that we know what happened. We should also ask for an immediate response from Moscow to clarify the situation."

"That sounds good to me," the President replied, "but we've got to handle this very carefully. Dotsenko is cagey, and a real pro at playing these diplomatic games. Let me know as soon as the time is set."

The meeting with Anatoliy Dotsenko at nine the next day shed little light on the situation. Dotsenko emphatically denied any knowledge of the incident. The Kremlin's official response delivered later that afternoon was equally unhelpful.

The President decided his only choice was to contact General Secretary Petrov directly, and the preliminaries for the call were initiated early the next day so that all circuits and players would be ready by the appointed time. The White House Chief of Staff and the Secretary of State were waiting with the President and the interpreter when the call came through.

"General Secretary Petrov, I am certain you know why I am calling, but to ensure that there is no misunderstanding, it concerns the destruction of our Star Wars satellite by the Soviet Union. Such action amounts to an act of war, for which Congress and the people will surely demand retaliation. I also want you to know that we consider the response delivered by Ambassador Dotsenko as totally inadequate. Could you give me a plausible reason for this violation of our agreement so that I can calm the fears of the American people?"

Petrov formally thanked the President for calling in the interests of preventing conflict, and reaffirmed that this too was the aim of the Soviet Union. He then repeated a paraphrase of the ambassador's response, emphasizing that no one had a weapon powerful enough to shoot down satellites from the ground.

"Mr. General Secretary, your country's actions have already stretched our patience to the limit. None of the evidence supports such a conclusion. I ask you again for an explanation of this very serious matter."

"Mr. President, we fully appreciate the gravity of this situation, and after Dotsenko called, I queried each department for information that would clarify the issue. However, none were aware of this incident, and I can only conclude that no such activity emanated from the Soviet Union. I also asked my scientific people for a possible explanation of how the satellite was destroyed, and they believe it was hit by a meteor shower."

"Mr. General Secretary, our scientists too have considered that alternative, but it was ruled out because the evidence did not support such a conclusion."

In reply, Petrov merely restated his position and added that, other than a meteor shower, he was at a loss to explain how the satellite was damaged.

"Mr. Petrov, I was hoping for a more illuminating discussion, but in view of your position, I must inform you of the following:

"The United States is hereby giving the Soviet Union formal notice that it considers the destruction of our satellite an extremely grave provocation. A written notification through diplomatic channels will follow.

"The United States will definitely take measures to counter this turn of events.

"The United States does not want war or an escalation of tensions, but we are fully prepared to take any action necessary to prevent or counter any further eroding of our defenses."

With that, the President indicated to the interpreter that he was terminating the conversation. Turning to the others, he shrugged his shoulders and said, "It looks like we lost round one. They know that we know, but as you heard, they're admitting nothing concrete. Nothing but a lot of rhetoric."

The President leaned back in his chair for a few moments and then continued, "I was afraid this was the way it was going to go; therefore, I made a list of things we should put into motion right away. First, no actions will be taken to alert or alarm the public—it will be business as usual. Second, Tom, I want you to fly to Houston to see the director of NASA, and make arrangements to launch the backup Star Wars III unit as soon as possible. Undoubtedly, he'll mention previously scheduled missions, but I prefer that he not be briefed on MONGOOSE. If he balks, tell him the orders came directly from me. If he needs an explanation to give his people, use the old excuse of a classified Department of Defense mission. Before you go, touch base with General Woods and brief him on the hot line call. Tell him to develop some contingency plans in case the situation deteriorates.

"Ray, I'd like you to do the same on the diplomatic side of the house. Now might be a good time to send someone to London to brief the Prime Minister on events thus far. You also could prepare messages to the other NATO countries that we can use if the need arises. Only include the items you think they will need, not all the details. I suppose you ought to get Al Yeager down here from the U.N. and give him the same briefing that's going to England. Due to the security considerations, the people involved will get limited help from their staffs.

"I'll see Walt Martin later today to talk about increased alert status for our military forces around the world, just in case the Soviets try to exploit the situation. The only problem with this move is developing a plausible cover story.

"Lastly, Tom, when you get back, I want you to keep a close eye on all areas of MONGOOSE, and keep me informed of any changes. I didn't like the tone and evasiveness of Petrov's answers, and I've got a feeling that this matter is far from over."

### The Kremlin

Viktor Petrov, President of the Soviet Union and General Secretary of the Communist Party, was having a troubled evening. Since the hot line call from the American president late that afternoon, he had had a sense of dread about certain plans he knew were pending. Although none of them had been officially approved, he knew the actors behind the scenes who were pushing for their adoption and could foresee a tough power struggle ahead. He didn't relish crossing swords with the Council of Defense, especially since his own position could be jeopardized if things went awry. However, he also knew he had little choice, and told his secretary to notify the special group within the Council of Defense of an important meeting at eight o'clock in the morning.

This "special group" was made up of ten individuals, most of whom had been selected by Petrov himself, primarily on the basis of political reliability. Others were there by virtue of their jobs or some specific expertise. Petrov had used this management technique frequently during his two years as General Secretary. It brought together just those people who could help solve the problem, and eliminated the useless debate and questions of those not concerned with the issue, or who could add nothing to it. Another important advantage was that it kept the number of people knowledgeable of the high-level discussions on any particular subject to a bare minimum.

However, even though most of the special group had been hand-picked, the General Secretary wasn't naive enough to believe that all of them could be trusted implicitly. Petrov was an astute player of the Kremlin game. His springboard into politics had been his highly successful career as a tank commander during World War II. By carefully allying himself with powerful patrons, and by skillfully manipulating friend and enemy alike, he finally achieved his goal of General Secretary in 1993.

Rather than contemplate the unpleasantness he would be facing at the meeting tomorrow, Petrov leaned back in his chair and reflected on the events that had brought him to a position of such power. He had been a well-established conservative in the party when Mikhail Gorbachev became General Secretary, and from the outset, the new leader's liberal policies caused considerable discomfort among Petrov's clique. He smiled to himself remembering all the workings behind the scenes to consolidate his small but influential right-wing faction while ostensibly supporting Gorbachev's various schemes for maintaining a presence in the Warsaw Bloc countries alongside flourishing democracies.

Taking advantage of the General Secretary's loosening hold, volatile movements against Communist rule gained widespread strength along the western frontier. Like falling dominoes, Poland, Czechoslovakia, East Germany, and Rumania ousted the Communist party, and their victories added fuel to similar trends in Bulgaria and Hungary. Foment was everywhere, yet Gorbachev refused to take Petrov's advice and use the Red Army to crush these insurgencies. Even the success of the Chinese in quelling the revolt in Tiananmen Square did not sway him. About the only thing he did that Petrov applauded during these turbulent times was taking the initiative to assume the powers of both the president and the general secretary. Petrov saw many possibilities reminiscent of the Stalin era in having one man hold the iron hand of control over both the government and the party.

Despite its popularity, Petrov was a keen enough student of politics to know that the convulsive lurch toward democracy at the turn of the decade was only a temporary setback. Just another example of Stalin's theory of ebb and flow. The weak regimes that finally emerged from the electoral process in these fledgling democracies had to struggle constantly to stay afloat. Rival factions besieged them from all sides, hamstringing any attempts by those in power to stabilize their fragile economies. Petrov recalled how the warm welcomes given to the early refugees by the NATO countries quickly turned to hostility when the trickle of immigrants became a flood. Shortages of consumer goods, unemployment, and discontent spread as the coalition governments wrestled with the mounting problems. Petrov did all he could to help his cause by making sure that subversive forces in these countries redoubled their efforts to spread discord and prevent the formation of a unified front.

The conversion to consumer production so clamored for by the newly vocal populace never really got on track because of the splintered demands for the available resources. When these liberal movements first started, there was much talk in the Free World about aid programs to underwrite efforts in this direction. However, as he predicted, the Free World's largess was more rhetoric than cash. The confused approach taken by the new democracies toward their problems nearly closed the door on any "Marshal Plan" that might bail them out. Petrov also had a hand in stirring up opposition to such a move by rekindling old fears of a unified Germany. In addition, his well-placed remarks on Russia's renewed interest in their traditional sphere of influence that encompassed Poland and the Balkans made some Western governments quite nervous. He settled deeper in his chair while recalling the comforting thoughts of how his diatribes against these upstart nations kept them from getting one ruble of Soviet assistance. Without foreign aid from either the East or the West, Petrov knew the days of these radical movements were numbered.

The maelstrom of events that swept through Eastern Europe during the first three years of the new decade were tailor-made to Petrov's personal career plans. Gorbachev was stretched to the limit in a never-ending battle to extinguish fires of insurrection springing up throughout the Soviet Republics. These continual brushes with rebellion did not set well with the old timers in the Politburo, and Gorbachev's credibility began to suffer badly. Adding to his woes was a significant lack of success in reestablishing a foothold for Communism in the Eastern Bloc nations. Gorbachev's star was setting, and with some adroit maneuvering behind the scenes, Petrov might hasten its demise. The breakaway nations and republics would continue foundering until a strong central guiding force was reimposed. Petrov was convinced that he was the man destined for this task.

As public and political opposition to the General Secretary grew, Petrov gradually broadened his influence among key groups in the

Kremlin, especially the military and the KGB. The offers by the West to help Eastern Europe were propagandized to the Soviet public as attempts to gain control of former Communist strongholds. Building on this premise, Petrov fanned into life the old Soviet animosity toward the West by veiled inferences to a gradual encirclement by traditional enemies. Once this idea was implanted, the next step was the declaration of the need to establish a buffer zone against imperialist advances. Gorbachev's problems with the Warsaw Bloc continued to grow as their demands far exceeded the Kremlin's willingness to give. In the late spring of 1993, events took an even sharper downward turn for the General Secretary. Petrov, now in a very strong position, sensed that the time to make his move had arrived.

In a midnight coup backed by army units loyal to his cause, Petrov replaced Gorbachev and announced the "resignation" or "retirement" of many top officials in the Central Committee. He immediately filled these key positions with his own supporters, who wasted no time in publishing new policies denouncing the liberalization movement. These words were backed up by artillery, tanks, and infantry, which moved swiftly to take over the Warsaw Bloc countries, meeting only token resistance. Now secure in the seat of unchallenged authority as both President and General Secretary, Petrov reversed all the gains made by Glasnost and created a new ice age in East-West relations.

\* \* \*

Petrov was now 70 years old, and the once military-trim figure had become somewhat fleshy with a heavily jowled face. Beneath a mane of white hair were a pair of dark, deep-set eyes that could still freeze one's blood. He was growing tired after a lifetime of political machinations, and age brought with it a tendency toward caution and avoidance of open confrontations with the Council of Defense. Nonetheless, since he had come up the hard way, he disliked failure on the part of his subordinates, and the penalty for a botched job was usually severe.

Sitting down at the conference table, Petrov acknowledged the greetings of the others with barely perceptible nods, and got right to his briefing. Afterwards, before any discussion got underway, he asked General Pavel Moskalenko a pointed question.

"General Moskalenko, you are in charge of all activity at our high-energy research facility at Zhigansk. Tell us what, if anything, went wrong with the test firing of the new weapon?"

Moskalenko was clearly ill at ease in such high-level company, and his nervousness increased with such a negatively oriented question. "Comrade General Secretary, we had no major problems with the test, and all things considered, we were quite pleased with the entire operation. The laser weapon itself worked perfectly; however, the aiming system needs some adjustments to ensure a kill on the first shot. As expected, the test used up our entire supply of the deuterium-fluorine isotope. Work is underway on the aiming device refinements, and should be completed in a week. The capability for full-scale production of the isotope has been developed concurrently with the building of the weapon. Everything is on schedule, and we should be able to achieve quantity production for sustained operation of the laser in about four weeks."

"That is not what I meant, General!" Petrov boomed. "What I want to know is, how did the Americans discover that it was our laser that destroyed the satellite? Your earlier reports indicated that the flash of light would only be visible for a second or so. How could they have seen something so brief and identified its origin from half a world away? One of the basic premises on which this project was approved was the anonymity of the Soviet Union, and now this has been compromised—apparently with ease! This situation is particularly disturbing after we have gone to all the trouble and expense of setting up that sham of a laser research facility at Sary Shagan a little over six years ago. After the American scientists visited there in 1989, I was assured that we had thrown them completely off the track. Can this problem be corrected?"

Moskalenko was now totally rattled, and looked imploringly at his scientific advisor for assistance. But, the latter was intent on reading his notes. "Comrade General Secretary, I really cannot answer your question as to how the Americans determined that the laser was ours. The very nature of the weapon requires a beam of visible light. Our original calculations took into account the short duration of the flash, the necessity of the observer to be looking at exactly the right spot at the precise instant, the effects of distance, and the possibility of cloud cover. The probability of detection when all these values are factored in is almost negligible. The chance of sighting the flash and determining its source from a military or commercial aircraft is equally remote. All I can say at this point is that the weapon is perfected, and only needs a few subsystem adjustments to become fully operational."

Petrov's next remarks were aimed at the entire assembly.

"Comrades, I have been giving this matter a lot of thought since yesterday, and want you to reassess our original plan for destroying the
Star Wars system. My reasons are as follows:

"We did not anticipate that the Americans would learn that the
satellite was deliberately destroyed. It was supposed to appear that the
satellite had had a complete internal failure.

"The Americans view this incident as an act of war, and our initial
concept did not include triggering a third world war.

"Our original plan was predicated on the Soviet Union's achieving a decisive advantage by the destruction of the Star Wars defense, in
addition to the simultaneous neutralization of the BMEWS stations just
prior to the launching of our missile attack. This concept depended
on the Americans not associating us with the failure of the first satellite. Also, while their reaction was forceful, it was less than it should
have been, if destroying that one satellite had disabled their entire system. Apparently, they have a redundancy built in, and Star Wars is still
mostly operational. All things considered, I do not think we achieved
the conditions originally planned, and this shortfall could cause the
Soviet Union to suffer unacceptable losses on the first missile exchange."

The General Secretary paused to see what reactions would come
from the more hawkish members of his staff.

Mikhail Volzhin, commanding general of all Soviet forces, and the
other military commanders were in a rare frame of mind. All of them
shared the same thought—they were furious with the General Secretary for weakening his resolve in this matter. The recent increase in
international tensions brought the military faction in the Politburo
back into prominence. Those in uniform viewed these events as a
long-overdue chance to regain power that had been lost to the KGB
and industrial cliques during the "Glasnost" period begun by Gorbachev in the previous decade.

Before the meeting, Volzhin had warned them, "Whatever position we take, I want the military to speak with one voice. We have too
much at stake to risk losing it all on a fragmented approach to the
problem. Our presentation must be coordinated, forceful, and emphasize the positive aspects of regaining a military parity with the West, or
perhaps even a superior position." So when Petrov paused, Volzhin
was the first to speak up.

"Comrade General Secretary, it is my considered opinion that we
should proceed with our original plan." Then, extending his fingers
to tick off the points, he went on. "First, if Star Wars is allowed to

remain operational, the Soviet Union would be extremely vulnerable. American missiles, with their superior accuracy, would deal us an unacceptable blow, while they in return would suffer relatively minor damage. And, with Star Wars operational, our major offensive threat is reduced to submarine-launched missiles. However, with their better electronics, the American hunter-killer submarines may negate or considerably reduce the effectiveness of this form of attack. Also, if our long-range bombers get airborne before the first missile exchange, they will be hard-pressed to penetrate the American air defense system.

"Second, we are fairly certain that Star Wars can still function with only a partial reduction in effectiveness, without the key unit we destroyed. Therefore, if we don't proceed, we have gained nothing.

"Third, the Americans will replace this satellite with a backup in the near future. The next launch of their Shuttle is scheduled in four weeks, and they are probably doing everything they can to move this date up. General Tolubko of our mission command expects they will have problems doing this because the mission profile must be reconfigured and the satellite's systems readied for operation.

"Fourth, if we allow the system to become fully operational again, we will once more be at their mercy and must acquiesce to their demands. Naturally, since they lost one satellite, we can expect them to react more quickly to any tampering with the system in the future. Therefore, we must strike decisively to neutralize Star Wars, followed up immediately with an all-out missile attack. Without Star Wars, the United States is helpless against our first strike, and we will crush them with one overwhelming blow."

Volzhin slammed the table with his fist to emphasize his final word, and paused to let these points register. Then, leaning over the table toward Petrov he continued, his voice even more charged with emotion. "There is one other point, Comrade General Secretary, that is of critical importance, and that is time. We must assume that the Americans will replace the satellite within four to six weeks. Once that occurs, they regain the upper hand. This, as we decided previously, is totally unacceptable. The current circumstances present us with an opportunity that is unparalleled in modern times—one that must not slip through our fingers."

He paused to look around the table. "We cannot ignore an opportunity to achieve our ultimate goal in one bold stroke. For this reason, we must carry out our original plan within the next month and a half. As soon as we have a sufficient quantity of the isotope fuel on hand, the other Star Wars satellites must be destroyed. Once this is done, we can expect a violent reaction from the Americans; therefore, we must nullify their entire missile warning system. This will be accomplished when the remaining satellites are destroyed, by specially equipped submarines positioned near the BMEWS antennas. Shortly after the first satellite has been knocked out, these submarines will beam high-energy radio waves directly at the antennas. Equipment on board will shift the frequency to match any countermeasures attempted. With their early warning system jammed, we are free to launch our strategic missiles with impunity.''

Petrov held up his hand to interrupt Volzhin. ''But, Mikhail, if I were in the American's place, the simultaneous destruction of the satellites and the jamming of the BMEWS sites would be sufficient provocation to launch a retaliatory strike. Such evidence would surely indicate that our missiles had been launched, and there would be no time for a hot line call. I don't see where jamming the BMEWS sites would be to our advantage. A nuclear war would be underway, and we have already decided that we cannot accept the damage of a missile exchange on equal terms.''

''Not so, Comrade General Secretary,'' Volzhin replied quickly. ''Since the sixties, the American public has developed an intense aversion to using nuclear weapons. This reluctance to employ these devices has even permeated their strategic doctrine. The President would never order their missiles launched until he was absolutely certain that ours were on the way. And, without the early warning system, he cannot be sure until the first missile strikes, and then it is too late. This policy of 'retaliatory strike only' is their Achilles' heel, and by our proper exploitation of it, they will be brought to their knees.''

Petrov, becoming irritated at what sounded like more polemics for foreign consumption, interrupted again. ''Marshal Volzhin, you have still not given me a good reason why the Americans will not strike back as soon as we attack their BMEWS and satellites. I cannot believe they will behave the way you predict, despite their aversion to nuclear war. How do you propose to exploit this factor?''

''Comrade General Secretary, a few moments ago I mentioned a small time difference between knocking out the satellite and jamming the BMEWS. Undoubtedly, the Americans are on the alert for such actions, and the event will be reported to the White House immediately. We will allow 15 minutes for the President to receive this news. Then you will initiate a hot line call to inform him of the following four points:

" 'We have not launched any missiles against the United States.

" 'We consider the presence of Star Wars an extremely dangerous threat to our national security. Rather than precipitate a mutually destructive nuclear war, our only alternative was to eliminate it. The device used to accomplish this is fully operational.

" 'We have also developed a means of nullifying your BMEWS. To assure you that this is not an idle threat, a demonstration is taking place at this time.

" 'I repeat, there are no missiles launched against your country, nor will there be, unless you choose to act irrationally. But should you launch your ICBMS, be advised that this new weapon can be used against missiles, as well as satellites.' "

"Once you have gone over these four points, you will let him know that with this new realignment in the balance of power, we have certain conditions for the maintenance of the peaceful status quo. This will require the withdrawal of American forces from Europe and the Far East, and the cessation of logistical and financial support of NATO."

Volzhin finished by saying, "Naturally, if the Americans acquiesce to these demands, the opportunities for additional conditions are almost limitless."

As Petrov and the others nodded in reluctant agreement, an aide to General Ivanovskiy, Chief of the KGB, came into the room with a memo. After reading it, Ivanovskiy addressed the General Secretary. "Apparently the Americans are not reacting according to Marshal Volzhin's plan, and our task might not be as easy as he describes. This report states that all American forces have been moved up to Defense Condition Four. The cover story for the public is a preplanned exercise of some sort. Their Strategic Air Command is probably on a higher status since more aircraft are on alert and training sorties are not being flown. In addition, their ballistic missile submarines have stopped their normal patrol routines, and are orbiting positions we have always regarded as probable launch points."

Volzhin glared at General Gorshkov and Admiral Batov, commanders of all air and naval forces. "Why didn't you two know of these events? We have been made to look like fools!"

The news also worried the General Secretary. "How does this turn of events affect your plan, Mikhail?"

"Until General Ivanovskiy shares his report with the military and we have analyzed it, I cannot give you a definitive answer," he replied irritably. He paused before continuing more calmly, "However, I do not think these actions by the Americans will have an adverse impact on our overall plan. We naturally expected some sort of reaction, but not to the degree that has occurred. Keep in mind, Comrade General Secretary, that such moves are resorted to as a matter of course in times of increased tensions, primarily to indicate a nation's resolve. Since we have had no reports of any NATO countries following suit, I am certain these actions are merely for show.

"Actually, comrades, their increase of readiness status makes some phases of our plan more easy to accomplish. Faced with the reality of no warning or no defense against our missile attack, they will no doubt abandon their allies and agree to our demands. Withdrawal of American forces will cause panic and paralysis in NATO, affording us a perfect opportunity to sweep across Western Europe with minimal resistance. We will inform them through discreet sources that their increased readiness status only compels us to do likewise. Under this guise, we can concentrate our forces for a quick thrust to the coastline. Having their missile submarines loiter around possible prelaunch positions only simplifies our problem. We can now group our hunter-killer submarines around these locations, and if they attempt to launch missiles, we neutralize them."

He looked around the group before summarizing, "As you can see, comrades, I don't think our plans should change simply because of some posturing by the Americans. We hold the upper hand, and their response only necessitates some allowable variances in our basically sound strategy. Comrades, time is of the essence, and we can't let minor problems interfere with something we have been waiting fifty years to achieve."

Petrov rose to indicate that the meeting was over, "Comrade Volzhin, your arguments are most persuasive, but such a bold move demands consideration. Let us see what develops in the next week, before deciding what to do about the other Star Wars satellites."

*CIA Headquarters*

Activity at the Central Intelligence Agency increased markedly after the satellite was destroyed. John Egbert sent his key agents a top-secret directive to query their most trusted contacts for information on a new antisatellite weapon. Researchers combed recent scientific literature for articles offering a clue to Soviet developments in long-range laser technology. Surveillance of the northcentral U.S.S.R. was stepped up.

These efforts generated reams of reports, but not much illuminating information. Based on what they knew thus far, Egbert was convinced that they should concentrate on the high-energy research facility at Zhigansk.

When the name *Zhigansk* was first run through the computer, the printout indicated they had an agent, codenamed SANDPIPER, working at the lab. Since their efforts to date yielded so little, he sent for SANDPIPER's dossier.

Egbert's "man in Zhigansk" had been recruited ten years earlier, and was employed at the middle echelon level in the research lab. His reports were considered reliable, and were sent as coded letters to a relative in Moscow. The relative was another agent with the code name BLUE JAY, who worked as a clerk in the Kremlin. After receiving a letter from SANDPIPER, BLUE JAY would make a drop for a CIA man from the American embassy. The information was decoded and sent by diplomatic pouch to Washington.

This roundabout method of communicating was probably the reason for a relatively thin report section in the file. But there had been no need for haste previously, since there had been little interest in the Zhigansk area. The infrequent letters to BLUE JAY also kept the KGB from getting too suspicious about information coming from a sensitive area.

One of the last entries showed that SANDPIPER had been sent an Emergency Flash Transmitter, a device used to send extremely critical information on an emergency basis. "He might be needing that gadget pretty soon," Egbert thought as he turned to SANDPIPER's reports.

The data from Zhigansk was sparse and lacking in details, probably because of the reporting method. The entries dealt with routine operations pertinent to research on using lasers and particle beams as weapons. There was no mention of any impending breakthroughs in either field. As far as equipment went, SANDPIPER's reports showed a large amount of electronic items that seemed normal for the work being done at Zhigansk.

One entry did look a little out of the ordinary. Regular shipments of steel liquid containers had been arriving at the facility for some time. The amounts were small at first, and then suddenly increased to carload-sized lots. But there was no mention of what kind of liquid was in the containers.

Egbert marked this item for reference later, since it seemed the most significant of all the entries. He also noted that the date of this last report was three months before the satellite incident. "This might tie in with DiAngelo's hunch about a deuterium-fluorine laser," he said half aloud, while scribbling a reminder to discuss these containers with DiAngelo at the next meeting.

The intercom buzzed and his secretary said the chief of the photo analysis section wanted to see him. "Good! Send him in," he replied, hoping that the satellite pictures of Zhigansk taken over the past two years would prove more informative than SANDPIPER's file.

The analyst lined up the pictures on the conference table and indicated that no significant additions had been made to the facility over the entire time period. He pointed to what he thought might be a new power generating station, adding that it might be nothing more than a backup for the existing one. Another new area consisted of a wide flat building in an X shape, separated somewhat from the main complex. This could be anything, he surmised: labs, storage, living quarters, or an administrative area.

Along with the photographs, he brought a set of overlays depicting infrared scans of the Zhigansk facility. Those taken recently showed a continuous hot spot in what had been a previously "cold" section of the main research building. The analyst implied that the emissions were too steady to be accounted for by the usual experiments in this type of installation, and showed Egbert comparison shots of American high-energy physics labs. The IR signatures coming from Zhigansk were steady and intense, looking very much like those associated with manufacturing or processing plants. The director wasn't sure if this information was pertinent, but made a note of it anyway.

As Egbert finished his review of the satellite photos, his secretary buzzed again to tell him that a representative from Dr. DiAngelo's office was waiting. He signed for the report on laser and particle-beam weapons that Carmen had promised to send over and told the messenger that there would be no reply.

The thick package contained quite a bit of scientific information, but the cover sheet had a synopsis in laymen's terms that had all the information he needed. DiAngelo reported that current technology limits laser and particle-beam weapons to short ranges—nowhere near the twenty-five thousand miles involved in the satellite kill. Both systems require large amounts of electrical power, and each is considerably more effective when operated in space, as opposed to on the ground, because of atmospheric attenuation. Theoretically, longer-range weapons require a quantum boost in electrical input; however, he doubted that this alone would achieve the twenty-five thousand-mile range.

The report also mentioned that some research had been done on using other than normal materials as base substances for lasers, but he had no evidence that these studies had reached the development stage. The most promising work had been with isotopes. The summary ended with a statement that such an advanced weapon would require no special facilities, but a larger size because of the need for extra power generation.

The CIA director reviewed all the evidence, but still could not put his finger on anything conclusive. His gut reaction was that the Zhigansk laboratory must be the key, but there was no hard data to support it.

"If only there was a more recent report from SANDPIPER," he thought. "But, if Zhigansk is the answer, the increased security usually associated with the development of a new weapon might be why we haven't heard from him."

This line of reasoning was reinforced by negative reports from all other agents, indicating that whatever the project, it was a closely guarded secret. Running over the flimsy evidence once more, he was still convinced that everything pointed to Zhigansk.

Only SANDPIPER could provide the needed information, and he must be contacted. Although it deviated from standard procedure, his agent would have to use the Emergency Flash Transmitter, since the White House was pressing for more information on MONGOOSE. The EFT was a new, miniaturized, yet very high powered radio transmitter that could send a page of text to a surveillance satellite in less than one-fifteenth of a second. The information would be stored in the satellite until the latter was queried by a coded signal from the CIA.

The decision made, he called the Deputy for Soviet Affairs to his office. Cliff Davis had been overseeing their Soviet operations for some time, and put in a lot of overtime keeping tabs on any issue that even looked suspicious. As he entered, Egbert asked, "Anything new on MONGOOSE?"

Davis gave the same answer as he had for days. "Nothing!"

"Cliff, I want you to send this message to BLUE JAY that he can relay to SANDPIPER:

Urgently need the following information at earliest possible date:

1. Has a new laser/particle-beam weapon been developed?
2. If so, give type and status.

3. Where is it located?
4. What is its basic power substance?
5. Critical components, if any?
6. Do you work on the new weapon?
7. Other information you think significant.

Reply with EFT in repeat mode.'

"It must be sent in the next diplomatic pouch, and instruct BLUE
JAY to get it to SANDPIPER by the fastest means available that won't
arouse suspicion."

The next twenty-four hours passed with no word from BLUE JAY.
The waiting game had never been his strong suit, and Egbert fumed at
the lethargic clock.

While waiting, he got a call from Harry Voit, his Deputy for Eastern European Affairs, who sounded quite worried and was very insistent on seeing him at once. Egbert told him to come right up. "Maybe
he's got something that will help clear up the MONGOOSE puzzle," he
mused. The deputy came in with a large rolled map, and a sheaf of
intelligence reports marked SECRET.

"Sir," Voit began, "we've been getting more and more reports
from stations monitoring message traffic in my area. At first, these
didn't appear out of the ordinary until the volume rose significantly
during the past 36 hours. Consequently, we started to plot some of the
activity on this map. These are intercepts of their armed forces network, and they all concern moves of military units, diversion of sup-
plies to staging areas, and the dispersal of fighter aircraft to forward
operating bases."

The CIA Director felt a shudder of fear as he digested the implica-
tion of the colored arrows on the map. All of them moved from inside
the U.S.S.R., or from within Warsaw Bloc countries, toward the border with the West. Without a doubt, this represented a massing of
forces in numbers that would overwhelm NATO in short order. The
size of the units involved, the type of equipment, and the huge
amount of munitions and material being stockpiled made it clear that
this was the initial phase of a battle plan to overrun Western Europe.
Even more unsettling were the notations next to some of the arrows—
missile and artillery units equipped with tactical nuclear weapons.

"If this is their reaction to our increase in Defense Condition, it
sure is overkill. They could have countered with a like response and
have achieved the same end."

"Yes," Voit answered, "but there's something else that makes it even more puzzling. If they just wanted to counter our higher readiness states, it could have been done more easily by a single message to all units. Look at these time/date groups at the end of the arrows. The one at the tail represents when the order was sent. The one at the head is when the unit is to be at the deployment base. Apparently they are in no hurry, since all the in-place dates are four to five weeks from now. We know from past exercises they've held that they can move a lot faster than that."

The deputy then added some more unwelcome news. "Another thing, Mr. Egbert, I don't think these are fake messages. We have received reports from agents throughout Eastern Europe confirming that military units are on the move—all in a westward direction. They also state that there appears to be no urgency to the moves, no massed exodus. This seems to reinforce the timetables shown on the map. An additional disturbing element in the reports from these agents is that conscripts who are at the end of their enlistment are not being demobilized. This bolsters even more the proposition that they are preparing for an all-out war."

Egbert nodded in agreement, and made some notes on the in-place times listed on the map. The earliest and the latest bracketed a one-week period a little over four weeks away. Apparently, something big was due to break around the first of September.

"This is good work, Harry. I want you to take it over to Walt Martin's office and let him take a look at it. From now on, I'd like you to concentrate on these intercepts, and coordinate all information with the Department of Defense. Hopefully, if we combine our information with theirs, we might come up with a composite situation map that could be invaluable if the balloon does go up. I'll give Martin a call to let him know you're on the way."

\* \* \*

Another twelve hours passed before Egbert was handed a message from BLUE JAY. His reply was that the request had been sent to SANDPIPER, and should be received no later than the 18th, Washington time—one week away.

The rest of BLUE JAY's message reported that high-level activity in the Kremlin had increased drastically during the past ten days. Tight security had been imposed, but nobody seemed to know why—and if they did, they certainly weren't talking. All his normal contacts for information suddenly dried up. He also noticed an increase of activity at the military bases on the outskirts of Moscow—those that made up the city's antimissile defense system. The message ended on a solemn note, saying that such measures had not been seen since the Cuban missile crisis.

## Zhigansk

Fedor Lushev was an extremely frustrated spy. After reading the letter that had arrived a day and a half ago from his contact in Moscow, he realized this was at last his big assignment. Its importance was underscored by the requirement to use the electronic transmitter that he had kept so carefully hidden during the past six months. Lushev had already prepared the reply and had it entered into the device, and everything was ready to go. Now all he needed was a chance to slip out of the village into the surrounding forest and activate the transmitter.

At first he thought the increased security that extended from the research facility to the airport, including the village itself, would be a problem. However, as was usual in a remote area with no apparent threat, the guards' initial fervor quickly paled, and had become only a cursory check now and then, or whenever their officers were looking.

It didn't take long to establish a time and a route that would get him into the woods undetected after nightfall. Eleven o'clock the previous evening, he had intended to sneak out of town and send the message, but late in the afternoon the first hitch developed in his plans. A heavy cloud deck moved in, and just before dark it started raining continuously. He had been in these parts long enough to recognize that this particular combination of wind and precipitation usually meant a lengthy period of bad weather. There would no chance of getting the required star sightings until this overcast moved out.

Sitting at the window in his drab apartment, Lushev cursed the lowering clouds and the now driving rain. His thoughts drifted to his job at the research plant and his present situation as an agent for the Americans, and once again, the stabbing ache in his gut returned. It was not the pain of guilt for being a spy against his homeland, but that of an intense hatred for a system that denied him his rightful place in the scientific community.

In graduate school, he had forgone the usual leisure times, and the relentless struggle with the books over so many years had finally showed signs of being rewarded. His advisors, both academic and political, had assured him that a prestigious research post would most certainly be his after his upcoming graduation. Lushev had made quite a few plans based on this promise, and both he and his fiancée were eagerly awaiting the posting. However, the job was not to be his. Instead, it was given to the son of a prominent party member, whose academic achievements qualified him for a position of laboratory assistant at best.

In a society where intellectual recognition was immutably tied to political affiliation, Lushev became just so much flotsam on the sea of academia. Lacking the proper entrée to the more desirable positions, he reconciled himself to a lifetime mired in mediocrity and uselessness, and went alone to this remote outpost in Siberia. Obsessed by this festering wound of dashed pride and ambitions, he became a relatively easy mark for a CIA recruiter, and shortly thereafter entered the black world of espionage. Now the time had come to realize his dreams of revenge, if only the rain would stop.

## Washington, D.C.

Eight days later Egbert was starting to get extremely edgy. He had been hoping that SANDPIPER might have gotten the inquiry early, now it was late.

A call had alerted him to the weather front in Central Siberia that was, in all likelihood, blocking SANDPIPER's transmission, but after two more days of waiting, the weather section still could not promise any breaks in the overcast until the 24th. The White House and the Pentagon kept pressing Egbert for news from SANDPIPER, and his repeated answer of "weather problems" was not getting a kind reception.

\* \* \*

On the morning of August 24th, the first item in his briefing folder was the weather report on Zhigansk, and today was the first time in a week it looked encouraging. The system was showing signs of movement, and on the latest satellite photographs, the cloud cover was starting to break up northwest of the research facility. The forecaster stated that the broken clouds should reach Zhigansk about dusk their time, and conditions should improve thereafter. If this prediction held up, SANDPIPER would have his first chance in over a week to use his EFT.

This news encouraged Egbert, but given their past luck, he mentally added, "If only there are no more problems!" Dusk in Zhigansk had occurred about two hours earlier, and if the variables shook out in their favor, they should be hearing from SANDPIPER at any moment.

The morning hours passed with agonizing slowness, and Egbert was thinking about calling for a sandwich when the phone rang. It was Cliff Davis, who fairly shouted, "Flash message from SANDPIPER! I'll bring it right up!" A few minutes later, the deputy arrived, breathless from his run up the stairs.

"SANDPIPER came through like a champ, but I don't think you'll like his report."

Egbert took the message from Davis, and indeed it was not what he wanted to see, as he read aloud the numbered responses:

> " '1. Yes.
> 2. Laser weapon—operational by August 30th.
> 3. New facility northeast of main plant.
> 4. Deuterium-fluorine.
> 5. Deuterium-fluorine isotope—decomposes if subjected to heat or shock—supply adequate but limited at this time.
> 6. Not directly—only on noncritical subassemblies.
> 7. Entire complex under extremely tight security—increased number of military at new facility.' "

As instructed in the original request, the message kept repeating itself until the tape ran out. This was an additional precaution to ensure that the complete text got through, just in case some portions were garbled or not received. Egbert immediately called all the MONGOOSE principles, and told them that SANDPIPER's message was in, and each would get a copy by courier.

Almost an hour later, Egbert got a call from Tom Whitney telling him to be in the Oval Office at five that afternoon.

# Chapter 3

## The White House

The President was visibly worried as he opened the meeting. Everyone was aware that September 1 was only days away, and that this was the key date in the Soviet's plans. The President was determined to decide on a course of action before this meeting was over. He turned to the Secretary of State, "Roy, what about recent diplomatic activity relative to MONGOOSE?"

"I really have nothing new to report on the diplomatic front. I talked to the Soviet ambassador once since he met with the Soviet President. That meeting was brief and cool, with nothing said about the satellite. My recommendation would be to avoid the use of force in this matter."

Carmen DiAngelo was next, and he looked a little sheepish as he stepped to the lectern. "Gentlemen, I have to admit that we were quite a bit surprised at the content of SANDPIPER's message. The Scientific Advisory Council had no idea that the Soviets had achieved such a significant breakthrough in high-energy lasers. Now that we know the base material is deuterium-fluorine, we can hypothesize how this weapon works.

"It has been known for some time that elements in the halogen family would make very powerful lasers, if their atoms could be raised to a higher energy level *and* held in this state long enough to be used in the lasing apparatus. The process involves packing more electrons into each atom of fluorine, and keeping them there until the newly created isotope can be used in the weapon. There is no difficulty in making the isotope—we merely bombard the basic element in a particle accelerator. However, the electrons added in this process are only stable for a few thousandths of a second. Then, the substance reverts to basic fluorine, with a corresponding release of energy. If this energy could be channeled into the lasing device, the resulting beam would be more powerful by many orders of magnitude than existing lasers. Somehow, this is what the Soviets have managed to do, possibly by adding deuterium to the process.

"SANDPIPER's report that the isotope is sensitive to heat and shock is consistent with this theory. Many unstable substances can be kept in elevated energy states by applying extreme pressure or intense magnetic fields, or by cooling them to temperatures approaching absolute zero. In many cases, a combination of these techniques are used.

"Although this type of weapon poses a serious threat to our security, an even more disturbing aspect is its potential for future development. It is only logical to assume that as the Soviet's refine the process for extending the 'shelf life' of this isotope, they will find additional applications for this weapon. It is readily apparent that such a possibility will complicate the business of defending our interests. I cannot suggest a defense against this weapon, nor would it be practical to protect our backup satellite by some sort of armor plating. This approach is not feasible because of the additional weight and the problems of making it work with the shielding."

John Egbert began his presentation next. "SANDPIPER's message has cleared up many questions we had a few weeks ago," he said and flicked the switch on the nearby slide projector. "We know the weapon was designed and built at Zhigansk, which is shown here on this enlargement of a surveillance satellite picture. This is how the facility looked a year ago, and the next slide will depict how it is today. Note this new structure, which according to SANDPIPER, is where the weapon is housed. The liquid shipments referred to in SANDPIPER's earlier reports are either deuterium, fluorine, or both. These are processed into the combination that powers the laser weapon. This processing operation probably explains the increase in IR radiation coming from this old section of the facility."

Carmen DiAngelo agreed, "That all makes sense, and the relatively modest increase in their electrical generating capacity also makes sense. My guess is that the new weapon gets its effectiveness from the isotope principle we discussed earlier. But, it also needs more electrical power than is available from the existing plant, hence the new addition."

Walt Martin's opening statement was, in essence, a call to arms. "If the United States does not answer Soviet actions of this sort by a like show of force, we will be coerced into agreeing to any terms they care to dictate. The map of Eastern Europe we have just seen convinces me beyond a doubt that the Communists could overrun the NATO countries, while holding the gun of World War III to our heads. This laser weapon is the key to the entire issue."

The President responded dejectedly. "Even though I hate to agree with you, Walt, the available information supports your point of view. In any event, we must consider the worst possible situation. What contingency plans have you developed thus far?"

The Secretary of Defense replied that all but the final details of their various options had been worked out, and the Chairman of the Joint Chiefs would brief everyone on the courses of action under study.

A somber General Woods spoke up. "Our analysis of the situation shows that if the United States wishes to maintain parity with the Soviet Bloc, decisive action must be taken. The unanimous decision of the Joint Chiefs is that this new weapon must be destroyed!" A murmur went through the room as the implications of such an action struck home.

"The question is not 'if' the weapon should be destroyed, but 'how,' " the general continued. "We can assume that this device is built along the lines of the laser generators we possess, and as such, is made up of electrical components, electromagnets, vacuum systems, and cooling apparatus. We must also assume that if any or all these various assemblies are destroyed, they could be repaired or replaced in a short time. But, the Achilles' heel of this weapon is their limited supply of the isotope. Producing this basic 'fuel,' to the degree of purity and in the quantity required, is a delicate and time-consuming operation. Without a stockpile of the isotope or the capability of producing more for a considerable length of time, the laser weapon is effectively neutralized. Thus, the objective of our plan is to destroy the new research building, located just northeast of the main complex." As he spoke, he pointed to the satellite photo of the Zhigansk research facility being projected on the screen.

"We do not think a small nuclear weapon would be appropriate for this task, since the heat and blast of conventional explosives should be sufficient to destroy the stockpiled isotope. The weapons used would be large enough to demolish the more fragile components of the refining process that creates the isotope. Using conventional explosives would also allow the Soviets to back out of this confrontation without losing face, since the explosion could be blamed on a mishap at the facility. Public opinion, particularly here at home, would be better served by avoiding nuclear weapons, especially given the delicate nature of this entire situation.

"Obviously, the method of accomplishing this is the major portion of the 'how' question. Three different approaches were considered. Having SANDPIPER sabotage the new facility was an option we discarded because of the time and uncertainties involved. Cruise missiles launched from a submarine in the Arctic Ocean was another possibility, but the pinpoint accuracy we are looking for relegates this choice to second place.

"The plan we feel has the best chance of success also has some undesirable aspects. If anything goes wrong, and indeed even if everything goes right, the involvement of the United States would be undeniable. We could end up with a great deal of public embarrassment, but given the stakes of this entire situation and the lack of alternatives, this is an acceptable risk.

"Another drawback in this plan is the very high level of danger to the individuals who would carry out the mission. Without going into the details, which are lengthy and complex, we recommend a strike by two aircraft specifically equipped for such a mission.

"A task like this presents hundreds of problems, and there are still a few unknowns in the equation. The final answers to some of these may not be known until the actual mission is underway. The one overriding reason why such a strike is our best course of action is that it offers the highest probability of target destruction. This high PK is due in large part to the use of simple, proven weapons, carried by an airplane with an excellent track record for reliability and performance. However, the most important factor by far in ensuring accomplishment of this mission is the presence of a man in the cockpit over the target area. Given a job of this importance, there is no substitute for someone who can make decisions and alter the mission as the situation dictates."

As Woods sat down, a deep silence settled on the room. The proposal amounted to a preemptive strike, an aggressive act of war—something that was totally foreign to the traditional strategic doctrine of the United States.

The President looked unsettled as he broke the silence. "My God, Walt, do you realize the political ramifications of this, whether we succeed or not? Except for about a half dozen countries, every member of the U.N. will be hanging the label of 'aggressor' on us!"

"We realized that would be one of the undesirable consequences

of this mission," the general responded, "but with the stakes so high
and the time so short, PROJECT MONGOOSE is the best way of resolving
this dilemma. The accusations of other nations be damned! If they are
too shortsighted to see which side their economic and military bread
is buttered on, then to hell with them! I am sure that after an initial
period of the usual outcries, they will realize the necessity for our
actions."

"I suppose you're right, Walt," the President answered solemnly,
"but I still don't relish these fair-weather friends raking us over the
coals." He shook his head then asked if anyone else had any questions.

"Yes," Tom Whitney replied. "General Woods, you mentioned
that this mission will involve just two aircraft. Given the distances to
Zhigansk from almost any direction, I would assume that they would
be bombers?"

"No, Mr. Whitney. Since speed and maneuverability are critical to
the success of this endeavor, our planning staff only considered a
highly modified version of a single-seat fighter that is currently in
operational status."

The Commandant of the Marine Corps spoke up next. "Regardless of the speed and maneuverability of these airplanes, Chuck, the
Soviets are just about on a par with us in the area of fighter technology. How do you propose to get through their radar net and keep
from getting shot down by the large number of interceptors they will
surely scramble against this mission?"

The general explained, "One of the modifications I just mentioned is a technique we've been working to perfect for quite some
time, and they think it's ready to go at last. We have finally gotten the
Stealth concept fine-tuned to the point where the aircraft cannot be
seen by opposing radar until it is very close to the station. Our latest
data indicates that we have achieved a significant improvement over
the Stealth technology that has been in use during the past few years.
In addition, we've upgraded the avionics with some new black boxes
that will give them an edge over the interceptors and the missiles
they'll be firing. In order to make things as difficult as possible for the
defense, we plan to run this mission at night and at low level. Time
over target will be just after first light."

"Won't the MiGs have a field day on the egress route in daylight?" Morrison asked.

"That's a definite possibility, Pete. Admittedly the egress leg is the
riskiest portion of the mission, and was the part that made us do the

most soul-searching. However, we have a high degree of confidence in the combination of the new electronics and the Stealth modification. Add to this the superior training our pilots receive, and our calculations show that the odds for the escape route are about fifty-fifty.''

The Secretary of State turned to Woods with a question of his own, ''Assuming this option is approved, and assuming the aircraft reach their target, how can we be assured that the weapon is destroyed? We certainly don't want to call their bluff with such a provocative move, only to find out they are still holding all the aces. Even considering the urgency of our situation, this move gives us no fallback position.''

Carmen DiAngelo stepped in to field Butler's question. ''As mentioned earlier, the key to this weapon system is the stockpile of the isotope. The destruction of this substance would render the laser weapon useless, even without the additional damage done by the explosion. And, there is a way to determine if the isotope breaks down to its stable state. The heat and concussion from the bombs should be sufficient to initiate this breakdown process, which once started, is irreversible and continues until the stable state is reached. As I mentioned previously, a considerable amount of energy is released as this isotope changes composition. This energy has a very distinctive wavelength that can be detected easily by an appropriate receiver on the strike aircraft. The device will illuminate a light in the cockpit, informing the pilot that a certain amount of this energy has been picked up from the target.''

The President still wasn't fully convinced, and he turned to the Chairman of the Joint Chiefs. ''General, I'm sure you've considered every facet of this plan, but it is extremely risky from the diplomatic standpoint, and sounds like a suicide mission. Also, do we have someone to fly this mission? If we ever have to use this option, I would only accept volunteers for such an undertaking.''

''I don't think finding crews for this mission will be a problem. Once this option came up, we made some discreet inquiries at selected bases. The wing commanders were told that we needed volunteers for an extended flight involving great danger, but of extreme importance to the security of the entire country. They were directed to first interview bachelors who were extremely well qualified in all phases of the tactical fighter mission. Only if none were found, or if no one volunteered, would they be permitted to interview married personnel. Each candidate was ordered to say absolutely nothing about the interview, whether they volunteered or not.

"Considering the fairly restricted area of our search, the response has been a bit overwhelming. Our problem became not one of finding crews, but choosing the best qualified. This process is in its final stages, and with your permission, Mr. President, I would like to brief the selected pilots on the entire MONGOOSE PROJECT, if we decide to exercise this option."

"Of course, General. However, I hope that such a briefing will never be needed. You apparently have a handle on your crew situation, but exactly what fighters do you plan to use, and are they capable of the long journey?"

"We do have a few unknowns in this area, Mr. President. I have a transparency showing the proposed route of flight for this mission. As you see, the trip will be extremely long, especially for a fighter, but the mission plan does call for a refueling after the strike aircraft have exited Soviet airspace and are over international waters.

"As to the airplanes, we have just two that we feel are capable of such a flight. These are experimental versions of a proven design that has been the mainstay of our tactical air arm for the past two years. The unknowns are related to the modifications being added to the airplanes. Their installation is almost complete, but the new systems have not been flight-tested in these particular aircraft. We are confident that these devices will function as their preliminary tests indicate, but we would feel a lot more comfortable if we could try them out in the air.

"In any event, these airplanes are the only ones capable of flying this mission, along with offering the crews a better chance of survival than any other fighter in our inventory. Therefore, if we must go, these are the airplanes we'll use whether the new systems work or not.

"One thing I should mention is that these modifications are in addition to the basic weapons system already in the airplane, which has been thoroughly tested. Thus, the mission aircraft will not be defenseless, even if all the new items fail to work properly."

The President glanced around the table and asked, "Gentlemen, we've heard what has been proposed. Does anyone have any different approaches, or anything to add to those presented?"

When he got no response, he continued. "I think we agree that the recommended plan should only be implemented after some extreme provocation by the Soviets, and when it appears that negotiations will no longer serve our purposes. I am still basically opposed to this type of move, since it is so alien to our traditions. However, with the stakes so high, we must assess every development with the utmost care, and not act precipitously on something that has such grave consequences.''

## Langley AFB

Major Bill Gates looked very much like the archetypical fighter pilot—just topping six feet, he had blue eyes, and very dark hair cut close to conform to Air Force regulations. At 35, he had a muscular build with no trace of the fat so common on someone who is starting the uphill grind into middle age. Keeping in shape had become a necessary part of his job because the rigors of flying air combat tactics demanded top physical conditioning. A total devotion to his job and a determination to keep one step ahead of the friendly competition had given Gates a somewhat serious demeanor.

During his four years at the Air Force Academy, Bill Gates had been driven by only one goal: to be a fighter pilot. Everything he did was focused on achieving a class ranking high enough to be selected for flight school. Gates proved to be a natural in fighters, and at each of his assignments was recognized as the one to beat in aerial competition. Specialized schooling in weapons and tactics followed, and by the time he reported to the First Fighter Wing, his reputation was well established. Thus, even though he had no idea what was in store for him, he knew that if it involved tactical flying, he could handle it, and probably better than anyone else.

At present he knew only that this trip had something to do with his mysterious interview with the commander of the First Fighter Wing at Langley. Colonel Birkner had called him up to his office late one evening, with no explanation. The timing of the call was certainly odd, since at this time of year they were only involved in routine training, with no special activities on the schedule.

Colonel Sam Birkner was seated at his desk as Gates walked in and saluted. The commander returned the salute halfheartedly and motioned him to a chair.

"Gates, before I say my piece, I want to go over some ground rules concerning this meeting. First of all, you're under orders not to mention this get together, or anything we talk about, to anyone: your commander, the guys in the squadron, your girl friend, no one! Is that clearly understood?"

Gates replied instantly, "Yes sir!" a little surprised at Birkner's brusqueness.

"Good! What I have to ask you will raise a million questions in your mind, but unfortunately I don't have the answers to your question, or even mine. Yesterday morning I got a top secret TWX from the Joint Chiefs ordering me to the Chief of Staff's office immediately. I was brought into General Cunningham's office, and briefed by the Old Man himself. He said the Joint Chiefs were looking for a volunteer for a highly classified mission, involving a large degree of risk. They need someone very well qualified in the F-24, especially in the air-to-air and air-to-ground mission. The only other information the general gave me was that the mission involved an extended flight in an F-24, and was of critical importance to the security of the nation.

"Bill, I've spent the entire day going over the records of every man in this wing, looking at total flying time, hours in the F-24, gunnery and bombing scores, wins and losses in fighter vs. fighter engagements, personal background, and any other experience that would be valuable on such a mission. As the reigning Top Gun of this wing, it's not surprising that your name is at the head of the list. There are some others here at Langley I have to talk to yet, but since you're the best qualified, I thought I'd give you the first shot.

"Before you answer, let me assure you that if you decline, there will be absolutely no stigma attached to your decision, and since you and I are the only ones who know about our meeting tonight, the outcome is strictly between us. I wish I could give you more information, but it wasn't given to me. Would you like a few minutes to think it over?"

"No sir, Colonel. Put me down as a definite yes!"

"I figured that would be your answer. I'll send in your name as our primary candidate, and if any others accept, I'll list them as alternates. Remember, don't mention this meeting to anyone—period! Also, I don't know what time frame the JCS has in mind, so you should hang pretty close to the base until we hear from the Pentagon."

The TWX approving Gates's selection arrived at Langley Communications Center about 1100 hours, and was delivered to the commander's office. A satisfied smile crept across Birkner's face while reading the message. He jabbed the intercom and told his secretary to have Major Gates report to his office right away.

When Gates came in and closed the door, Sam Birkner handed him the message and offered congratulations. "I knew we had the best man for the job, and it looks like the JCS agreed."

A tingle of professional pride and excitement ran up Bill Gates's spine as he read the TWX:

> Major William Gates, SSAN 158-11-3216, 94th Tactical Fighter Squadron, will proceed immediately to Andrews AFB, Maryland, to participate in PROJECT MONGOOSE. Travel will be by the most expeditious means available. Upon arrival, report to Special Operations Command Post. Full flying gear for winter and summer required. Project priority is one.

He silently agreed that the JCS had definitely picked the best man, because if this hush-hush mission involved flying the F-24, his credentials proved that he was at the top of the heap.

The wing commander continued, "I've checked this afternoon's flying schedule, and the only B model in the lineup is from the 71st. Called Hank Lawson and said I needed the bird for a priority mission to Andrews. Told him to have one of his guys file the flight plan and be standing by at the airplane, ready to go. He squawked at losing the sortie, and started to bleed about the importance of the scheduled instrument ride, but I cut him off by saying I didn't have time for a lot of talk. The weather's no sweat, so if your stuff is ready, you can launch in about an hour."

"My bag's already packed, Colonel. The only thing left to do is to pick up my flying gear from the Personal Equipment Shop and throw everything in the plane. I should be ready in an hour with no problem."

"Good! I'll have my staff car follow you home if you want to drop off your wheels. By the way, when I talked to the 71st, I didn't mention the name of the project, so if whoever's taking you up has any questions, say I'm sending you to the Pentagon for a tactics briefing or something. Given the security of this thing, it would be best not to mention PROJECT MONGOOSE, unless it becomes necessary to get where you're going."

"Don't worry, Colonel, I'll have a song and dance ready in case he's curious. Those 71st guys will believe anything!"

"I don't know what the JCS has cooked up for you, but it's important, and I'm sure you can hack it. The whole thing probably won't be a piece of cake, but it sounds exciting enough that I wish they'd let some of us old heads volunteer."

"Colonel, I've got a sneaky suspicion that before this trip is over, I'm gonna wish that someone like you were along."

The two shook hands as Birkner said, "Good luck, Bill, and Godspeed!"

A half hour later, Gates had picked up his clothes and was back at the personal equipment section. It didn't take long to pack his cold weather gear, and since everyone else was either briefing or eating lunch, there were no questions about the winter flying equipment.

It bothered him that he couldn't call Maryann in Chicago, and tell her he was going TDY. He didn't have the answers to her natural questions of where, how long, and why, and this would only generate more questions and perhaps an argument.

Maryann and Gates had known each other since high school, but things had not gotten serious until three years previously. He was visiting his parents in Tomahawk, Wisconsin, over the Fourth of July, when he ran into Maryann at the fireworks display. Friendship blossomed into something more, and grew over the intervening years. His hectic schedule and her new position as account executive precluded any immediate plans for settling down. Nonetheless, Gates knew deep down inside that this relationship was special.

He had recently been giving some thought to the possibilities of getting married, and intended to explore the subject when they saw each other in a couple of weeks. He knew, however, that it would take a silver-tongued orator to convince Maryann that the Air Force life would be her cup of tea. She had often mentioned that service wives must have a terrible time with all the moves and uncertainties associated with the military. But he also knew that with her personality and enthusiasm, she would definitely find a place in the fighter squadron family.

The one problem he might have was the possibility that she would not be willing to give up her more settled way of life, and might ask him to leave the Air Force instead. Somehow Gates could not imagine a sedentary existence in a nine-to-five job. But his imaginings were also beginning to suggest the undesirability of not having Maryann at his side in the years to come.

He thought about the irony of being brought into PROJECT MONGOOSE just as his own life might be about to change in such a major way.

As he headed for the door, one of the PE technicians took his bag and asked, "Need a lift to the flight line, Major? Goin' on another TDY?"

"Yeah. Got to go up to the Puzzle Palace and help straighten things out."

Once in the step van used for transporting crews to and from their airplanes, Gates told the sergeant, "I'll be going to the B model down in the 71st's area." When they turned into the row where the two-seated F-24 was parked, he noticed that Bob Mills was just finishing up the preflight inspection.

Mills glanced up from the wheel assembly he was checking as Gates got out of the van, and shouted a "Howdy" over the ever-present noise of a busy flight line. Gates waved and climbed up the boarding ladder to stow his gear in the electronics bay. When everything was tied down, Mills was standing at the foot of the front cockpit ladder, and couldn't resist a little dig. "Things going so bad with the Hat and Ring gang that they have to snivel time from the 71st?"

Gates expected something like this because of the keen rivalry between their two squadrons. Flying time was the currency by which much of a fighter pilot's net worth was measured, and to lose a mission, particularly to someone in another unit, was a bitter pill to swallow. Although no reply was necessary, Gates thought it best to keep things light before Mills started to prod him with questions as to why he was going to Andrews.

"Somebody's got to keep an eye on what your ragtag outfit is doing," he grinned. "Believe me, I'd much rather be riding in some 94th iron, but this was directed by higher headquarters and you guys had the only B model on the schedule. What's it like between here and Washington?"

"Just some scattered middle stuff, winds aloft out of the west about 50 knots, Andrews is wide open with light and variable surface winds. The boss said to get you up there in a hurry, so I filed direct at ten grand. If we don't run into any delays, I'll just shut down the left engine to let you out, and press right on back to Langley."

"Sounds o.k. to me. Let's crank 'er up."

Once Mills and Gates were strapped in by the crew chief, idle chatter ceased and everything became very businesslike. Checklist items were clicked off rapidly in both cockpits, and following protocol, Gates took over the operation of the radios and navigation systems in the back seat. He quickly copied down and read back the clearance from Ground Control.

By now, Mills had both engines fired up and was just completing the poststart checks. Ejection seat safety pins were pulled, shown to the crew chief, and stowed as the chocks were pulled. With only a slight touch on the throttles, the big fighter started taxiing toward the active runway. Gates went through the weapons system checks more from habit than from an anticipated need for the radar or ground-mapping capabilities. Despite his comments to Mills about the 71st, the radar and its subsystems were performing right up to specs in all modes.

Mills asked for a switch to tower frequency as they neared the active, and called, "Langley Tower Alpha November Two Five, number one for zero seven." They answered quickly with a clearance into position, and for takeoff.

Regardless of his time in the F-24, Gates never tired of the thrill of getting airborne in an airplane with such dazzling performance. After completing the runup checks and noting that everything was in the green, Mills left the throttles at 100 percent power and asked if he was all set. The bird seemed eager for flight, straining against the brakes in anticipation, as Gates responded quickly, "Let 'er roll."

Inside the cockpit, the ear-splitting screech of the engines was reduced to a muffled roar and a mild airframe vibration. The jet lurched forward as Mills released the brakes, and almost immediately both pilots were slammed into their seatbacks by the instant acceleration from the afterburners. They lit with a dull boom as Mills moved both throttles outboard and forward to the stop. The airspeed indicator suddenly came alive, as the needle quickly jumped past one hundred knots and continued upwards at an increasing rate.

Mills lifted the nose gear off at one hundred seventy-five knots, and the mains were clear a second or so later. It now became a contest between the pilot and the awesome acceleration of the two Pratt and Whitney turbofans. Mills increased the back pressure on the stick to maintain control of the airspeed, as his left hand hit the gear switch to the UP position. This technique was necessary to keep from accelerating beyond 250 knots before the wheels were up and locked, otherwise the gear doors would be ripped off by the airloads.

Once the airplane was cleaned up, Mills chopped the burners, but even under military power, it only took a few seconds to reach the initial climb schedule of four hundred knots. The remainder of the flight into Andrews was quite routine, with both pilots busying themselves with the usual navigation and reporting procedures.

During a lull, Gates felt another twinge of regret at not being able to tell his parents about being selected for MONGOOSE. He knew his father would be quite proud, and in a small town like Tomahawk, everybody that was anybody would soon know the full story, particularly the crowd at the Bridge Tavern. But, all the questions without answers would undoubtedly cause more worry than pride, especially for his mother. In any case, he decided it was best that he couldn't tell them about the mission until it was over.

Thinking about his family brought back into sharp focus what Colonel Birkner had said about the dangers associated with this project. He knew that technique-wise, he could handle just about anything even a tough mission could offer. However, the way Birkner had emphasized the risks caused a flash of apprehension in the back of his mind. What if the flak was so intense as to be impenetrable, or if the number of interceptors launched against him was so overwhelming that escape was impossible? More than the fear of death was the fear of failure at something where he was regarded as one of the best. The number of guns and missiles fired at him or the numerous airplanes trying to down him would never be known to anyone here at home. If he didn't make it back, the only comment from his peers would be, "He didn't hack it!"

Another item that bothered him almost as much was the timing of this whole thing. Here he was, just getting ready to do some exploratory work on popping the question, when he gets sent off to God-knows-where for God-knows-how-long. The thought of possibly not seeing Maryann again added to the blossoming second thoughts coursing through his mind. "The Air Force is a prime example of Murphy's Law," he grumbled to himself, "if something can happen at the worst possible time, they will ensure that it occurs just then."

However, all of these feelings were a trifle late since he was committed, and things had probably progressed to the point where he couldn't back out. On the other side of the coin, his professional pride would never allow him to change his mind at this late date.

The JCS had been notified of their departure, and since weather was not a factor, Andrews Approach Control had been told to expedite their recovery. When Mills reported over Patuxent River TACAN, he was cleared immediately for a straight-in approach to runway zero one right. Mills greased it on the runway following the GCA, in spite of the much higher gross weight caused by the large amount of fuel still on board.

"Not too bad for a 71st type," Gates commented in mock praise of the good landing, as Mills held the nose off the ground for maximum aerodynamic braking.

A "Follow Me" truck was waiting as they turned off the active, and led them to a parking spot in front of Base Operations. Gates safetied his seat and unstrapped as they taxied in, while Mills was getting his clearance back to Langley from Ground Control. After the crewchief crossed his wands over his head for the "Stop" signal, the left engine was stopcocked and a ladder was hooked over the rear canopy rail.

Gates handed his gear to the airman standing at the foot of the ladder and secured all the loose items in the back seat. When he was clear of the airplane, the combustion starter on the left engine roared, and in less than thirty seconds idle RPM had been reached. Gates gave a thumbs up sign while mouthing "Thanks for the ride." Mills nodded in return, signaled for "Chocks Out," and was quickly taxiing out to the active.

When the F-24 cleared the parking slot, a staff car waiting alongside Base Ops started moving in Gates's direction. The driver got out, saluted, and inquired, "Major Gates?" He nodded while returning the salute, and the driver loaded his bags into the trunk.

"Sir, I'm to take you to the Special Operations Command Post."

Driving through the base, Gates noticed that Andrews still looked very much the same as on his previous short trips to the Pentagon. Since it was the headquarters for the Air Force Systems Command, an unusually large variety of aircraft were parked on the flight line. Each one was probably a research vehicle for some of the spooky projects AFSC was involved in. Also scattered about were National Guard fighters, MAC transports, and a conglomeration of Navy and Marine aircraft, reflecting the assortment of other units also stationed at Andrews. Even though the base was over fifty years old, it was kept up beautifully, as was common with major command headquarters.

Gates's AGO card was scrutinized closely by an air policeman outside the command post; however, when he mentioned PROJECT MONGOOSE, things started to hum. The duty officer was called immediately, and in a few moments a balding major opened the door and held out his hand.

"Hi, I'm Jerry Shacker. My shop is the CP here, and I'm sure glad you made it. The Pentagon has been on the horn three times since you landed, asking if you had checked in yet."

Shacker steered him into a small room saying, "We'll use my office. It's more comfortable than the Situation Room, and a lot more private. Coffee's on the table there if you want some."

Gates declined as Shacker handed him a TOP SECRET envelope with the remark, "This was hand-delivered by a full bull from the Pentagon yesterday morning."

Gates tore open the envelope and read the short directive it contained:

TO Major William Gates, SSAN 158−11−3216

FROM JCS

SUBJ PROJECT MONGOOSE

Maj. Gates will remain on Andrews AFB until further notice, utilizing BOQ reserved in his name. He will be available at all, repeat all, times for contact by this office, by means of telephone and/or alert radio to be provided by the Special Ops CP. Upon notification by this office, Maj. Gates will proceed immediately to the Office of the Air Force Chief of Staff for project briefing. Transportation will be by helicopter from Andrews Base Operations. Backup will be by staff car with driver experienced in the Washington area. All personal and flying gear will be brought to the Pentagon.

"Nothing too difficult about this," remarked Gates as he handed the message to Shacker. "I guess I'll need an alert radio from you guys, and then just hang tight until I get a call. Can you set me up with a driver that knows his way to the Pentagon? According to the one that picked me up, I'm to keep the car, but I'll need help in getting over to the Puzzle Palace."

"Can do," answered Shacker. "I'll notify the Motor Pool to have someone on standby, and here's a list of restricted numbers for the Command Post, and my home phone, in case you need anything. Be sure to let me know if you run into a snag on anything, and I'll see what can be done."

"I appreciate that, but I plan to keep a low profile, so I doubt there will be much I'll need."

Shacker took a radio from his desk drawer and Gates saw that it was the standard hand-held set he was used to. "If anything changes, I'll let you know."

Shacker had been in the business long enough to know better than to ask what the project was all about, but as he shook Gates's hand on the way out, he said, "Good luck with the mongoose!"

*STRATCOM*

Jim Crawford sat in STRATCOM's control center scanning the status board and noted that everything was in the green. He jotted a notation in his hourly log and started thinking about all that had happened in the past few weeks. Suddenly the harsh shriek of an alarm klaxon

shook him from his reverie, and the status board for Star Wars IV
started flashing red. He yelled to the crew chief to switch the satellite
to backup power in case the auto transfer failed, but it was no use. The
technician replied that the manual transfer had no effect, and the satellite was completely dead on all channels. Crawford sat there in
stunned disbelief as the transfer was tried once again, but the crew
chief looked up from his console and shook his head.

Since the first satellite was destroyed, the standing order for all
shifts was to call General Cox immediately if anything unusual occurred. The commander was sleeping soundly and it took quite a few
rings before he answered. After hearing the news, he said he would be
right down. Cox told Crawford to call the White House Chief of Staff,
the Secretary of Defense, and the Chairman of the Joint Chiefs and
report to them what had happened, and that he would get back to
them with a complete report after checking the control center.

*　*　*

At six A.M., the President was notified that a hot line call would be
coming through within an hour. He couldn't believe that the Soviet
leader would be calling to explain last night's satellite destruction, so
he instructed Roy Butler and Walt Martin to report to the Oval Office
immediately. The two cabinet officers barely made it to the White
House in time, when the hot line phone on the President's desk
buzzed.

Viktor Petrov came on the line, and with the exception of saying
hello, there were no other amenities. Even the translator's voice
sounded grim, with the Soviet General Secretary rumbling in the
background like a distant thunderhead. He wasted no time with diplomacy, but launched brusquely into a diatribe against Star Wars.

"Mr. President, the Soviet Union can no longer exist under the
threat to our security posed by your Strategic Defense Initiative. For
that reason we have taken the steps we feel are absolutely necessary to
remove this Sword of Damocles from over our heads, and thus rectify
a situation that we find completely intolerable. I want to personally
assure you, Mr. President, that the Soviet Union does not intend to
take any additional strategic action—we do not plan to launch any missiles against the United States.

"You are no doubt aware by now, that we have developed a new
weapon that nullifies the Star Wars system. I also want to assure you
that this technology can be used against targets other than satellites,
such as airplanes, ships, vehicles, and incoming missiles. Because of

this new weapon, the balance of power between our nations has shifted decidedly toward the Soviet Union. This, in turn, makes the present an auspicious time to reaffirm what we have believed to be our destiny for many decades. In brief, Mr. President, from this point forward, the Soviet Union considers its sphere of influence as extending over the entire area of Western Europe.

"In this light, and in order to prevent an escalation of tensions beyond the point already reached, we have some conditions for the maintenance of this status quo. These are in essence: deactivation of the remaining Star Wars units, removal of American forces from Western Europe, and cessation of all logistical support to the NATO countries. Our ambassador will deliver a more detailed communique concerning all this, later in the day."

The President's fury was controlled, but barely, as he replied tersely. "Mr. General Secretary, your proposal is nothing more than nuclear blackmail, and I reject it completely. Our strike force is still intact and ready, and we certainly have no intention of deserting our allies. Why should we acquiesce to such outrageous conditions?"

"Your response is a natural one, Mr. President, and anticipated," Petrov stated. "However, let me point out a few things that may alter your thinking on the subject. First of all, you have no defense against our missiles, now that Star Wars is no longer operational. Second, you know that we outnumber you by a considerable margin in the number of missiles available for an initial exchange. Third, you will have no warning from your BMEWS, since we have developed a capability to counter your early warning system. To convince you of its effectiveness, we have arranged for a demonstration that should be taking place now. We also have been tracking your missile submarines quite closely, and have surrounded their positions with attack submarines. These vessels will counter any launch actions your submarines take, by the immediate use of force.

"Mr. President, I am sure you can deduce from these facts that the United States would be decimated if a missile exchange should take place. You will suffer irreparable damage in both casualties and property, while we, with our defenses and warning system intact, will weather the storm."

The President realized that much of what Petrov said was true. Without Star Wars, BMEWS, and the Trident submarine force, the country would indeed end up the loser in a missile exchange. There were, however, two possible fallacies in Petrov's reasoning. The American hunter-killer subs were available to protect the Trident fleet, and the actual effectiveness of the countermeasures directed at BMEWS might be less than expected. Knowing that gaining time was essential, he attempted to push the General Secretary as far as he could.

"Mr. General Secretary, I am appalled at the Soviet Union's callous disregard for our agreements concerning peaceful coexistence; however, I will carefully review the document your ambassador will deliver. I am sure you realize there will be much to consider from both a foreign and domestic viewpoint. You will have our reply on these issues when they have been thoroughly discussed."

"Mr. President, I can appreciate the scope of what you must do; however, our timetable is firm. If I do not have your reply within ten days, it must be interpreted as a refusal, and we will proceed accordingly. Good-bye, Mr. President!"

After hanging up, the President turned to Tom Whitney, who had arrived during the call.

"Tom, scrub my schedule for the rest of the day, and prepare some notes to brief General Woods on Petrov's demands. It looks like PROJECT MONGOOSE is far from over, now that these lunatics have forced our hand. Also, make sure that no one else gets wind of this latest development for the time being, and get Woods over here as quickly as possible."

The Chairman of the Joint Chiefs arrived by chopper in less than half an hour, and Whitney went over the details of the General Secretary's ultimatum with him in detail. Woods was amazed at the audacity of the Soviets, but had to admit that if they were to follow through with their threats, the U.S. would be totally at their mercy.

Then Woods brought some disturbing news. "On my way to the helipad, I was handed a Flash Report from STRATCOM. It states that all BMEWS sites experienced a high level of electronic jamming at 1305 Greenwich time, which was during the hot line call. The jamming was very effective, rendering all detection and tracking circuits useless. This is a preliminary report and, therefore, quite brief. Each of the sites is equipped with a frequency analyzer to investigate just such countermeasures. However, the evaluation of this data will take a little time, and will only tell us the type of transmitter used. Without eliminating the transmitter, I doubt there is any quick fix that will nullify the jamming."

The President asked, "Where is the jamming signal coming from? Inside Russia?"

"I'm no electronics expert, Mr. President," Woods responded, "but I don't think the jammer is located in Russia. A signal strong enough to disrupt our equipment would have to originate fairly close to the BMEWS site. It's my guess that it came from a trawler or submarine equipped with a highly directional antenna."

The President mulled this over and then said, "It appears that the Soviets weren't bluffing about their capabilities, which only lends credence to Petrov's threats if we refuse his demands. General Woods, can the Navy do anything to keep these jammers from operating?"

"I'm sure they can, Mr. President, but for an exact picture of the naval situation, I'll get Admiral Sullivan over here with an updated status map. That will show the current positions of our ships and theirs, and let us see just what our options are."

Getting a nod from the President, Woods called the Chief of Naval Operations. "Pat, we need you in the Oval Office immediately, and bring along your latest situation map. I'll send the chopper back to pick you up."

The President turned to the Secretary of State after answering his intercom. "Roy, Pauline says the Russian ambassador insists on seeing you. He has some extremely urgent documents that must be delivered immediately. Probably the formal demands that Petrov mentioned. Use the office across the hall in case he gets talkative, and get back here when you've looked over what he brought."

Then, to Walt Martin he continued, "I suppose Petrov's timetable refers to their occupation of Western Europe during the early fall. We ought to bring our forces there to a maximum state of readiness next week, and also advise the NATO countries of a probable move by the Soviets. I'm sure they are aware of the Communist troop movements, but I doubt they know of the September 10 deadline."

"I'll get those messages out right away, sir, and use the Soviet buildup as a reason. For now, I think we'd better not mention PROJECT MONGOOSE unless we hit a major snag with one of the NATO countries. If that occurs, you probably should call the head of state concerned and convey the urgency of this action. Telling them about MONGOOSE at this point would only generate a lot of questions, necessary explanations, and probably a bit of panic, all of which would be counterproductive with time so short."

"I agree, Walt—that's the best way to handle this. Do you have any more information on the strike plan we discussed the other day?"

"Yes sir. Two pilots have been selected, and are on call over at Andrews. They still don't know anything about MONGOOSE, or that each other are involved. General Woods will brief you on their qualifications."

When Woods finished describing the two men who had been selected, the President said, "Both of these men seem very highly qualified. If we have more with similar credentials, wouldn't a larger force provide a greater certainty of target destruction?"

"Mr. President, a doctrine we have used quite successfully for many years is that we fight as we train. These pilots are accustomed to working in pairs, in order to provide mutual support for each other. Also, by using only two airplanes flying at high speed and extremely low altitude, we have a good probability of slipping in beneath their radar net. If they do get an occasional contact on the two specially modified aircraft, it should be so weak and intermittent that it will most likely be dismissed as clutter and not arouse suspicion. A larger number of unmodified aircraft would almost guarantee discovery, and reduce the probability of target destruction to nearly zero.

"Having only two aircraft also increases our chances of avoiding infrared and sound-detection systems," he continued, "since multiple aircraft would be picked up easily by either of these methods. Another reason for not enlarging the strike force is that two airplanes can carry all the weapons needed to destroy the target and still provide a redundancy factor. Thus, there is no need to risk additional personnel."

As Woods finished, Roy Butler returned with the Soviet demands and distributed copies. "It's fairly straightforward—doesn't say much more than Petrov did on the hot line, just fills in some of the details. The bottom line is they want us to roll over and play dead as far as Europe is concerned."

After reading his copy, Walt Martin made a proposal. "From the looks of this, the Soviets have laid all their cards on the table, and it's time for us to act. Mr. President, I suggest we start the ball rolling on PROJECT MONGOOSE."

"You may be right, Walt, but I want to hear what Admiral Sullivan has to say first."

A few moments later the CNO arrived and spread out a large situation map on the table. Even though it had been drawn up hastily, it was clear that the Soviet leader had spoken the truth. The U.S. missile submarines were in their launch positions, but two Soviet hunter-killer subs were near each one.

The Chairman of the Joint Chiefs made marks on the chart about 50 miles in front of each BMEWS site and then asked Sullivan, "Pat, under emergency conditions, how fast can you get attack subs to each of these three locations, and out to counter those Russian boats shadowing our missile subs?"

The CNO studied the map before answering. "Well, figuring that we'll have to match the Soviets one for one around the missile boats, it's going to take every attack sub we've got in the Atlantic, including a couple that just arrived at Groton for routine maintenance. Just eyeballing the distances involved, I'd say the last boat would be in position no more than sixty hours after we give the launch order."

At this, Martin spoke emphatically. "Mr. President, given the obvious intentions of the Russians, I'd recommend we initiate this deployment immediately. We'll be in a much better bargaining position with these forces in place, and they can always be recalled if things turn out for the better."

The President answered quickly, "Admiral, take the necessary steps to get these submarines moving at the earliest possible moment. I can't overemphasize that time is extremely critical in this operation. Once they are underway, General Woods will have further orders concerning their mission as things become clearer at this end. The main thing now is to get them pointed in the general direction of the positions indicated."

After the CNO left the room, Woods spoke, "With your permission, Mr. President, I'd like to fill in Admiral Sullivan on the latest developments with PROJECT MONGOOSE. He looked a little puzzled as he left."

"Certainly, General, I didn't intend for him to work in the dark. Give him the latest details on what has happened, but caution him that it should go no lower at this time."

Then, speaking to the entire group, he continued, "Gentlemen, we've arrived at a point where a decision must be made. We are aware of the pros and cons of implementing PROJECT MONGOOSE, and with time so short, I don't think a debate is in order. However, I would appreciate your opinions before I make the final decision."

While he looked at each man in turn, Tom Whitney replied first, "I say we go ahead with it." Martin was quick to concur.

"I'd say we launch MONGOOSE, Mr. President," Woods added.

The Secretary of State agreed reluctantly.

The President nodded. "Good! I had decided that this was the way to go, but it's heartening to have unanimity in such an unprecedented step. My decision is that we proceed with PROJECT MONGOOSE. Walt, will you and General Woods take care of putting the wheels in motion?"

"With pleasure, Mr. President," Martin answered.

# Chapter 4

*Andrews AFB*

Gates found himself dozing through the final innings of a fairly dull game between the Mets and the Phillies. He had been at Andrews for two days killing time by reading magazines and watching television. The oppressive heat of August still cloaked the Washington area on the first of September, and this didn't make his eyelids any lighter. Sitting there staring blankly at the television, reminded him of being on alert waiting for the scramble horn to blow. Each time a phone rang in the hall or in an adjacent room, it brought him bolt upright in his chair. He had been rooting for the Phillies, but they were falling hopelessly behind when another phone jarred him back to reality.

"Major Gates, this is Captain Daniels at the Command Post. The Office of the Joint Chiefs just called. A chopper will pick you up in front of Base Ops in fifteen minutes. Leave the car keys and the radio with the duty officer—we'll pick them up later."

"Roger, I'm on my way," Gates answered as the first traces of adrenaline peeled away the lethargy of the past couple of days.

When Gates arrived at Base Ops, the Pentagon helicopter was just settling on the VIP helipad out front. He hustled out to the open door of the chopper. The pilot kept the engine running, so after Gates strapped himself in the seat, the bird lifted off and headed west. In less than ten minutes, the craft thumped solidly onto the pad at the west side of the building near the Joint Chiefs' office. As the turbines whined down to a stop, a full colonel ducked under the rotating blades and opened the cabin door.

*The Pentagon*

"Major Gates, I'm Jack Benning from the JCS office. The boss wants us over there right away. Don't worry about your gear; I've got some people here to bring it down."

Gates gave a quick salute before shaking the outstretched hand, and then scrambled out of the helicopter to follow Benning into the maze of hallways. The colonel walked at a brisk clip, which made small talk a little strained. "As usual," thought Gates. After all the waiting since he was first approached about this project, time now seemed to be of the essence. "Typical Air Force—hurry up and wait!" he said to himself as Benning opened a door leading to a small office.

"Grab a chair for a few moments, Major, while I see if the general is tied up."

A few minutes later, Benning poked his head in and motioned for Gates. The surroundings in the adjoining offices became much more elegant as they went in to meet General George Cunningham. Gates was glad his uniform was fresh from the cleaners as he snapped to attention and saluted. Although he figured he was involved in something important, he was surprised at being in the office of the Old Man himself. General Cunningham returned the salute and shook Gates's hand, as Benning introduced them.

"Major Gates, it's a pleasure to meet you. The guys from TAC have been saying a lot of good things about what you're doing down at Langley."

"Thank you, sir. I've had a lot of top-notch help from all the folks there. It's a great outfit."

The general motioned him to a chair, and as he sat down, Gates noticed that Benning had left.

"I suppose you're wondering what PROJECT MONGOOSE is all about. I realize you haven't been exactly overwhelmed with information, but this is an extremely sensitive matter that had to be kept under very tight wraps. The Chairman of the Joint Chiefs wants to brief you personally on MONGOOSE, and we'll be heading down to his office shortly. Right now we're waiting for the other member of the team. He arrived about the same time as you, and Colonel Benning is bringing him up now."

The general noted the slight look of surprise that flashed over Gates's features when he mentioned the additional team member. However, it was encouraging from a security point of view that even the principles didn't know others were involved.

"I don't think I'm stealing any of General Woods's thunder by bringing you up to speed on that aspect of the project. You have been selected as the lead pilot; however, in an operation of this importance, we needed some redundancy to ensure success. Therefore, Major Ken Brock has been chosen as your wingman. He's been at Nellis for the past few years. Ever met him?''

"Yes sir. I've worked with Ken on the ground at tactics conferences, and against him in the air during Red Flag missions."

"Good. Starting with General Woods's remarks, you'll be briefed as a team. Even though we've staffed out all the details pretty well, we'd welcome any suggestions that either of you might have."

There was a courtesy knock at the door, and Colonel Benning came in with Brock, and introduced him to the general.

Cunningham motioned in Gates's direction and said, "I guess you two don't need any introduction."

"No, sir," Brock replied as the two shook hands warmly, "I've known Bill for some time."

Brock was a little shorter than Gates, his dark eyes and black hair reflecting his mother's Southern Italian heritage. His only deference to the fighter pilot's image was a thick mustache carefully trimmed to Air Force specifications. He too was in good shape, but Brock really had to work at it. His fondness for pasta forced him to wage a constant battle against a tendency to develop a gut if his resolve faltered. His happy-go-lucky attitude, good sense of humor, and easy disposition quickly made him "one of the boys" in every new assignment, aided considerably by his being a very tough competitor in the air.

Cunningham rose saying, "We'd better get down to General Woods's office immediately."

Woods was waiting for the MONGOOSE team when they arrived, and Cunningham introduced the two fighter pilots to the Chairman of the Joint Chiefs. Woods was friendly, but very businesslike, as he started his briefing.

"I suppose you are bursting with curiosity as to what you've gotten yourselves into, and for now, I'll just say that the mission is going to be a tough one. You have been selected because of your across-the-board expertise in the tactical air mission. General Cunningham will cover the specific details down in his shop, but I wanted to meet you and to personally give you the background on how PROJECT MONGOOSE came about. There is a considerable amount of risk involved in this mission, but we feel that it has a good chance of success. We also want you to know that the security of the entire nation hinges on its success, and that's why we picked the best in the business. If either of you have any second thoughts about this project I'd like to know now. You'll be excused without prejudice, and no more will be said about it."

Both Gates and Brock replied, "No, sir," almost in unison.

"Good," Woods continued. "I didn't have any doubts, but I still had to ask."

The Chairman of the Joint Chiefs then began unfolding the story of the destruction of the first Star Wars satellite and the efforts to verify the overt action by the trip to White Sands. As he talked, he passed around photographs of Star Wars III and asked them to note the damage. The general didn't give them time to ask questions, but went right on with an explanation of the theories concerning the new Soviet weapon. He continued with the details leading to the firm conclusions that the Soviets did indeed have such a device. The abortive attempts to clarify the issue with the ambassador and the General Secretary were mentioned, as well as the chilling news from BLUE JAY and SANDPIPER that illustrated Soviet intentions. Woods kept going with a description of the information presented by the CIA and the Scientific Advisory Council during the meeting at the White House. He wound up with the news that a second Star Wars satellite had been destroyed, and a summary of the demands made by Moscow on the hot line.

"Gentlemen, we are faced with a very tough problem. We cannot allow our Star Wars satellites to be shot down at will, nor can we acquiesce to their conditions. As I mentioned, we believe there is a way to destroy this weapon, and thus neutralize the overwhelming advantage the Soviets have right now. After considerable discussion with key advisors, the President has decided that a limited preemptive strike is our only way out of this dilemma."

Woods stared intently at their faces to see what impact the words *preemptive strike* would have, but other than a slight arching of the eyebrows, Gates and Brock remained impassive.

Feeling more comfortable with the selection of these pilots, he continued. "We've had some of the best people in the business working on the particulars of this mission. It will not be an easy task. What it boils down to is a pair of aircraft penetrating into the heart of Siberia, and surgically removing the facility where the weapon is located. Your selection was based strictly on experience in the F-24 and expertise in all phases of the fighter pilot's mission. Major Gates will lead and Major Brock will fly wing."

He noticed the trace of disappointment flash across Brock's face at being named wingman, so he tried to soften the understandable blow to this fighter jock's pride. Looking at Brock, he went on, "Like most missions flown by people at your level of experience, there is no absolute leader or absolute wingman. Just.like air-to-air combat, the guy who gets the visual has the lead and makes the bounce. The same procedure will apply here. The one who recognizes a situation that requires action as a flight, will call the shots until it is resolved.

"One other general item. The weapons carried by each aircraft are powerful enough to do the entire job by themselves. The reason two of you are going is to increase the probability of getting the ordnance on target. Therefore, once you cross the Chinese border, if anything should happen to either aircraft, the other will continue to the target alone. I know this decision runs contrary to our current doctrine of mutual support, but on this mission, the target *must* be destroyed.

"I've said my piece, and you two have a lot of information to absorb in a very short time, so it would be best to get started. The tentative mission date is six days away, and between now and then you have considerable ground to cover, literally and figuratively. General Cunningham has been with this project since the beginning, and he can answer your questions in a lot more detail than I can. Good luck and good hunting!"

Gates and Brock were completely dumbfounded over the enormity of what they were involved in, as Cunningham hustled them back to his office. A million questions flashed through their minds, along with some serious doubts that such a mission was even possible, and about whoever could have thought it up. Fly through China *and* the Soviet Union all by themselves with a load of weapons? How could an F-24 make a flight that long? What did he think their air forces would be doing while we sauntered through? We'll be picked up at least a hundred miles from the coast and be sitting ducks for the rest of the trip! How do we get out after hitting the target? Woods didn't mention anything about refueling but it has to occur somewhere. Why won't there be any escorts to help keep the fighters off our backs? Nothing was said about SAM suppression or ECM—are we going in there naked? Suicide Mission! loomed large in each pilot's eyes.

Before closing the door, the general told his secretary to order some sandwiches and coffee since they would be working through the dinner hour.

"Make yourselves comfortable," said Cunningham as he hung up his uniform jacket. "After you've heard what we'll be adding to General Woods's remarks, you will certainly view this whole thing as a staggering task, which it is. There were quite a few times during the planning stages when we were ready to scrub the whole mess. Everything we did seemed to scream at us that we were attempting the impossible. But then things finally started to fall in place, and the numbers began to look better. Our people here, and any other military or civilian agency involved in MONGOOSE are at your disposal, and will work around the clock to make sure this project succeeds.''

He took two envelopes from a safe marked TOP SECRET. ''These packets contain all the mission data we've been able to put together up to this point. Some of it is a little sparse, and a lot is based on nothing more than educated guesses, but it's our best shot and certainly better than playing it by ear. I've got a copy of what you've just been given, and for the next hour or so we'll go over the whole nine yards, and try to answer your questions.'' He paused a moment for them to absorb his words thus far.

''What I'd like to do now is to go over the entire scenario of what's going to take place once you leave here. The first item is your orders, and by design they are fairly general since we don't want to tip our hand until the last moment, if at all. They are signed by General Woods, and give you the highest priority to do whatever is necessary to accomplish the mission. You are authorized direct access to the scrambler network in case you want to talk to us for any reason. If you should have to use these orders to get something accomplished, they also direct all commanders to give you maximum support with no questions asked.

''Once you're through here, the helicopter will take you back to Andrews, where one of the Special Operations jets is standing by to take you to the coast. There are sleeping accommodations on the airplane so you can get some shuteye during the trip, and I'd certainly advise that you take advantage of the sack time. You've got a heavy day tomorrow with a lot of information to absorb, so we want you bright-eyed and bushy-tailed.

''Your destination is the Lockheed plant at Burbank, and more specifically, the famous ''Skunk Works'' that you've undoubtedly heard about. The folks at Lockheed have been working for some time on two highly modified versions of the F-24. Although they were originally intended as test vehicles for some new equipment, they are tailor made for the MONGOOSE project. Externally, they look about the same as the F-24s now in the fleet, but from what they're saying at

Lockheed, they have quite a few advantages over the production models.

"The guys at the Skunk Works will give you a thorough briefing tomorrow on all the particulars of the new equipment installed. But in a nutshell, these birds have new engines that produce greater thrust, yet are more economical on fuel than the current engines. They've finally got a workable version of the Advanced Fighter Technology Integration tied in with the variable camber wing, which should give you some enhanced capability for combat maneuvering. Another gadget they've been tinkering with for a number of years is the Visor-Mounted Sight. The final bugs have been worked out of this system, and you'll get a chance to use it before it's introduced fleetwide. These planes have one big item that make them ideal for this mission. The whiz kids at R & D have come up with something that looks exceptionally promising in the area of a Stealth capability for a fighter.

"This new development is a marked improvement over the technology used for the F-117 back in the mid-80s, in that we haven't sacrificed most of the qualities needed for a multirole tactical fighter. But convincing the Appropriations Committee to o.k. this project took some doing, since the high costs and skepticism that surrounded the B-2 program were all too fresh in their memories at the time."

Cunningham buzzed his secretary, "Betty, call Colonel Dumont and tell him to come up here right away with the MONGOOSE briefing."

Turning back to Gates and Brock, he continued, "These new additions to your aircraft will undoubtedly be a great help on the mission; however, there is one fly in the ointment. The new systems have been checked out in the air on other airplanes and have completed extensive ground checks in the F-24. The one thing we haven't had time to do is to flight-test them in the F-24. The area of primary importance here is the actual cruise-control figures on the new engines. The ground-test data looks great, but until we see how they run in the air, it's nothing but a bunch of theories. To pull this mission off, we needed a fighter with extremely long legs on the deck, and if the preliminary figures are correct, we've got a winner in this modified F-24.

"The mission profile calls for a nap-of-the-earth penetration from the south, into the East Siberian Uplands, and then an egress straight north to the Arctic. Colonel Dumont planned the strike route and will go over it in detail as soon as I'm finished. As you can imagine, this is a tremendous distance to travel at low level, but we are confident that it can be done.

"The three legs of your trip across the Pacific will be run under

mission conditions so that we can get a handle on some actual numbers dealing with fuel consumption, range, and fuel management.
Tuesday night you'll leave Burbank for Hickam, and although the distance to Hawaii isn't that far, it's long enough to get a good checkout
on the fuel transfer systems.

"I know most fighter pilots would rather take a whipping than fly
at night, but we've got our reasons for that, too. These modified F-24s
have a little different external appearance than the standard models in
operational squadrons. The differences aren't too noticeable to a
casual observer, but to the trained eye, these aircraft stick out like a
sore thumb. Also, anything coming out of the Skunk Works is of interest to the opposition, so if they have someone keeping an eye on the
place, we're hoping the darkness will obscure these changes.

"There is another reason for the nighttime departure that has a
more direct bearing on mission success. About five hundred miles off
the west coast, the missile cruiser *Chicago* will be returning from Pearl
Harbor to San Diego, and your flight path should take you right over
her position. Last Thursday, her sailing orders were amended to
include a period of increased radar surveillance, and the maintenance
of logs detailing any unusual surface or air contact. About fifty miles
from her position, you will turn off all navigation lights and lock on to
the *Chicago* with your radar. Note the time at the fifty-mile point, and
keep your speed constant while steering to pass directly over the ship.
The whole idea is to see if she does pick you up on radar, and if so,
how far out. We're pretty sure the Stealth mod will get you very close
to the ship before they get a good paint, and by that time, you'll be
nearly in their clutter area.

"You'll depart Burbank together, but should go through the
ship's radar coverage about ten miles apart, which will give the *Chicago* two cracks at picking you up. We'll ask them to transmit the
radar logs by normal reporting channels soon after you've passed, and
by the time you reach Hickam, we'll have analyzed the report on the
effectiveness of the Stealth mod.

"When you're fifty miles beyond the cruiser, note the time and
get your lights back on. Something else you can try while inbound to
the ship is the visor sight. Granted, the large target should present no
particular problem for the system to acquire and track, but it will give
you a chance to exercise this new gadget and get used to it.

"I mentioned that the trip to your deployment base would be
under mission conditions, but that only applies to altitudes and airspeeds. Unfortunately, this whole affair caught us a little short, and we

don't have enough extended-range drop tanks with the Stealth mod to allow you to jettison them when empty as you will on the actual mission. However, if any fuel problems develop on your trip across the pond, a tanker will be accompanying you all the way to bail you out. We've got reliable range factors, with and without tanks, so we should be able to apply these to the fuel figures you come up with and get a good idea of the difference that actually dropping the tanks will make. Fill in your flight data cards as you go along, and have the Comm center at Hickam send us the information immediately. We'll apply the conversions and have any changes ready before you flight-plan the next leg.

"There will be a team of maintenance specialists, including factory tech reps, waiting for you at Hickam. Ground Control will be instructed to take you to a secluded hangar where this team will be waiting, so follow their directions carefully. After you debrief with maintenance, Colonel Dumont will call me for any new information or instructions. Hit the sack in time to get a full eight hours of rest.

"Your takeoff from Hickam is scheduled for twenty-four hundred hours that night, but I want you at the flight line two hours before that. We'll have the updated fuel and range figures waiting for you, arranged in a line number format, corresponding to the line numbers on the flight planning card—just another precaution to minimize attention to this mission, in case the bad guys are monitoring our Comm net. Check over the new flight planning data and be certain that it all makes sense, just in case something gets screwed up in transmission. If you have any questions give us a call.

"Your call signs for all deployment legs will be CORONET RED One and Two. Here again, we're hoping that, by using call signs normally associated with transpacific ferry missions, your flight won't seem out of the ordinary."

Cunningham's secretary announced that Dumont had arrived, and their sandwiches were ready. "Good," answered the general. "Have Jack come in, and I guess now's as good a time as any to eat." Dumont entered carrying a large rolled map and a thick manila folder. Gates and Brock were introduced to Dumont, although they were not total strangers, having worked together a year ago on a tactics conference.

"The next leg of your trip will be from Hickam to Anderson Air Force Base on Guam. After getting some rest, you'll head up to Kunsan Air Base on the west coast of Korea. Compared to the other two jaunts, the last trip should be a welcome relief, since it's only about seventeen hundred miles. Regardless, this will be another low-level flight to give all systems one last shakedown before the big event. Kun-san is the closest base to Commie territory where we have a good handle on security. It's a long haul between Hickam and Guam, and this leg will be a perfect dry run for the actual mission. Again, you'll be making the trip on the deck—about five hundred feet, and at night.

"If any problems develop, the tanker with Colonel Dumont aboard will be following your route to top you off, should any tank system fail to feed. For problems other than fuel, Midway and Wake Island will be the abort points.

"About an hour into the flight, you'll be approaching a carrier task force from Pearl Harbor, deployed on a scheduled exercise west of Hawaii. Given the variety of ships and their sensitivity to air traffic, we should get an excellent check on the Stealth mod. The Chief of Naval Operations will send a directive to have all aircraft recovered, including helicopters, by your estimated departure time from Hickam. This hold on flying activity will allow you to penetrate their airspace without having to worry about a midair. It will also allow the task force's radar operators to concentrate on outside traffic, since they will be under similar orders as the *Chicago* while you're within their coverage. The same 'lights out' procedures will apply as on the first leg.

"We'll have to file flight plans for all segments of the trip, just to keep everything as normal as possible and minimize questions. Your route on both legs after Hickam is direct, with the exception of a very slight dogleg around the southern end of Japan. We will notify the air traffic control centers you'll deal with that this is a priority mission, so there should be no changes or delays with your clearance.

"File your altitude as 'classified,' but you'll be given a special IFF code to squawk en route. This will be a discrete code not normally monitored by the navy; however, just in case some swabbie is playing around with the interrogators, turn your parrot off as soon as you leave the center's frequency. After you've gone through the task force's coverage area, it's o.k. to turn the IFF back on.

"Undoubtedly, there will be some problems with the traffic control centers because of your altitude. With you on the deck, they will lose radio and IFF contact with you a lot sooner than they will expect to. If they start asking you a bunch of questions, just give them the old 'You're garbled' or 'my receiver's intermittent' routine. We'll have one of our people at each center to field any questions in case anyone gets too curious. The same thing goes when you're approaching Hawaii, Guam, Japan, and Korea.

"Jack Dumont will be contacting you from time to time for fuel status and position reports. This will give us another check on fuel and distance calculations, but more importantly, he will act as a radio relay in case you need to get information to us or the centers.

"Weather is something we'll have to play by ear. Unless you run into low-level turbulence or thunderstorms, you should be able to stay at the programmed altitude for the entire trip. However, if things get too hairy, ease it up to where you're comfortable until the situation improves. Between your radar altimeter and the terrain-following modes of the radar, you shouldn't have any difficulty in maintaining clearance from the ground or any other obstacles. Check out the autopilot before getting down to your en route altitude, to see if there are any glitches in the system.

"Weather on the run into the target will be more of a help than a hindrance, since it will give you something to hide in. The systems on the F-24 are proven entities as far as the nap-of-the-earth flying is concerned, and if the weather turns sour right down to the deck, LANTIRN will be the key to pulling this job off. Therefore, be absolutely sure that this unit checks out perfectly before takeoff. Because of the critical nature of the MONGOOSE mission, a failure of the LANTIRN system will not be cause for an abort. If this occurs, it becomes a case of 'Ya pays yer money, and ya takes yer chance!' You'll have to fly at the minimum en route altitudes for each segment of the trip. Flying that high will increase the risk of being picked up on Soviet radar, so as soon as the cloud cover permits, get back down on the deck.

"One team member at Kunsan will be a weather type from a special detachment that provides weather information to the National Command Authority. These guys have access to data from highly classified satellites and sensors, allowing them to brief on weather behind the Iron and Bamboo Curtains on close to a real-time basis. Just before takeoff, the latest ceiling and visibility reports for each leg of the flight will be loaded into the on-board computer. Then, by using an auxiliary channel on your cockpit CRT display, you can call up the weather information for the leg you're on and the next.

"The target run is a lot more detailed, so Colonel Dumont will give you the particulars. His shop worked out the flight planning data for the entire trip, as well as analyzing where your high-threat areas will be. Do you have any questions on the trip from the States to Kunsan?"

Gates and Brock shook their heads as Dumont uncovered a large map of eastern Asia. Standing out in stark relief to the various features was a black line running from the Yellow Sea, just west of Korea, straight north through Manchuria and eastern Russia to an X in the middle of Siberia, and then to a spot in the Arctic Ocean.

Up 'til now, the details of the mission and the distances involved had impressed both pilots deeply. Not an enjoyable task, but one that could be done. However, seeing a chart with a course line that crossed the interior of what had recently become very hostile territory brought some of the harsher realities of PROJECT MONGOOSE into sharp focus.

Normally, missions against a target such as this would involve a slew of aircraft: lots of bomb carriers, air-to-air birds to handle the enemy fighters, some Iron-Hand types to take out the SAM sites as they came on the air, chaff dispensers to mask the route, and possibly even an AWACS. All of these aircraft were strangely absent as Dumont tried to sell them an odd bill of goods: an on-the-deck penetration of hostile territory, through a maze of defensive radars (and undoubtedly a swarm of interceptors scrambled against them), to a target where an act of war would be committed that could trigger a nuclear exchange.

Even if they did reach the X undetected, which was not a very realistic assessment of the Communist defensive network, once the target was hit, the cat would be out of the bag. Every available fighter would be used to block their egress and, with the knowledge that the interloper had just destroyed their key to world supremacy, the pursuit for a revenge kill would be relentless. How did the brass expect them to defend themselves against such odds, with just the limited number of missiles and the gun carried by the F-24? And even more important, just two against so many?

Cunningham had mentioned a bunch of new innovations that had been put in the mission aircraft, but both Gates and Brock felt that a lot more details on these items would have to be forthcoming to quell their freshly rising doubts. The Soviets would certainly realize that if an enemy aircraft was able to slip by their defenses for so great a distance, it must be something special, and they would spare no effort to get their hands on it, or at least its wreckage.

By this time, both pilots were thinking the same thing: "That Stealth mod better be damned good!"

General Cunningham settled in the leather chair behind his desk, and nodded at Dumont to start his briefing.

"Gentlemen, your target is the high-energy physics research facility located on the Lena River, here at Zhigansk. This line will be your course from Kunsan into the target, and out to a refueling point over the Arctic Ocean.

"Before starting, I'd like to explain why this specific route and direction were chosen. The relative proximity of the target to the northern coastline of Siberia might indicate to you that a strike from that sector would be more feasible. This option was considered, but the time involved in getting a carrier task force into position was much too great to fit the time constraints of this mission. Other reasons were that our carriers do not normally operate in these waters, and the number of ships necessary to support such an operation would undoubtedly tip our hand. Even if the Navy could make it timewise, the pack ice would compel them to operate very close to the shoreline. This would make them a sitting duck for every weapon the Soviets have in that area.

"Another option was to run the mission out of Alaska. However, the chances of being picked up by the Soviet air defense network would be greatly increased, since the flight path would take you between two very sensitive coastlines. Also, there are more fighter bases in this area than along the route shown on the map.

"This option was selected because you'll be flying behind the radar net, once you make the initial penetration just north of the Yellow Sea. Although getting into China will not be an easy job, we feel that their equipment and level of training are not on a par with that of the Soviet Union. In addition, once you're a couple hundred miles inside Manchuria, you will only encounter air traffic control radar, and they won't be looking for targets at extremely low level with no transponder return. We also feel that an attack from this direction would be less expected than one from the Arctic, Alaska, or up through the Sea of Okhotsk.

"There will be no clearance, either normal or tactical, filed for the departure from Kunsan. Our people will be in the tower with authority to give you precedence over everything except an act of God, so you shouldn't have any delays in getting off. You will use navigation lights only until you're over the water, then you'll go totally blacked out. Your IFF will be off for just about the entire mission, unless you have an emergency just after takeoff and you have to recover in Korea. From Kunsan, you'll head northwest for one hundred ninety-six miles to intercept the 124-degree line of longitude. This line represents your actual track to the target, but you may want to ease off to one side or the other now and then to take advantage of the terrain as a shield from their radar. The dogleg after takeoff keeps you over open water, so you can stay as low as possible while going through the North Korean radar coverage. These people are always a little more nervous than anyone else, so they might be watching their scopes a bit more closely.

"You'll cross the Chinese coastline twenty miles west of the mouth of the Yalu River. This is an easily distinguishable landmark that can be seen on your ground map radar. Make sure that your LANTIRN system, radar altimeter, and search and track radar are all working once you turn north. Getting to a point two hundred miles inland will be one of the tougher parts of the entire mission, and the lower you can get, the better your odds are. If cloud cover and visibility permit, you might even go visual and get a little below the LANTIRN minimums. But, do not push it to the point where you'll be scraping the treetops. We didn't have time to analyze every mile of your route for anything less obvious than major power lines and prominent peaks and valleys. We have to assume that items like TV and radio transmission towers will be located along your route, so don't crowd your minimums unless it's absolutely necessary, and keep an eye on your radar.

"During the briefing I'll mention some significant landscape features you may find useful as checkpoints along the way. However, since there won't be any practice runs to see how they look on your radar and LANTIRN, we've come up with the next best thing. Three-dimensional models were constructed from satellite photos of the area. These models were placed on tracks and moved toward a radar set and then a LANTIRN pod to record an approximation of the imagery you should see on the scope and the Heads Up Display as you approach each one. The pictures were then enhanced and sharpened by a computer, which also produced a sequence of graphics representing each of the checkpoints as seen from varying distances.

"These images will be stored in your aircraft computer just before you fire up at Kunsan, along with a program that allows you to view them in real time with respect to your airspeed. Each picture will have your ideal track superimposed on it, and thus act as a reminder of which valley or bend in the river you should be crossing at certain points along your route. This should eliminate any need for referring to the strip map as you go along, and let you concentrate more on flying the airplane.

"Navigation shouldn't be a problem with the Inertial Navigation System and another piece of equipment that the Skunk Works put in just for this mission. This is the Global Positioning System, which uses satellites to perform the same functions as your INS. Either one of them can get you to the target, but on a mission like this we felt a backup system was in order. Each aircraft will have the complete flight profile entered into its computer, which should help if both of these systems fail. However, this backup information will be based on dead reckoning. Therefore, as a hedge against everything turning into a can of worms, update your position in this system as you cross each checkpoint.

"Your track takes you over, or very near, many large cities, and if there's a low deck of clouds above you, the glow from their lights will silhouette your birds against the overcast so try to avoid flying directly over as many as possible. Go around any you can. Some of the cities, particularly Shenyang here and Skovorodino up here, have commercial airports nearby. These facilities mean more radars and more low-level traffic, so give them an especially wide berth.

"Just beyond Shenyang, you will pick up a section of the Great Wall of China on your radar, running southwest to northeast across your track. This section is known as the 'Willow Wall,' and once you're past it, you'll be through the toughest part of the air defense network. From the wall north for about the next four hundred miles, you'll be over the Manchurian Plain, where the countryside is comparatively flat. While this should make the flying less exciting, it will also leave you more exposed to radar, so the name of the game here is to keep 'er down as low as you can.

"About seventy-five miles north of Ch'ich'ihaerh, you're back into more mountainous terrain, as your track roughly parallels the Greater Khingan Range. The tops of these hills are about five thousand to fifty-five hundred feet. Angling in from your right will be another line of hills known as the Lesser Khingan Range, which run about twenty-four hundred to twenty-six hundred feet high. So, as you approach the Soviet border, you'll be flying into the narrow end of a funnel formed by these two ranges, which should provide some good cover from their radar.

"By now, your centerline or wing tanks will have gone dry. Drop the empty tanks immediately to reduce drag; however, make sure you punch them off in a desolate area. We don't want a lot of commotion stirred up because you flatten some farmer's house with a couple of drop tanks. Being so low, you won't be able to see a great distance in front of you to pick the most desirable spot for the tanks. Just head for an area that doesn't have any lights and hope for the best. The same procedure will apply when the other external tanks feed out.

"Even if the Chinese suspect you're in the area, it's almost a sure bet they won't forward your track to the Soviets. They haven't been on the friendliest of terms in this area because of numerous border incidents. And, unless the Stealth mod is a total failure, their tracking information will be minimal at best. Their penchant for not wanting to lose face will undoubtedly keep them from passing on anything that cannot be verified by both sides.

"The border between Manchuria and Russia is formed by the Amur River, which runs in a general east-west direction where you will cross it, and should be a good radar target. About fifty miles north of the Amur, is Skovorodino, whose commercial airport is just north of town. Stay east of track until you are well clear of this area. After the dogleg around Skovorodino, you'll be picking up the Stanovoy Mountains on the scope. They cross your track at roughly a 60-degree angle, and the tops run about seven thousand feet.

"Don't worry about remembering all these numbers," Dumont said in an aside, "they will be in your computer, and will be shown as Maximum Terrain Altitudes for each route segment. As a backup, they'll also be marked on your strip maps." Then he continued tracing the route.

"The Stanovoy Range is quite rugged, with plenty of places to hide from their radar, but conversely, it will result in a bumpy ride if you stay low enough to avoid detection. Things don't improve for the next one hundred sixty miles after crossing the Stanovoys. You'll still be in fairly mountainous terrain until you pass Aldan, beyond which the hills gradually get lower all the way to the target. Aldan is fifty miles east of your track, so don't expect to see much more than a glow from their lights at your altitude. However, they do have a commercial airport, so keep your eyes peeled. A couple of MiG squadrons are based there.

"Your next major checkpoint is the Lena River, which you'll cross near the town of Markha. This is a big river, and you'll be crossing where three other rivers join the Lena, which will give you some good land-water contrasts to check your position. Over the Lena, you will be forty-three minutes from the target, and there would be a good time to get your ECM equipment in Standby. The jammers are an improved and miniaturized version of what we now carry in external pods, and cover the frequency bands of their GCI, SAM, and AI radars, as well as voice communications. But remain in Standby until you know you're being tracked by radar. If the Stealth mod works, we don't think they'll be getting a return large enough to be utilized by SAM or airborne radar guidance systems. The procedure is to keep them guessing as to your exact position until they actually have an eyeball on you, and then hit them with the jammer across all bands.

"Nineteen minutes out from the target, you'll cross the Vilyuy River, which runs east to west in that area. From here on in, the terrain is pretty flat, with some nine hundred-foot hills on your left. When you're sixty miles from the target, you should start picking up the Lena River again, angling in from the right. Your armament system should now be set up for the drop so that your full attention can be devoted to target acquisition and aiming, when it comes into view. Just short of the IP, Brock will close up to a five-mile in-trail position, which should result in a thirty-second separation between bomb releases. This will keep the bombing pattern fairly tight, while providing enough delay for the smoke from number one's bombs to clear the target. Then, number two can make any sighting adjustments required.

"Your route has been timed to put you over the target just after dawn. In this way we maximize the darkness as a cover for the ingress, and still give you the proper light for a visual weapons delivery. This mission will cause quite a stir on the foreign relations scene; therefore, our primary goal will be to restrict the damage to the new building at the research facility. The timing of the attack should ensure that only a small number of people will be at work, and thus keep casualties to a minimum. But—and this is important—if cloud cover or enemy action precludes the pop-up delivery technique, use any mode you can, including LANTIRN.

"We realize that some modes of attack may not give us the surgically precise removal of just the target building, and might result in peripheral damage to other structures. However, target destruction is of paramount importance, and if this is accomplished, we can deal with the political consequences of any overkill. The research facility is northeast of Zhigansk on the west bank of the Lena, three miles from the edge of town, with a single road leading from the main gate toward the city. It's far enough from town so you should have no difficulty picking it out. This group of buildings in the center of the facility is the main research area, and is not, repeat *not*, your target. What we are going after is this one-story, X-shaped structure northeast of the main buildings. This is where the laser weapon and its isotope fuel are located.

"The weapons you'll be carrying are powerful enough to level the entire building, which is exactly what we want. However, we don't know just where the weapon is located in the building. Common sense dictates that it would be in the middle, so for openers, the primary aiming point will be the center of the X.

"Brock, when you roll in for your run, should you notice that lead's bombs have hit the center and one side of the target, shift your aim point just a little toward the other side, to ensure that the whole building is knocked down. If Gates's shacked the target, put your bombs on top of his. Should weather force a LANTIRN delivery all the way, both of you aim for the center of the target.

"A note of caution during the approach from the IP and the identification of the research facility: Ten miles to the south of Zhigansk, is another town of nearly the same size, called Uolba, also on the west bank of the Lena. Make sure you don't confuse the two. The best way to be positive is that Zhigansk has a commercial airport located west of town. As you can see on this photograph, the concrete runways stand out pretty well against the surrounding grassy areas.

"It is highly unlikely that the Soviets would allow any overflights of the research facility by commercial or military aircraft, especially since they've developed this new weapon. Therefore, it's a good bet that you won't be bothered by anyone in the traffic pattern for the airport.

"The next part of the mission adds a wrinkle to the normal weapons delivery procedures you've been accustomed to. After pickling your bombs, modify the pullout to establish a level, 360-degree turn to the left around the target at two thousand feet indicated, with a minimum of 45 degrees of bank. I know this sounds crazy, but unless you're under attack by interceptors or are running into heavy flak, it's got to be done. As General Woods explained, the stability of the isotope fuel can be upset by shock and heat. The blast effect alone will be more than enough to do the job, and whatever fires are generated will help accelerate the reaction. However, the National Command Authority has to be absolutely sure that this isotope has changed to the lower-energy state that makes it useless in the weapon. The decomposition process releases a significant amount of radiation that can be picked up by specially built detectors. This flash of radiation is the only positive indicator we will have that the isotope has been destroyed. This information is critical to our discussions with the Kremlin after the mission is over.

"The three-sixty around the target will allow the detector to record the characteristics of the radiation pulse. It will be mounted on the upper left side of the fuselage, just aft of the leading edge of the wing, which is why the turn must be to the left. The intensity of the radiation pulse diminishes rapidly as it travels outward from the target so, to get data our scientists can analyze, make your turn as tight as you can. The blast and the heat should trigger the breakdown of the isotope almost instantly, but if they have it well protected, it may take a few seconds to develop. Therefore, play the turn to give the detector about a twenty-second look at the target after the bombs go off. Your weapons will be fitted with eight-second delay fuses to give you time to get from the drop point into your orbit. This will be the only variation from their normal high-drag configuration.

"Because of the circle around the target, number two will have to play his roll-in until lead has finished two-thirds of his orbit. When number two calls 'rolling in,' lead will ease off his turn slightly to give number two a clear run at the facility and enable lead to keep a visual on him during the bomb run. Lead will break out of his turn once two has passed, pick up the egress heading, and if circumstances permit, make some mental notes on the damage to the building. After two finishes his twenty-second look at the target, he will break out of the orbit and get in trail with lead on the egress heading.

"Everyone back here, including the President, will be waiting for word on how the mission went. For this reason, the Skunk Works installed a light in the cockpit that is connected to the radiation detector. If the device picks up a level of radiation that indicates the isotope's decomposition, the light will come on, letting you know the mission was a success. After you get within radio range of your tankers, transmit the codeword ROSEBUD if the light came on in either aircraft. If neither of you get a light, then transmit CARNATION. The tankers will relay the code to the National Command Authority immediately, so they will know how to plan their next move.

"By now the Soviets will undoubtedly have reacted. It's a good bet you'll have a fight on your hands during the egress leg, and since it will be daylight, your chances of being spotted are greatly increased." Dumont then mapped out the egress route—including a short dogleg to the northeast, west of the Verkhoyanskiy mountain range—and the dangers it posed.

"After reaching the Laptev Sea, you'll most likely encounter the stiffest opposition from Soviet fighters. They'll have everything with wings looking for you, and without any terrain features for you to hide behind, their radars will get a fairly clean look at you for the first time. The game plan will be to stay low and rely on the Stealth mod to keep the interceptors and their missiles from getting a good lockon. If you're in the barrage mode, GCI sites will find you by triangulating on the jamming signal. So, don't use that feature unless you're in a clear air mass, and the opposition has a visual on you. The same goes for the UHF Comm jammers. Don't give them anything to home in on and get to a point where they can launch an IR missile. The gate stealer and angle deceiver circuits in your ECM gear should prevent a radar lockon until they're almost on top of you. If any of them get a tally ho, he'll undoubtedly be used as a trailer and you'll soon have lots of company in your six. Take advantage of any cloud cover near your altitude to prevent them from getting an eyeball on your flight.

"The general strategy once you hit open water is to keep them confused as to your exact position, while opening the distance between yourselves and their recovery bases. If we can pull this off long enough, they'll hit Bingo Fuel and have to head for home plate. Without any weather to cover your egress, we don't get a break until you hit the permanent ice pack, which should start about three hundred miles off the coast. Should you have fighters trailing you, get down as low as you can over the ice, which will look like rough ground to their radar. Since these MiGs will have been launched from the mainland, they'll really be hurting for fuel by this time and the nearest runway will be at Zemlya Bunge on the New Siberian Islands. This is a civilian field, but the runway is long enough to be used in an emergency.

"The farther you get from the coast, the more desperate the Soviets will become, and given the traditional mindset of their hierarchy, we cannot rule out last-ditch suicide attempts to ram your aircraft. Therefore, keep an eye on each other's six to prevent some kamikaze type from sneaking up on you.

"Your refueling point is at eighty degrees north and one hundred thirty-five degrees east. About a hundred miles from the refueling point, start a cruise climb to thirty-five thousand feet, and give your tanker a call. If enemy fighters pick you up during the climb, you won't have enough fuel to do anything about it. To counter this eventuality, your tankers will be accompanied by eight F-24s with their own tankers and an AWACS to control the whole show. The AWACS will be monitoring your frequency and, when they have you on radar, will broadcast the position of any Soviet fighters and vector you to your tankers. But because of the Stealth mod, you'll have to turn on your parrot about two hundred miles from the rendezvous and squawk a special code assigned.

"The task force will be orbiting in an east-west racetrack pattern, and when you're close to hooking up, they'll start a turn toward Alaska. The fighters will be south of the refueling point by about seventy-five to one hundred miles, ready to engage anyone following you. The tankers earmarked for your flight will have their fin and rudder painted red to avoid confusion. The new engines run on an exotic fuel that will only be carried by the marked aircraft.

"After you get topped off, the rest of the trip into Eielson should be no sweat. A debriefing team will meet you to remove the radiation detectors and get a few brief facts before they take off for Andrews. The remainder of your debriefing will wait until you've had a good night's sleep.

"It seems like I've been talking forever, but we had a lot of ground to cover. It's a lot to swallow in a short time, so if you've got any questions, sing out. All the major points we've gone over are in your mission packets in one form or another."

Both pilots looked a little bewildered as the enormity of the task began to take shape in their minds. General Cunningham could see the doubt on their faces and the wheels turning in their heads now that their mission had been fully explained. Glancing at the clock he realized it was time to get these people on their way to California.

"Gentlemen, what you've heard must sound like a staggering task, and as you fit the pieces together in your head there are bound to be some questions. There are no hidden agendas on this project, and if you need some information, or even think you need it, we'll get the answers if it's humanly possible. Colonel Dumont will accompany you to Kunsan, and should be able to field any questions on the finer details of the flight. We'll be standing by here for anything that needs to be researched further.

"The chopper is waiting down on the pad, and all your gear has been loaded. At Andrews, the Special Operations bird will be ready to leave as soon as you're on board. That airplane is a tanker that's been plushed up with sleeping and eating accommodations, along with extra communications gear.

"You'll be getting into Burbank about three o'clock A.M. their time, so stay in the sack for a few more hours. The steward will get you up at six and will have breakfast ready. Your briefing with the engineers at the Skunk Works is scheduled for eight o'clock. Jack has some STOP pills in case you have trouble sleeping on airplanes, although I think you'll find these accommodations pretty inviting."

General Cunningham got up and shook hands warmly with each

pilot. Then, while exchanging salutes, he remarked, "There have only been a few times in history when the future of a nation hung on the actions of one or two of its champions, and this is certainly one of those situations. I know we've got the right men for the job, and all I can add is that our prayers will be with you all the way. Good luck, and to paraphrase an old Irish blessing: May you have a tailwind all the way!"

## Andrews AFB

There wasn't much conversation on the trip to Andrews, as Gates and Brock stared out the windows, their minds half a world away. A myriad of "what ifs," "maybes," and "how abouts" whirled through their heads, as they sifted and weighed the odds on each phase of the mission. Each had to admit that, based on what they heard thus far, the people working for the Chief of Staff had done their homework. It was a well-thought-out concept, and, with a lot of luck, they just might be able to pull it off. Cunningham's briefing answered a lot of questions they had after first learning of the mission, but then again, it also posed quite a few more.

"Do you really think they've got an F-24 that will go that far unre-fueled?" Gates asked Brock over the roar of the chopper's engine. "I've flown some ferry missions that distance, but we were at altitude and weren't carrying any weapons."

Brock took a more cavalier approach to the problem, even though he too had his doubts. "It does sound a little strange to me, but I'm sure they wouldn't have gone to all the trouble of laying on this mission if some computer type hadn't figured it all out. They'll probably fill in more of the details at Lockheed tomorrow."

"Maybe so, but they make it all seem just a little too pat. Like it's something we do every day. Did you notice that the fighter opposition wasn't emphasized?"

"Yeah! Might be that we'll get an intell briefing before we launch to cover that little oversight. I bet there will be a passel of them, but with all these new gadgets the Old Man told us about, we should be able to handle them."

"What if some of these thingamajigs don't work as advertised?" Gates cautioned. "That quick check with the Navy on the way to Kun-san doesn't sound like the complete answer to me."

"Well, it sure beats no check at all," Brock quipped. "Possibly the Lockheed people have run some tests on this stuff that will help us out. I don't imagine these mods could be all that complicated."

"If the mission timetable is as tight as they say, everything they throw at us tomorrow will have to be a take on the first run-through. Sure hope we get it all."

"No sweat G.I.! We'll hack it!"

\* \* \*

This was indeed the Super Bowl of the fighter business, and Brock reflected on how he had gotten into such a predicament. He had grown up in Trenton, New Jersey, and after watching numerous airshows at nearby McGuire AFB, was hooked on flying fighters. His mother would have preferred law or medical school, but soon realized his interest was in the skies. Always a good student, he had no difficulty at the Academy and easily won a flying school slot. He was in his element with every facet of the tactical air mission, and soon made a name for himself in the tough competition of weapons meets. His first love was the air-to-air game, and when approached about an assignment to the Aggressor Squadron, he jumped at the chance. Flying air combat tactics against different fighters every day was like dying and going to heaven. His success against pilots in Red Flag exercises resulted in an unofficial bounty being placed on his head by every squadron participating. Even with an assignment most fighter jocks only dream of, the lure of PROJECT MONGOOSE was like a siren's song.

\* \* \*

At Andrews, Jack Dumont gave them each a STOP pill after they settled into the transport, and both downed them without comment. Knowing what a heavy day they were facing tomorrow, they realized that some sack time was essential. However, it still took the dose of Seconal to quiet the whirligigs of thoughts about the upcoming mission.

# Chapter 5

*Washington, D.C.*

As he made his way to the White House for a meeting with the President, Roy Butler was still not convinced that they had made the right decision in authorizing PROJECT MONGOOSE. He had to give the boss a "how goes it" briefing on his efforts to blunt the Soviets' demands through diplomatic channels, and his news was not good.

"Well, Roy, what's the latest from Foggy Bottom? Any progress with Dotsenko?"

"No, Mr. President, I'm afraid not. I went over to his office this morning to see if some one-on-one discussion might get them to soften their stand. However, it was a repeat of the other day when he delivered Petrov's message. It's my guess that he must be under very strict orders from Moscow on this one, since there is absolutely no give and take at all. He sounds like he's reading from a script, and cannot ad lib one iota. I've known Anatoliy for quite some time, but in this matter, it's like dealing with a stranger."

"I really didn't expect them to change their tune since they're in such a strong position, and all I can say is to keep trying," the President replied. "Walt Martin was here this morning with an update on the Warsaw Bloc troop movements. Things still don't look good since they're continuing to build up the forward bases. I was hoping against hope that all this might be a feint to get our attention and make us cave in to Petrov's demands quickly. But from the way things look, they aren't going to pull back and will be in position on schedule."

He then broached another topic. "What's this I hear about one of your people at our embassy in Moscow?"

"I was just coming to that. One of our attachés has been accused of spying by the Soviets and has been declared persona non grata. Naturally, all the charges are ridiculous and easily refuted, but with the current state of things, it would be much less trouble to just send him home.

"This type of action has been a standard ploy whenever tensions heat up between the two of us. Perhaps we should counter with a similar move. Lord knows we shouldn't have to try too hard to pin something on one of their KGB agents listed as an 'economic advisor.' "

"That's probably worth pursuing, Roy, but don't let it interfere with your trying to get to Dotsenko."

"No, I'll stay on top of that and have someone else take care of the spy setup. Did you see this morning's summary of *Pravda*?"

"Yes. I imagine you're referring to that major speech Petrov made to the Supreme Soviet, where he blasted us again for deploying Star Wars. For the life of me, I can't figure out how he sells that line about the U.S.S.R. not being able to exist in a world threatened by U.S. domination."

"It's a mystery to me, too. Just before I left the office, Al Yeager called me from the U.N. to mention that the Russians have been making loud and abusive speeches in both the Security Council and the General Assembly that mirror the party line in *Pravda*. Any special instructions for him?"

"No. I don't want him to say anything that might bring MONGOOSE into the picture, so he'll have to concentrate on rebutting their arguments with our usual counters. Something he possibly could use to throw them off balance is an item Walt Martin mentioned. He's been getting reports of Soviet fighters buzzing our civilian and military aircraft and making provocative runs along the NATO borders. Incidents like that ought to give him some ammunition to hammer them for upsetting long-established treaties and arrangements."

"I'll pass that along, but from my point of view, it sure looks like they have the potential for calling all the shots in this mess. Although I hate to admit it, our only chance seems to depend on the success of PROJECT MONGOOSE."

### The Skunk Works

The MONGOOSE team was awakened at 6:00 A.M. Pacific time and after showers and shaves, a breakfast of steak and eggs was waiting in the forward cabin. Seeing the menu, the aircrew smiled to themselves at another aspect of the detailed planning behind this mission. They had already started them on the low-residue high-protein diet that was de rigueur for pilots flying fighters across the pond.

At a quarter to eight, a car was waiting for them, and a few moments later they were producing orders and ID cards for the security guards at the Skunk Works.

Their guides led them down long hallways around the circumference of the hangar, to an office labeled "Flight Operations." Inside they met Frank Ryan and Mark Krause, two Lockheed test pilots who had been working on the improved F-24s. There was an immediate empathy between Gates and Brock and the Lockheed pilots—the same type of affinity that has naturally developed between flyers since the dawn of flight. Warm handshakes and introductions were exchanged, then the Lockheed team got down to business.

Ryan gave them a rundown on how things would proceed during the day. "Before we begin, I want to emphasize that none of these modifications have been flight-tested in these particular airplanes. So we can't tell you positively that these systems will perform as designed in the F-24. Individually, the systems work very well, and our job was to test the integration of these mods with the F-24's airframe and weapons system. Based on what we've seen in the simulators, and the ground checks we've run, everything looks A-O.K.

"My job here at Lockheed centers on the areas of engines and airframes, so I'll handle that portion of the briefing. Mark Krause is our resident expert on weapons systems, so he will cover the items that fall in that area. I figure it will be a lot easier to do all this down in the hangar, where you can see and touch the things we're talking about.

"Tomorrow morning we'll have the latest projections on fuel consumption, power settings, and range profiles for all altitudes. Short of actually flying the mission, we feel that this data is the latest and most accurate on this particular engine installation."

Going down to the hangar, Gates felt they were entering hallowed ground. There, some of the most imaginative concepts in military aviation were brought into being under the guiding genius of Kelly Johnson—the F-80 Shooting Star, the F-104 Starfighter, the U-2, and the SR-71 Blackbird. During the mid- and late eighties, this group had also played a major role in the development of the Advanced Tactical Fighter, which eventually resulted in the F-24. The new airplane was still in limited operation when work was started in Burbank to incorporate emerging technologies that were not finalized when the F-24 design was frozen for production.

One final security check, and they were admitted to the main hangar. This was the sanctum sanctorum, where so many of the country's ultrasecret projects went through final assembly and were readied for their quantum leap into the record books of flight. An F-24 sat in each half of the hangar, surrounded by test equipment of every description and what seemed like miles of electrical wiring and cables. The aircraft were unmistakenly F-24s, yet a closer look cast doubt on this first impression. The sharper angles and harsher lines of the original model were softened by subtle nuances that were discernible, yet not obvious, to someone familiar with the aircraft. The birds looked right, but the summation of many small differences added an unfamiliar dimension to the overall picture.

Ryan noticed Gates looking at the airplane quizzically, and understood his expression. "She does look a little different than the stock model, but then again not really, and I'll tell you why in a minute."

Turning to his partner, he said, "Mark, why don't you and Ken go through the weapons system on this one, and Bill and I will cover the airframe general on the other?"

Krause replied, "Sounds o.k. to me," as he motioned Brock up the ladder to the cockpit, while Ryan and his charge started across the hangar.

"The reason these planes don't look *exactly* like your standard F-24 is the blending concept that is part of the Stealth modification. Wherever possible, the hard angles and flatplate areas have been redesigned to lessen the radar reflectivity of the total airframe. Small sections of sheet metal have been replaced by pieces formed with a slight curvature in those areas where our analysis indicated a strong radar return. This technique does not reduce the total reflective area of the airplane by a large amount, but every little bit helps.

"One of the major areas where this method was utilized was in the engine intake ducts. The energy bounced back from the compressor is so strong and so distinctive that radar analyzers can be programmed to compare this signal with that of known engines stored in its memory bank. Thus, they will not only be able to pick you up on their radar, but will also know the type of aircraft you're flying. To keep this information from the enemy, the walls of the ducts have been altered slightly to incorporate subtle curves. These act as reflecting surfaces for the incoming radar beam, forcing it to hit the compressor face at a very specific angle and causing a phenomenon called *total internal reflection*. What happens is that the reflected beam is bounced back and forth between the walls at such angles that it never escapes out the front of the duct. Eventually, the energy of the beam dissipates to a point where it is too weak to be picked up by the opposing radar, even if it did escape from the duct. Thus, the radar beam has been effectively 'swallowed' by the engine inlet, resulting in a quantum gain toward the Stealth concept.

"While all this is good, a fighter still presents a large amount of flatplate area to enemy radars. The problem was to make this appear as a very weak target, or no target at all. A solution that has looked extremely good when tested on other planes is a thin plastic film embedded with carbon fibers and bonded to the skin of the airplane. These tiny fibers are cut to a very precise length that is a function of the wavelength of Soviet radars. They look and function like those used in chaff bundles. The big difference is that, while the fibers used for chaff are cut in lengths to maximize the radar return, those used for the Stealth covering are cut to minimize reflected energy. The result is the virtual absorption of a large portion of the radar energy hitting the Stealth covering. To date, we have not been successful in achieving a total disappearing act for the aircraft we've tried it on. Nevertheless, the stuff is so good that what reflected beam there is has been weakened and diffused to where it appears as clutter or noise on the enemy scope, if it shows up at all.

"Like any other system designed to fool radar, its effectiveness breaks down if the opposing radar is very close. During some tests, we did find a way to beat the Stealth system. If we got an eyeball on the target and could get behind him, we would drive in with a slight angle off from the stern and always got a lockon outside minimum launch parameters for the missiles. A few missions were flown using radar systems that had been modified to perform like those in Soviet fighters, and the results were the same. With no visual, or if the target was in the weather, we had no luck at all at the ranges encountered in the usual GCI setups. Even the beam approach with a stern conversion resulted in no contacts until the very final stages of the intercept, with us dead astern and speeds synchronized.

"Along with the film, we have made extensive use of deep-sectioned radar absorptive material in all leading and trailing edges. These are small sections of nonreflective material with a V-shaped notch built into each, so that the open end of the V faces outward. The sides of the V are stepped in such a manner that radar waves entering the V are reflected back and forth between the sides, and in essence, captured.

"Another problem we've had in trying to make an aircraft stealthy has been the cockpit area. There is no way of eliminating the sharp angles and flat surfaces there without adversely affecting pilot safety and access to controls. What we've done is to coat the Plexiglas with a thin film of indium-tin oxide, which allows ninety percent of the light to pass through, but effectively bars radar waves.

"The next modification will show you just how important incremental reductions in reflected energy can be. We know that the muzzle of the Gatling gun is another significant offender in this area. Therefore, the gun port now has a sliding cover that is blended in with the 'softened' outlines of the airframe. When you select GUNS on the armament panel, it pops back out of the way until you run out of ammunition or select another type of weapon.

"In summary, the Stealth mod has proven very effective in reducing detection ranges in a SAM environment to inside the minimum-launch range of the missile. The same holds true in the air-to-air business, but only for long-range armament such as our AMRAAM.

"So far we've only talked about denying target information obtained by radar. We've had indications that the Soviets are worried about this Stealth concept, since they've been unable to figure out a way to counter it. To fill this gap in their defenses, they have intensified their deployment of infrared detection and tracking systems. Up 'til now, we haven't been too successful in masking the hot sections of a jet engine and the exhaust plume behind the aircraft. Let's go around to the tail section, so I can explain another mod that shows great promise in this area."

As they walked to the rear of the aircraft, he continued. "One of the most un-F-24-like things about these airplanes is the rectangular tailpipes, with the bulges at the rear. These additions are a movable nozzle for the STOL system that I'll get into later. But, if you'll look up the tailpipe, you'll notice that the turbine section is noticeably farther away than what you've been accustomed to. These nozzles are longer than the aft section of conventional jet engines, which effectively puts the hot section 'deeper in the hole,' and consequently harder to see by opposing IR trackers. The combination of the extended tailpipe and the smaller cross-sectional area at the rear results in a much narrower cone of IR visibility. We've run ground checks on this setup and found that you have to be just about dead astern of the target to get a good IR lockon. Spotlighting was very difficult at angles off much more than ten or fifteen degrees, and if you did get a lockon, steering information was fairly erratic. The virtual lack of a good IR signature because of this modification is another major contribution toward Stealth operations.

"Notice that there are flush-mounted lights along both sides of the fuselage, and on the top and bottom surfaces of the wings. These contain high-intensity lamps that bathe the entire airplane in a tinted light. When these are used to illuminate the standard white/light gray/dark gray camouflage scheme, it creates an effect of blending the colors of the aircraft with the color of a bright sky or a cloud deck. While no panacea, this blending effect—we call it the Chameleon System— will work against someone scanning large areas of the sky quickly, but not focusing on any one segment. The lights on the top produce a whiter shade of light than those on the bottom. The selection of light sets is made from the cockpit, but just for the on-off function. The intensity of all lights is controlled by sensors that vary the brightness automatically according to the available sunlight."

He spread his hands and said, "That's it for the Stealth mod," then continued. "I mentioned the STOL capability as we were discussing the engine nozzles, and I might as well elaborate on that right now. If the airplane flies anything like the simulator, this mod will really surprise you on how well it works. Steeper, slower approaches, at higher power settings, can be accomplished very easily. All you do is select the Land Mode on the control panel and sight over the nose at the spot where you want to touch down. Rate of descent is more a function of throttle than anything else—pretty much like an exaggerated carrier landing. One of the additional goodies we got with this mod is a full thrust-reversing capability on landing. The throttle quadrant has extended slots below the idle stop for each power lever. Small T-shaped safety locks beneath the handgrips must be lifted to allow the throttles to enter this range. As each throttle passes the idle stop, it trips a microswitch that opens the thrust deflectors on each engine nozzle. Further movement of the throttles increases engine power in the thrust reversing mode, resulting in additional braking action. This, coupled with your standard antiskid wheel brake system, shortens landing rolls considerably, and is particularly effective on wet or icy runways.

"The most important item in this package really adds a new dimension to the air-to-air game. Not only does this nozzle have the capability of deflecting exhaust gases downward for STOL operations, but it also can deflect them upward for a vectored thrust augmentation in turns. The added turning rate generated by this vectored thrust can provide that last bit of advantage that can make the difference in a hard maneuvering fight. Early tests on the thrust vectoring nozzle indicated that the system was too sensitive and reacted too quickly.

We've put a limiter switch in the system to keep it from operating unless there were at least three G's on the aircraft. They also slowed down the reaction rate of the actuators, and the system works as smooth as glass now, with no tendency to bring on the JC Maneuver.

"All nozzle systems have a fail-safe feature built in. Should any component malfunction, high-pressure air will automatically lock the nozzle in the straight aft position with the reversing doors closed. The only time this could produce a touchy situation is on a STOL approach, where it might require some fancy stick and rudder work to transition to normal flight.

"The venetian blind arrangement on the end of the tailpipe has two functions. First is the thrust vectoring capability I've just talked about. The other is that these vanes are also a part of the Stealth modification, in that they help suppress radar reflections from the turbines. The horizontal slats are made of a radar-absorbent material known as *reinforced carbon-carbon*. Basically, it's carbon fibers in a special matrix baked at very high temperatures until the mixture carbonizes. The finished product can be worked almost like metal, and from the tests run so far, it really reduces the radar return in the stern area.

"You'll have the normal internal fuel load on the F-24, plus the regular conformal tanks mounted along the engine ducts. The centerline tank and the external wing tanks are a little different than those used throughout the fleet. These are considerably longer for streamlining purposes, and hold more fuel. All operating procedures are the same.

"The engines in these birds are quite different than the standard PW-5000s used in the F-24. These particular engines, plus a couple of spares, are examples of a technology that matured too late to be used in operational units. The metallurgists at Pratt & Whitney developed a process in which molecular composites could be used in selected parts of the engine, where temperatures become critical. They utilized this new technique to make combustion chamber liners and turbine blades that allow the engine to be operated at 2,000 degrees Fahrenheit. This is about 200 degrees hotter than the standard engine, which translates into more thrust. New fuel nozzles were installed to produce a flame pattern that burned hotter, in order to take advantage of the increased EGT limits. Since we're getting more push from an engine with the same weight, better fuel economy at cruise settings is a bonus.

"As these modified engines were being developed, it became apparent that a new fuel would be needed to enable them to reach their maximum potential. The old JP-4 just couldn't produce the temperatures required, without upping the fuel flow to the point where range and endurance suffered. What they settled on is a slightly altered version of JP-7. This was the stuff used back in the '70s and '80s for the SR-71 Blackbird, which had a boron derivative as an additive. A hotter burning temperature resulted, plus a few other features that made it ideal for the Blackbird's mission. We've changed the mixture around a little, and came up with something that is perfectly suited for these new engines.

"The combination of the modified engines and the slightly modified fuel resulted in some impressive performance figures. Test data indicates that you should be able to cruise at low level, holding normal tactical airspeeds, at fuel flow figures that are just a little higher than those you previously saw at altitude. Take the airplane up to 40,000 feet, and the fuel flow looks like you're in idle. We've had to rework the Digital Electronic Engine Control to take into account all these new operating parameters, but as far as the throttle end of the system is concerned, everything works the same.

"The operation of the variable camber wing hasn't been changed—everything is fully automatic in response to control inputs. The big news is that we've finally coupled it to the canards and have come up with an integrated system that offers some outstanding advantages. This mod has finally raised the canards to a full-fledged member of the flight control system. Until now, they've only been used as trimmers for the stability augmentation system. The new integrated package brings them into play as major control surfaces in every maneuver the airplane performs. During normal flying, including acrobatics, the canards require no special actions by the pilot, since their movements are controlled by the flight control signal processing unit, and they work with your elevons and rudder. However, in a hostile environment, an option is available that allows you to fly in ways that were never possible before, except on research planes like the AFTI/F-16.

"By selecting Combat on the flight control panel you not only have access to a vectored thrust capability, but that switch also activates the Decoupled mode in the flight control system, and this lets you do some pretty fancy maneuvering, all made possible by the canards. The first is called *lateral translation*, which means you can move the airplane sideways while the nose still points directly forward, and no rolling motion is introduced. This mod is great for moving in and out of formation, or easing the pipper to one side or the other during a dive bombing run. This movement is controlled by the rudder pedals, but be sure to feel this system out initially because it can generate up to thirty knots of lateral velocity. It is also possible to point the nose either right or left while maintaining your direction of flight. This is like a yaw, except there is no change of heading. Pointing to either side is also accomplished with the rudders, but to stay on the same flight path, you must depress and hold a new button on the stick grip. These same two functions are available in the vertical plane, and the pointing action is achieved by fore and aft stick movements, plus the Point button on the stick.

"Vertical translation brings into play another control that will probably take a little getting used to. The throttle linkage inside the quadrant incorporates a pressure transducer that reacts to a twisting motion applied to the top of either throttle. This moves the aircraft up or down without raising or lowering its nose. I'm sure you can appreciate how handy the vertical pointing or translation capability would be in a hard turning fight, when you're inside missile launch range but just can't pull enough lead to let them see the target.

"The control actions needed to perform these moves nearly always result in the surfaces working against each other, in sort of a cross control situation. The net effect is increased drag, so expect a slight loss of airspeed when you're maneuvering in the Decoupled mode."

"What about the effect of the Decoupled mode on weapons trajectory?" Gates asked.

"The old adage still applies—don't release in a skid, or when using this system during a translation. It takes a little getting used to, but the important thing to remember if you need to nudge the pipper a tad is to first make your move, then release the flight control system back to normal, and *then* hit the pickle button.

"I've saved the most unique feature of this system until last, and if you ever get in a combat situation with these birds, I think you'll find it a real life saver if the bad guys get lucky. As an example, let's say you're in a hassle, and you catch a good burst in the tail area that tears up the rudder pretty bad and blows off an elevon or jams it in a deflected position. Normally, the emergency procedure for battle damage of this nature would be a nylon letdown. However, when the flight control computer senses this condition, it immediately repositions all the remaining control surfaces to compensate for the effect of the damage. This will happen before you recover from the shock of being hit, and once the computer has things under control, it also analyzes what the airplane is capable of, with the banged up tail. The computer then flashes a battle damage report on your status screen, showing you the damaged system, and enumerating the general maneuvers that the airplane cannot perform. These will be in terms of maximum bank angles, maximum G's, and so forth.

"There are limits as to how much the canards, variable wing, and the other control surfaces can compensate after one of them is shot out. If you take a bad hit, the available control surfaces may be maxed out, and still not give you a really controllable aircraft. But if they can hold things together even for a short while, it will allow you a little decision time to come up with some better answers as to what you should do next.

"That just about wraps up my spiel, and it looks like Mark is finished with Ken, so I guess it's time to swap places."

## The Pentagon

The budget meeting General Woods was chairing was beginning to bog down in repetitious arguments. A heated debate between service representatives was suddenly interrupted by the insistent ringing of the scrambler phone on the table behind Woods's chair. Spinning around, he answered it somewhat abruptly. It was George Cunningham and he sounded quite agitated.

"General, I've got to see you at once. We might have some big trouble with MONGOOSE!"

"OK, George, meet me in my office in five minutes."

The Chairman arrived just before Cunningham, who rushed in followed by a slightly bewildered Tech Sergeant who was a little flustered at suddenly being in such high-level company.

"General, this is Sergeant Gazzola, who works down in the situation room."

Gazzola saluted quickly and then sat down in the chair indicated by Woods. "General Woods, last night I was in a tavern I go to occasionally, and was sitting at the end of the bar next to a line of booths that have high dividers between them. I hadn't been there fifteen minutes when Sergeant Dunaway came in with a guy I didn't know. Dunaway is a brand new man in the situation room who works the shift following mine. Since I didn't really know him and the two were engrossed in conversation, I thought it best not to say anything as they passed and sat down in the booth behind me.

"I normally don't eavesdrop on conversations, but the place was quiet and they were as close to me as you are. I overheard Dunaway telling the other guy that he had some valuable information for sale that would be of vital interest to the other guy's country. The guy asked how much the sale would involve, and I heard Dunaway telling him that he was sticking his neck out a mile, and wanted a million dollars in cash. The other guy laughed and said an amount that high would only be paid for information from the uppermost levels, and from someone with established credentials. Dunaway told him that what he has to offer is of vital importance and concerns something very critical that will happen around the first of the month. The guy said that he'll have to discuss it with his superiors, and told Dunaway to call the number on a card he gave him, at exactly five forty-five this afternoon. Dunaway said that was a good time since he gets off work at five. Then they both left without bothering to finish their drinks.

"I thought about it all night. I mean, I could hardly believe what I thought I was hearing. And then to be sure, I checked Dunaway's picture in our files, and it's the same person. General, we've been setting things up for PROJECT MONGOOSE in the situation room and were briefed that this was a very sensitive item. After hearing that conversation in the bar last night and checking the picture this morning, I felt that someone higher up ought to know."

"Sergeant Gazzola, I can't tell you how much we appreciate this. You have certainly done the right thing, and have helped out in an area of the utmost importance," Woods replied, then turned to Cunningham.

"George, arrange to have Sergeant Gazzola on some other assignment than the situation room for a while, just on the off chance that Dunaway might recognize him. Talk to Dunaway's crew chief and have him keep a very close eye on him for the next few days, and don't let him near any classified information. Maybe some orientation work around the building in general might be better than the situation room. But we don't want to let on that he's under suspicion, since that may cause him to panic and blow the whole thing by defecting or something. Then talk to the security section and have them provide a plainclothes Air Policeman to trail this guy until the CIA or FBI takes over. I'm going to call John Egbert now and let him know what happened. I'm sure he'll want one of his people keeping Dunaway under surveillance."

* * *

The CIA chief immediately had one of his top agents on his way to the Pentagon. After looking over Dunaway's personnel file, the agent drove out to where the security man was keeping an eye on Dunaway's apartment.

Dunaway had made only one stop on his way home from work, he was told. He had made a short call from a phone booth in a gas station, jotted something on a note pad, then went straight to his apartment, and had been inside since. Egbert's man settled down in his car for what would be a long evening until his relief arrived. It would be another hour or so before his partner could check in, so he had the security man watch the rear of the apartment complex until that time.

This was still a marginal operation since it would be at least 10:00 P.M. before all the required legal paperwork could be obtained for a wire tap. Even though the CIA had reacted quickly, he realized that if Dunaway had any information to pass to the Soviets, he'd have plenty of opportunities before all players were in position. In the meantime, his orders were to keep Dunaway under constant surveillance, photograph anyone who contacted him if possible, and make his report directly to Egbert at the end of his shift.

All that day and through the night, the CIA in conjunction with the FBI and the Pentagon were delving into every scrap of information they could dig up on Dunaway's past. However, neither his personnel file nor the top secret background check required for working in the situation room yielded any insight on why Dunaway's life had taken such a radical turn.

The next morning while his crew chief was giving him an orientation of the building, Dunaway kept complaining of feeling ill and finally asked his supervisor for the afternoon off. Dunaway went directly to his apartment and stayed there, making the CIA tail wonder if perhaps he were sick after all. However, John Egbert wanted to be sure. He had one of his men, dressed as a gas company repair man, knocking on the subject's door within an hour of Dunaway's return.

Dunaway answered the door quickly, fully dressed. The agent flashed his repairman's credentials and gave Dunaway a story about numerous complaints of gas leaks in the building. He asked Dunaway to sign a form stating that his appliances were troublefree. While Dunaway was signing the form on the clipboard, the agent glanced into the room and noted that the sergeant had been busy at a typewriter. The kitchen table was littered with typed and handwritten papers, and an open briefcase containing more of the same was on the floor next to his chair. After handing back the clipboard, Dunaway slammed the door, and the sound of typing started almost immediately.

Acting on this report, Egbert doubled the surveillance in and around the row of buildings containing Dunaway's flat. He knew that things had to happen soon if the information was to do the Soviets any good, and he dare not allow Dunaway to elude him and make contact with the Soviets without his people being on the scene.

### The Skunk Works

As Gates walked across the hangar, his mind was whirling in its attempt to absorb all this new information, and just how it would fit into the mission at hand. The realities of what they were facing made anything other than the "worst-case scenario" seem like a waste of time to consider. He felt sure his life would depend on just how well all these new mods worked and how effectively he could employ them when the chips were down. Passing Brock midway between the airplanes, he noticed that his wingman seemed deep in thought—no doubt pondering the same unknowns that were flooding his own mind about the next few days.

Mark Krause was waiting at the foot of the ladder to the cockpit, and said, "Climb on in and get comfortable—I'll do my talking from the outside."

Gates acknowledged the remark with a smile and mentally wiped the slate clean to ready it for another deluge of information, no less critical than the last to the success of PROJECT MONGOOSE.

Krause noticed his detached manner, and tried to ease his concerns by remarking, "The stuff Frank covered in his briefing is a little overwhelming when you have to swallow it in one gulp, but I'm sure once you get these planes in the air, all the pieces will fall into place quickly. There aren't too many different things here in the cockpit. But, there are a couple of new or modified switch panels to operate the systems Frank talked about." Gates listened intently as Krause pointed out the various controls available to the pilot.

Although the number of new developments was impressive, Krause still had more to show. "The really big news, as far as the weapons system goes, is that we finally have a Heads Up Display that depicts the complete tactical situation in front of the aircraft. The usual information such as heading, airspeed, climb and bank angles, G loading, altitude, and weapons aiming references are still available in the attack mode. Targeting data from the LANTIRN system is also presented as before. The improvement that will really water your eyes is the Pictorial Format, which is part of the Navigation mode. This is a radical step forward in presenting large amounts of tactical information to the pilot in a very condensed form. Multiple sensors in the wingtips and fuselage pick up friendly and hostile electromagnetic radiations from three hundred and sixty degrees around the aircraft. This 'passive' data is sent to a Central Processing Unit, where it interfaces with similar information from 'active' sources such as the radar, LANTIRN, forward-looking infrared system, and the Identification Friend from Foe unit. The CPU continuously analyzes these inputs and compares them with information stored in its memory bank. It looks at information from either navigation system to see what the intended track should be. All this data is synthesized and projected onto the wide-angle HUD in what is known as the Pictorial Format, with the added feature of it being in 3D. This latter goodie is made possible by the holographic projection system in the HUD.

"What you see on the combining glass is a full color picture of what you could, or should, see in the hemisphere in front of the airplane. Colors are as they would be, with the earth shown in brown and the sky in blue. Physical features such as cities, rivers, mountains, airfields, and so forth are depicted by a gray shading. The horizon line raises, lowers, or tilts in response to aircraft dives, climbs, and banks. A black silhouette of your aircraft is in the lower center of the picture, with a green ribbon extending from its nose to show the projected flight path across the ground."

Gates's look of surprise at these high-tech developments did not go unnoticed by Krause. He couldn't resist a touch of the dramatic, so to emphasize his point, he pushed the Nav button on the HUD pedestal. A light flickered once across the combining glass, and then just as advertised, the Pictorial Format appeared, looking like a watercolor painted in multicolored light.

"This is the level of intensity you'd use at night, but the image can be changed by the brightness and color knobs on the side of the pedestal." To illustrate, he turned the controls up, and the picture glowed in vibrant hues that would be discernible in even the strongest sunlight.

"Pretty neat stuff, huh?" he commented in response to Gates's wide-eyed reaction to this new system. "But you ain't seen nothin' yet! You're watching a demonstration tape, but all it does is feed in data that would normally be coming from the active and passive sensing systems. The images are all generated by the on-board computer. The picture now only shows the geographic features, your plane, and its flight path. But tactical missions are usually flown in pairs, and let's say you're flying wing on this sortie. Your leader would be off to one side and a little ahead of your position; therefore, he should also be pictured in the display."

Krause signaled a technician who threw a switch in response. "And there he is, off to your left and displayed as a green silhouette, showing his position in space relative to your airplane. Note that the silhouette of his fighter is smaller than the one representing yours, which gives perspective to the display. If you moved up on his wing or fell farther back, the green image would increase or decrease in size accordingly. Also, if you change sides, or go high or low with respect to the leader, his silhouette will move to show your position in relation to him. Any other friendlies in the area would be shown in the same manner—green images located on the display where you would expect to see them visually.

"Since the F-24 will operate in a combat environment, the system can also show enemy threats, both from other aircraft and SAM sites. If it can be picked up by your radar or is transmitting some form of electromagnetic radiation, the Pictorial Format will display it."

Krause signaled the technician again, and new colored symbols appeared on the HUD. "These small silhouettes represent enemy fighters, again depicted in an appropriate size to give the illusion of distance, and will move as do the actual targets. They are also shown at the correct azimuth and elevation from the black symbol representing your aircraft. Notice that the one with the greatest angle off is colored yellow, while the one more directly in front of your flight path is shown in red. This is the way the system shows the level of danger to your airplane. The computer has analyzed the position, speed, and direction of the one off to the side, and after comparing these values with the same for your bird, has determined that he is not a threat at this time, but should be regarded with caution. Hence the yellow color. If the geometry of the problem changes, his status could be upgraded to one of potential danger. The same analysis was performed on this other target in front of your flight path, and since he is in a position to attack, he represents the greater threat and is colored red.

"The same color scheme is used to show threats from SAM sites, and these are depicted as domes over the launch complex. The width and height of these domes are scaled to represent the effective range of the radars at the site. If the green ribbon showing your flight path does not touch a dome, the latter will be shown in yellow—again denoting caution. If your track does intersect a SAM dome, the Pictorial Format will show it in red. Should you be in a highly defended area with SAM sites all over the place, it may not be possible to reach your objective without flying through some red domes.

"Let's also assume that your ECM gear is a little under the weather, and the SAM radar operators can work through the jamming and lock on to your plane. The higher PRF needed for a lockon will be detected by your sensors, and the dome around that site will start flashing. They will switch to a still higher PRF for missile guidance, just before the SAM is fired. The fact that you have been selected as the target will be shown by the red symbol flashing more rapidly. When the SAM is on its way, a red flashing strobe will appear on the display. One end of the strobe will be on the silhouette representing your airplane, and it will be angled to the edge of the combining glass to show the relative bearing of the SAM. The idea is the same as the old RHAW scopes—to give you a direction to turn to put the missile off your wingtip for evasive action.

"An added wrinkle of these F-24s is a set of IR sensors linked to the radar detectors around the airplane. These act as a backup system, designed to pick up SAM exhaust plumes and provide a warning strobe on the HUD. It works pretty well on SAMs, but we haven't had enough time to evaluate its ability to detect the smaller exhaust trails of air-to-air missiles. In a hassle, I wouldn't count on it to give you the same kind of warning as the radar sensors."

Gates interrupted him. "This looks like great stuff for things happening out in front of the aircraft, but most of the time the guy that nails you is the one who sneaks into your six without anyone getting an eyeball on him. Does the system have any capability of showing a threat in the rear hemisphere?"

"Was just about to get to that," Krause replied. "Aircraft behind your beam within thirty miles, either friendly or hostile, that illuminate you with their radar will be shown on the HUD. These symbols will appear at the very edge of the display, at a position that is relative to their angle off your tail. Unknowns will be in yellow unless the sensors pick up something that indicates an immediate danger, such as a stepped-up PRF or a very high closing rate. Should a radar missile be fired at you from the stern area, a red flashing arrow will appear at the edge of the display pointing toward your aircraft. Friendly birds behind you will also be shown. But, by a combination of known radar frequencies and the IFF, their silhouettes will be green.

"Just about all the rearward warning system is triggered by radar of one type or another being picked up by the sensors. So, a bad guy could sneak up behind you with his radar in standby and launch an IR missile. Therefore, the old lookout doctrine and mutual support are still important. However, if he presses in for a gun attack using his ranging radar, the system will pick him up. In this case he would appear as a red silhouette with a dashed arrow pointing at your plane.

"I know Frank Ryan is enthusiastic about the Stealth mod, and it does work quite well. However, it's not perfect, and a GCI site with a peaked-up radar should be able to pick you up at about ten miles. An airborne radar would have to get in to about five miles, since they don't have the power output of a ground installation. For this reason, it's helpful to know where the GCI sites are located. If your sensors pick up a radar in this bandwidth for about a minute, the computer can triangulate a position on the site. When it does, a yellow X will appear on the Pictorial Format, so you'll know where to fly to stay outside the ten-mile radius. If the signal is lost for a minute, the symbol will disappear, which helps in nap-of-the-earth flying to let you know when you're below their coverage."

Krause then went down the ladder to get something from under the airplane. As he climbed back up to the cockpit, he had what looked like a regular jet helmet. Gates noticed that this model seemed a little thicker over the forehead than the standard issue helmet, and the cord for the electrical connections was a bit heavier.

"This is something we've needed for a long time, and I'm sure you can appreciate its advantages in a hassle. This helmet has been modified to incorporate the Visor Mounted Sight, which is located beneath the visor housing. Just inside the hard shell of the helmet is a small fiberoptic projector, mounted a little above your right eyebrow. When the visor is down, this unit projects half-inch cross hairs on the surface of the visor, just in front of the pilot's eye.

"This device really comes into its own in a hard turning fight while you are maneuvering to get in someone's stern quarter for an IR missile attack. If your target is really laying on the G's and you can't get your bird cranked around where your Sidewinders can get a look at him, you'd normally have to keep maneuvering for a shot. But with this sight, all you do is turn your head until the cross hairs are on the target and hit the acquisition switch on the radar control handle. The computer now knows the relative bearing in azimuth and elevation, and slews the radar and missile antennas around to look in that direction. Once the missiles see the target, you'll get the usual growl in your headset and if you're inside launch range, you can fire. Updated missiles with the movable IR heads also have the capability of guiding earlier in their flight than the usual Sidewinders. This permits steering out the large initial correction that will be needed, before settling down to terminal guidance."

Gates interrupted him again. "Will this system work the same if I'm only loaded with radar missiles?"

"Just about. The only difference when you're firing launch-and-leave or beam riders is that you must have a radar lockon to supply the missile with launch parameters. This system has another feature to make it easier to get a lockon while in a turning fight. Again, put the cross hairs on the target and hit the acquisition switch to get the antennas looking at the target. But this wouldn't result in a lockon, since the range gate has to be placed over the target return on the radar scope. This normally means taking your eyes off the target and looking at the scope to achieve the lockon. Not so with this mod. If you depress and hold the acquisition switch, you not only get antenna slaving, but now a range gate will automatically keep running out to three miles and back again along your radar beam. The gate will lock on to any target it encounters, just like the ranging radar used with the gun. You'll know the system has locked on when the cross hairs start to flash. After a few practice runs for each type of missile, I'm sure you'll find that it's a lot easier than the older method, particularly with radar missiles.

"One final thing about the radar is a new gadget that is really part of the Stealth concept. When you lock on to a target now, the power output of the radar is automatically reduced to the minimum needed to track the target. As your range decreases, so does the transmitted power, which will make it a lot tougher for their radars to home in on your signal."

He finished by saying, "That's all I've got as far as the weapons system mods are concerned, so unless you have some questions, we'll call it a day."

Gates shook his head and replied, "Not now, but I'm sure once everything starts to settle in, I'll have quite a few."

"No problem," Krause answered as he started down the ladder. "We'll be standing by, and if we don't know the answers, we can certainly dig up someone who does."

Gates climbed out of the cockpit feeling that he had reached the saturation point with respect to critical information. He and Krause met the other two near the door, and Frank Ryan had a few final remarks.

"We realize that you've been hit with an awful lot of information in a very short time. Granted, it would be nice to fly these airplanes a few times to try the new systems out, but with your departure set for tomorrow night, we simply don't have the time. Our F-24 simulators have been updated with all these mods and are equipped with a projection system for realistic visual effects for nap-of-the-earth missions, air-to-air combat, and STOL operations. We've got some canned missions that will give you good practice in using the vectored nozzle and reverse thrust features, as well as the new HUD pictorial, the Decoupled mode, and the visor sight. These machines have been reprogrammed for the new engines and the exotic fuel. The technicians will be at your disposal for as long as you want, and will run any or all of the canned missions you think will be helpful."

* * *

Lunch at the Skunk Works cafeteria went fairly quickly, with a lot of questions being answered and "what-if" situations resolved. Heading for the simulator, Gates and Brock felt much more comfortable with the new things they had learned during the morning. The rest of the afternoon they tried out the new systems in increasingly more difficult situations, with particular emphasis on the pictorial HUD.

Except for giving a pointer here and there, and answering a question or two, the Lockheed pilots had a relatively slow afternoon. They were impressed at how quickly the Air Force types picked up these new concepts and applied them effectively during the simulated missions. They did so well that Ryan and Krause threw in a couple of variants not called for in the script, and these too were taken in stride and handled properly. By the day's end they agreed that their "students for the day" were indeed two sharp throttle benders, and should have no trouble dealing with whatever PROJECT MONGOOSE demanded.

# Chapter 6

*Burbank, California*

Gates and Brock were up early the next morning to review the mission information given to them at the Pentagon. During dinner the night before, they had agreed there would be no need for additional simulator work, and their time would be better spent discussing the new systems. The talk mostly centered on how to optimize the Decoupled Mode and visor sight system during the fight that would develop once the Soviets found them out. Despite Ryan's sales pitch for the Stealth mod, they knew it would not guarantee a free ride, and sooner or later their aircraft would be picked up by one defense system or another.

Jack Dumont met Gates and Brock at the Flight Planning Room with the mission packets. Knowing that all fighter pilots felt they could do any job better than anyone else, he anticipated their answer to his comment, "I suppose you guys want to check over the flight plans we've drawn up for the mission?"

"Yeah. We thought we should throw an eyeball over them to see if you Pentagon types still know how it's done," Gates returned.

"Ok, here's all the information we've gathered up. The weather and winds look good, and the only new item for this flight is the abort procedure. Because of the priority of this mission, the good bird will not deviate from the flight plan to escort the plane with problems. After you've finished checking our figures, we'll go to the simulators where the PE guys will make the final adjustments on the cross-hair image for the visor sight."

Walking to the simulator building, Brock remarked, "You know, ever since we found out how far we're going, I've had a few reservations about making it at low altitude. I assumed someone had flight-planned it out, but it was reassuring to see the numbers fall into place on the no wind calculations."

"Yeah," Gates answered. "I felt the same way. I just hope some engineer didn't drop a decimal point when he was computing those fuel-consumption figures. They look too good to be true."

"Oh ye of little faith!" Dumont remarked as they went into the simulator room, then admitted, "We felt the same way the first time we saw them at the Pentagon, but they're the result of an awful lot of testing in a variety of airplanes, so we feel confident of their accuracy. The only unknown is the actual performance data in the F-24."

It didn't take long for the adjustments to be made on the visor sight, and when the pilots and specialist were satisfied with the installation, it was time for lunch. Dumont, in the meantime, called the Pentagon for an update on MONGOOSE, but was told there had been no change and to proceed as scheduled.

Lunchtime was the pilots' first opportunity to relax and take a deep breath. By one o'clock they were back in their room to pack, and when everything was loaded, they each took a STOP pill and hit the sack.

*CORONET RED*

Jack Dumont was at the Flight Planning Room when the two pilots arrived at 2200 hours. He handed each a copy of the low-level wind charts between California and Hawaii, with the forecast for Hickman noted on the bottom.

"It looks like the weather guessers are sticking to their guns," he said. "These updated winds are just what they called for on the forecast I got this morning. You'll have about a seven-knot tailwind component, and I figured your time en route at four plus forty. The PE guys brought over your helmets, and if you've got everything you'll need from your gear, I'll have the crew chiefs stow it in the aircraft. Do either of you have any druthers on which one you'd like to fly?"

Neither pilot had a preference, so Dumont assigned the plane closest to the front of the hangar to the flight leader, and then called the crew chiefs to pick up the gear for loading. The pilots checked the direction of the actual winds for each leg and agreed with Dumont's assessment of a seven-knot tailwind component. After calculating

ground speeds and fuel consumption, they entered all the data on the
cards used to load the aircraft computer.

Gates knew that when dealing with someone of Brock's experience, a flight briefing was hardly necessary. They were both professional fighter pilots and thus were expected to take any mission in
stride without dwelling unnecessarily on routine details. However, old
habits prompted by regulations die hard, so Gates went over a few
items, more to fill the briefing square than to impart any great revela-
tions to his wingman.

"We'll meet on Ground Control channel and get the clearance
copied before firing up. When you're all set, give me a nod and we'll
crank on my signal. We'll take the active and line up together, and use
a ten-second interval on takeoff. Stay in trail once we're airborne and
call 'locked on' at five miles. We'll remain in the five-mile trail until
the center loses us, and then you can back out to ten miles for the rest
of the flight. At that time we'll go to our discrete frequency, but
should monitor the en route channel, just in case. We'll do our bit
with the Navy and jot down the times that the Pentagon wants. After
that, we just grind it out until we're about a hundred miles from
Hickam, where we'll go over to center's control for recovery.

"If there are any problems en route, we won't abort as a flight.
The airplane that has difficulties will be on his own to the best abort
base, or to a ditch point. If it looks like a ditch, the low-level mission is
off, and the bent bird should climb to a good bailout altitude, squawk
emergency on the IFF, and punch out when things start coming
unglued. The other will press on at low altitude according to the flight
plan, with no orbiting of the ditch point.

"We ought to check out every system we can, although it won't
be much of a test for the terrain-following radar. It's about forty-five
minutes to wheels up, so we better saddle up our horses."

Preflight was next, and both pilots were surprised that the Form 1
carried no open writeups, which was unusual on an airplane of the
F-24's complexity. The Skunk Works had been working overtime to
clear up the minor discrepancies and overdue inspections that normally have to be lived with in an operational squadron. The actual preflight was equally rewarding—each one was clean as a whistle inside
and out, with no leaks and every gage sitting "in the green." The
external fuel tanks resounded solidly when thumped, and a visual
check confirmed that they were brim full.

As Gates signed off his acceptance of the aircraft, he could feel the
first twinges of excitement starting to build with the realization that

PROJECT MONGOOSE was finally getting off the ground. Just before boarding, Jack Dumont came over to shake his hand and wish him good luck. Gates thanked him and said, "See you in Hawaii," as he started up the ladder to the cockpit.

Strapping in didn't take long with the help of the crewchief standing on the ladder. The huge door that covered the entire front of the hangar started upward slowly, and two line tugs scurried underneath trailing towbars. When one was attached to the nose gear strut, Gates felt a slight jerk as the tug started to pull his plane out onto the ramp. His feet automatically went to the top of the rudder pedals so that he could ride the brakes in case they were needed.

The trip was only fifty yards to a spot where two clusters of ground support equipment waited to launch the pair of fighters. He noticed that the entire area was not lighted as well as an Air Force ramp. Glancing around, he saw that floodlights and light carts were available, but none had been turned on. Then, remembering General Cunningham's briefing about keeping a low profile, he understood the lack of illumination. Scanning the myriad lights along the perimeter of the airport, he casually wondered if the spaces between them hid a pair of unfriendly binoculars observing their preparations for flight.

Once chocked, Gates signaled for external power, and to load the flight data into the computer. A soft red glow from the instruments and edge-lit panels filled the cockpit as he quickly went through the prestart checklist.

"CORONET RED, check in!"

"Two," Brock replied immediately, in the old tradition of the wingman answering in as few words as possible, at the instant his leader's transmission ended.

"Burbank Ground, this is CORONET RED Flight, standing by for clearance."

The controller also followed tradition and spewed out the clearance like an auctioneer trying to raise the bid. The two jocks, however, had long practice in the art of copying clearances, and both would rather be boiled in oil than commit the unforgivable and ask for a repeat.

"Roger, Ground," Gates called back. "CORONET RED cleared Burbank to Hickam, direct, altitude as requested. Climb on course to three thousand feet until cleared by Departure Control for altitude change. Contact Departure Control on three six zero point six after takeoff. Report crossing the three four five slash one six of Los Angeles VORTAC. Squawk code eleven hundred on transponder. Contact

VORTAC. Squawk code eleven hundred on transponder. Contact Honolulu Center on three one seven point five when one hundred miles east of Hickam.''

''Readback is correct, CORONET RED. You're cleared to taxi to runway three three, altimeter three zero zero two, visibility five miles in haze, winds light and variable. Contact tower before taking the active.''

Gates glanced at his wingman, who immediately gave a nod indicating that RED Two was ready to start engines. Gates then gave Brock and the ground crew the ''wind 'er up!'' signal, and the roar of the air cart rose to a scream as the crew chief hit the valve open and gunned the blower engine to full RPM. The kinks in the air hose leading to the left engine straightened as the charge stiffened it out, and the number one tachometer started climbing steadily. At ten percent, he pressed the ignition button and moved the outboard throttle into the idle detent. Gates was still not used to seeing the higher readings on the Exhaust Gas Temperature gage, made possible by the modified engines. The needle stayed in the green, however, as the RPM accelerated smoothly to the idle setting.

The crew chief scrambled beneath the airplane to switch the air hose to the right engine, and when he reappeared, Gates signaled for number two, and the start procedure was repeated. When the right engine stabilized, he flipped the generator switches on and signaled for the disconnect of the air and electrical ground power carts. The remaining instruments stirred into life as he went from the left console to the right, turning on each aircraft and weapons subsystem.

The crew chief came on the intercom, and they went through the pretaxi check of the flight controls, variable camber wing, speed brakes, and boundary layer control. After the inertial platform was aligned, Gates went through the BIT checks for the radar, HUD, and LANTIRN systems. He was surprised to find that each one checked out perfectly, which was unusual for an airplane that had just gone through so many modifications.

Brock was waiting when he looked over, and gave him the ''thumbs up'' sign to show he was ready to taxi. Gates eased in the power, while the crew chief motioned him forward, but the aircraft seemed hesitant about moving. His momentary concern faded with the realization that all the extra fuel on board put him just under max gross weight for takeoff.

Taxiing the airplane required a deft touch once it did get moving, since it had a marked tendency to keep rolling in the same direction.

Turns had to be anticipated well in advance with respect to braking and steering in order to keep the beast on the taxiway centerline. They hadn't gone far when a "Follow Me" pulled out in front of Gates, to lead them through the unfamiliar taxiways to the active runway.

"RED Flight—go tower!" Gates called as they approached runway 33, and instantly heard his wingman reply, "Two!"

"Burbank Tower, CORONET RED Flight, number one for the active."

"Roger, RED Flight, cleared on and off. Winds three zero zero at four knots. Contact Departure when airborne."

Gates rogered the clearance and began moving the heavy airplane onto the right half of the runway. Brock followed quickly and taxied to the other half, just off the leader's left wing.

Once his wingman was in position, Gates gave him the runup signal and pushed the throttles to the full military stop. The RPM wound up rapidly, and the Exhaust Pressure Ratio settled down well within limits. All other gages were "in the green," so he released the brakes and moved the throttles outboard into the afterburner range. Both burners lit normally; however, the expected burst of acceleration was absent, as the heavily laden fighter seemed reluctant to pick up speed in the usual way.

After the taxiing problems, Gates expected a less than spectacular takeoff, so he let the F-24 cook along and kept pressure on the throttles to ensure against any creepback. He felt better when the line speed check at the three-thousand-foot mark of the runway was just what he had calculated.

At about the sixty-five-hundred-foot mark, the nose was light enough to lift off, but it took another fifteen hundred feet before the main gears finally cleared. He hit the retract switch immediately, and as the gear folded into its wells, the bird began responding more like he was accustomed to. It still required an experienced hand on the stick to maximize the balance between acceleration and rate of climb during the aerodynamic changes when the gear came up and the flaps retracted.

"This thing sure handles like a dog with all this extra weight," Gates thought as he chopped the burners at 300 knots and continued climbing to 3,000 feet, where he let the speed build to 500.

"Two tied," Brock called, indicating that he had locked his radar on the lead aircraft.

"Rog!—go departure," Gates answered, and checked the flight in with the radar controller. Los Angeles spread out on all sides like a sea of lights; however, every second was spent checking their radar for contacts or trying to get a visual on traffic called out by the controller. Both pilots kept their heads on a swivel until the coastline flashed beneath their wings and the city lights gave way to the inky combination of sea and midnight sky that stretched to the horizon.

Gates adjusted the power to maintain five hundred knots indicated, and slowly started the aircraft down to five hundred feet. The radar altimeter was checking out very closely with the barometric instrument, so he set its warning light to come on at four hundred feet, just in case he slipped below his planned altitude. At leveloff he nudged the throttles forward just a tad to keep the airspeed pegged, and was pleased to note that the fuel-flow indicators stayed at what seemed like unnaturally low readings.

It wasn't long before the center called and reported that CORONET RED had faded from their scopes, and was cleared to en route frequency. RED One rogered the call, and took the flight over to their discrete frequency to call the tanker following their route at thirty thousand feet. Jack Dumont answered and asked for a status report on both aircraft. All systems were Go, and Dumont told them to report their time and fuel remaining over the first checkpoint.

Gates glanced at the inertial panel, and saw that they were only fifty miles from that position. The course needle was centered and the miles were clicking off at better than eight per minute, so he decided that now was a good time to try out the autopilot. Getting a deathgrip on the stick in case the system had some engage transients, he first switched on attitude hold, and then added altitude hold. The auto system took over as smooth as glass, with only a barely perceptible jump in the stick; however, he kept a tight hold on it in the event some spurious signals happened through the circuitry.

Satisfied that all the "black boxes" were working correctly, he selected the full Terrain Following mode. The automatic system showed no signs of acting up as the mileage indicator wound down to zero, so he switched hands on the stick and jotted down the time and fuel remaining. They were right on the money time-wise, but the fuel figures planted the first seed of concern in his mind. He was about four hundred pounds below their estimate, in spite of the fuel-flow gages indicating almost where they should be.

"CORONET RED—fuel check! Lead has thirty-two eight."

Brock answered crisply, "Two has thirty-two eight fifty."

Jack Dumont quickly acknowledged their calls. "Roger RED Flight, copy your states."

Gates tossed the fuel figures back and forth in his head, looking for some obvious answer for the difference between actual and planned. "No particular problem right now," he thought, "but if these variances indicate a trend, things could get quite close on the longer flights."

The next checkpoint was two hundred miles away, and this leg would determine which way the trend was going. During a long fifteen minutes, Gates paid more attention to the fuel counter than to the primary flight instruments. The course needle finally swung, but now he was registering six hundred pounds less than planned, and Number Two indicated that he was only a hundred pounds better off.

Although Gates had hoped for more encouraging news, it appeared the trend was in the positive direction. He concluded that the new external tanks and the heavy fuel load resulted in a slightly aft CG during the early portions of the flight, causing them to fly on the back side of the power curve. He made a mental note to suggest they try feeding out the external wing tanks first on the next leg. This might ease the aft CG condition earlier in the flight, and keep them closer to the desired position on the power curve.

The pass over the cruiser *Chicago* went without incident, except for a large amount of consternation that it caused among the radar surveillance crew. MONGOOSE's overflight left them totally baffled as to how two jet fighters could get within ten miles of the ship without being detected.

*   *   *

Aboard the tanker, Jack Dumont almost let out a yelp when he read the decoded message from the *Chicago*. From all indications, the Stealth mod passed its initial test with flying colors. He wanted to call RED Flight with the good news, but the game plan strictly forbade any extra transmissions, especially concerning Stealth.

Thus far, everything was going as planned, except for the fuel-consumption figures. Dumont also thought that the shortages were caused by flying on the back side of the power curve during the early part of the mission. He expected that as the planes lightened up and were flying more on the step, the fuel figures would look a lot better.

*   *   *

Approximately three hours into the flight, Gates felt the first signs of weariness setting in. Flying at five hundred feet afforded no opportunity to relax, being so close to the water, and the lack of terrain obstacles introduced an aspect of boredom. There was little to do but fly basic instruments, with one eye on the radar altimeter. The seat had become like a piece of granite, and he squirmed around to find a slightly more comfortable posture, but without much success.

As on all long flights, he silently cursed the designers of ejection seats for their failure to devise something more amenable to the human anatomy. Idle threats though, since he knew that a cushion of any kind would be disastrous in the event of an ejection. The resiliency of the cushion would allow the seat to gain too much speed before his body started moving with it, resulting in a compression fracture of the spine.

The remainder of the flight into Hawaii would have been fairly routine were it not for some nasty jostling they received when going through a front. Not too long after breaking out of the weather, both fighters were on the ground at Hickam, and parked in a remote section of the field.

### Hickam AFB, Hawaii

By the time both pilots had debriefed with the maintenance people, Jack Dumont had arrived.

"Good mission, you guys. Any problems with the front?"

Like all fighter pilots, Gates and Brock rarely admitted that bad weather was anything more than a nuisance, so they replied nonchalantly, "Naw. It got a little bumpy at times and we hit a lot of rain, that's all. Any word on how the Stealth mod worked on that cruiser?" Gates asked him quickly.

"I think we've got a real winner with this one," Dumont replied enthusiastically. "According to the report, you first appeared on their scopes at ten miles, and the blips were somewhat fuzzy and indistinct. However, they felt that you were trackable, and if a fighter was close by, they could have completed the intercept.

"I called some of the electronics types on the secure voice net, and we came up with a plan for a more interesting test over the carrier task force tomorrow. Since there will be a good number of ships in that group, we are going to cluge your sensor system with a temporary program, so that the electronic identifiers of certain ships will be designated as hostile. With this fix in place, your HUD will display each of these radars as a yellow X, just as if it were an enemy GCI site. We're also going to try another temporary mod that will cause these X's to flash if your flight path will take you within twenty miles of the site. Using the projected flight path ribbon on the Pictorial Format, you'll fly so as to avoid those radars depicted as unfriendly.

"If this test works, the overflight will serve two purposes: first to recheck the data we got from the *Chicago*, and second to see if avoiding hostile radars by twenty miles will get you through undetected. If this proves to be the case, we'll make that mod a permanent fix."

The two pilots looked at each other and nodded, indicating their approval of the plan. Taking some papers from his briefcase, Dumont said, "I copied down your times and fuel figures, and everything looks pretty good. We'll crank in a correction factor for the first few legs, and I think we'll come out pretty close on tomorrow's mission. Let me have your flight data cards, so I can check my figures before sending the report to the Pentagon.

"I imagine you two are ready for a shower and a hot meal. The steward on the tanker is standing by to whip up something, and has a couple of beers iced down to wash the trail dust out of your throats. You'll be sleeping on the bird today, since it offers the least chance of any disturbance. After you eat, there's a staff car available if you want to go anywhere, but report back at noon for crew rest. Same schedule as last night: brief at ten and wheels up at midnight."

Neither pilot had any questions, so Dumont dropped them off at the tanker, and then headed to the base communications center to send his report to Washington.

* * *

Although the dinner sirloins were exceptional, Brock was wishing it were a big dish of pasta. His boyhood had been spent in the Chambersburg section of Trenton, which was solidly Italian, and his mother followed her family's tradition by not sparing the spaghetti.

Given her excitable nature, he was glad he wasn't able to call her before leaving the Nellis Complex for Washington. However, Angela was a different story. They had met just over a year ago and had been seeing each other quite steadily ever since. He knew that soon after he left, she would have called the squadron and be given the nonanswer of "He's gone TDY to the Pentagon." Not knowing what was going on was bad enough, but not being told he was leaving meant that Brock had some tall explaining to do when he got back.

Although this would cause a temporary flap, Brock was not overly worried about the consequences. Unlike Gates, he had experienced no inclinations toward plighting his troth. He liked Angela quite a bit, but for the foreseeable future marriage was not on the agenda. Both were free and, although they enjoyed each other's company, neither seemed ready to change the way things were.

Brock's mother had met Angela on a visit, and the two had immediately taken to each other. Since that time, whenever he called home there was the inevitable question: "Why didn't he settle down with that nice girl?" Up 'til now his ready answer had been that the numerous TDYs and assignments to remote bases would not make for an ideal married life. However, he knew that someday he would most likely get a tour in the Pentagon, and then would have to dream up another answer to fend off his mother.

# Chapter 7

The following evening, Gates and Brock had the wheels in the well right on schedule, as they headed out toward Guam, thirty-three hundred and twenty miles away. This leg would be the acid test, since it was almost two hundred and fifty miles farther than the run from Korea into the target and out to the refueling point.

The DME read four hundred twenty five miles from Hickam when Gates pushed his mike button, "RED—go blacked out."

Brock came back with a quick, "Rog."

Lead switched his radar to long-range search, and he soon started picking up returns from the outermost ships in the task force. Gates had never seen a naval group of this size deployed for battle, and he was surprised at the number of blips on his scope and the wide area they covered. Soon, images representing the ships were projected on the HUD, and his airplane's sensors began separating the friendlies from those designated as "hostile" by the temporary fix.

The projected flight path on the HUD showed him passing near or over at least three of the "bad guys." The twenty-mile minimum radius from the first "enemy" ship was going to be violated if he didn't do something soon, so he eased in a slight correction to the right. The computer calculated the geometry of the new problem, and in a moment the first yellow X stopped flashing. However, his change of direction caused the other two X's to start blinking.

"And I thought this was going to be a breeze," he said to himself as the difficulty in avoiding these radars became clear. To escape detection, he would have to fly an arc around each "hostile site," which amounted to a continuous S course over the entire task force. The key to success would be his ability to judge the twenty-mile radius from each X and keep the flight path ribbon centered between the two closest to his position. However, each time he took up a new heading to solve the immediate problem, the X's representing radars farther away would flash ominously.

"The only way we're going to manage this is to take them one pair at a time," he thought, while nudging in a bit more aileron to keep the ribbon from drifting toward the ship at his two o'clock position. "It's a good thing real GCI sites aren't located as close together as these ships."

Gates could now see the lights of the picket ships, looking like stars resting on the black water ahead, so he flipped the radar over to intermediate range to get better target resolution. The new picture made it easier to pick out the carrier at the center of the formation. The flagship was about twenty degrees port at thirty miles, and added one more complication to his problem of avoiding the "hostile" radars. There was no way he could make a straight run at it from his present position without causing a lot of yellow X's to start flashing. He would have to keep arcing around the radars until he was almost abeam the carrier, and then make a hard turn to cross her at right angles to the flight deck.

While maneuvering past the last "enemy" ship between his bird and the carrier, Gates switched on the activating circuits for the AMRAAM and Sidewinder missiles. This was a good chance to check out the new sight, so after making sure that the Armament Master Switch was in the Off position, he lowered the clear, nighttime visor on his helmet. The cross hairs were too bright at first, but twisting the intensity knob brought them to a more comfortable level.

The ship was still sixty degrees port when he selected the stations for the AMRAAMs and turned his head to center the cross hairs on the carrier's lights. It took a few tries to get the sight settled down long enough to hit the acquisition switch on the left stickgrip.. The sight worked as advertised, as the radar and missile antennas slewed left and locked on to the target. Noting the green lights on the weapons panel indicating that the missiles had their launch parameters, Gates switched over to the Sidewinders. Immediately there was a loud growl in his headset, confirming that the IR seekers were also homed in on the target.

As the last yellow X slid off the bottom of the HUD, RED One rolled out of his turn and headed straight for the flattop. Spotting another escort ship at his two o'clock position, he turned to put the cross hairs on the smaller ship, and hit the action switch again. The system immediately acquired the new target, but a large red X started flashing on the combining glass, indicating that he was too close to the target for the radar missiles to guide effectively.

Satisfied that the visor sight was working properly, Gates turned his attention to the enormous bulk of the carrier, which was rapidly filling his windshield. He knew they must have picked him up by now, and the bridge would be notified of a low-level unknown in the area. Time for one quick check of the altimeter to make sure he was at five hundred feet before the flight deck swept beneath his wings and was gone.

The darkness swallowed him again, seeming even more intense after flying through the relative glare of the carrier's operating lights. He rolled the bird over in a steep right turn to correct back toward track, but as soon as he leveled out, the HUD was once again alive with flashing yellow X's.

"More fun and games," he muttered while taking the necessary evasive action to still the symbols for the nearest radars.

"Aircraft that just overflew U.S. task force, identify yourselves!"

The transmission on Guard channel startled Gates, as much for its absurdity as its unexpectedness. "You idiot," he thought. "If someone just buzzed the admiral's flagship, he wouldn't be dumb enough to stick his head in the noose by giving you his call sign."

The message was repeated three more times, each with additional emphasis. Apparently the admiral was quite disturbed, most probably because someone flew over his entire task force with only minimal detection.

Neither Gates nor Brock replied, but Dumont was anxious about a possible compromise of the mission's security if the ship was given an answer.

"CORONET RED, make no reply!" came over their en route frequency, and Gates clicked his mike twice in acknowledgment.

They exited the task force area close to their intended track, so Gates only had to put in a small correction to bring them back on course. The needles centered just before reaching the next checkpoint, requiring a gentle right turn to resume the planned track. Checking the fuel remaining, he was pleased to see that the revised consumption figures made a big improvement. All the S'ing through the task force had cost a little gas, but nothing worrisome.

The only thing they didn't have a chance to check out com-

pletely, which along with Stealth would be critical for the mission, was
how the Pictorial Format worked at low level over the ground. Even
with a good report from the task force about Stealth, keeping it low
would still be crucial in getting to Zhigansk. The trip from Anderson
to Kunsan was only a relatively short hop of seventeen hundred miles
or so, but like the other two legs, it was entirely over water, even for
the run up the Yellow Sea along the west coast of Korea. Since fuel
wouldn't be a problem on this trip, they might make more money by
crossing Cheju Island just south of Korea, and then heading directly
for Pusan. After hitting the coast, they could turn northwest toward
Kunsan and get the benefit of crossing as much of Korea as possible.
Gates had spent a tour there while he was a captain, and he knew that
the rugged landscape across the southern part of the peninsula would
provide a good check of the HUD display and the terrain following
system.

The more Gates thought about this wrinkle in their flight plan,
the better he liked it. He made a note on the margin of his mission card
to discuss it with Brock and Dumont after they landed.

## Anderson AFB, Guam

Touchdown was on schedule, and thirty minutes after the airplanes had been turned over to the maintenance crews, Dumont
charged in excitedly with a sheaf of papers in his hand.

"An hour before we started down, I got the analysis of the radar
report from the task force. The guys at my shop consider the Stealth
mod a roaring success! None of the ships that we designated as hostile
to your computer reported any good contacts on your flight—certainly none that would have been usable in a "for-real" situation. Flying the twenty-mile arc around these radars looks like the answer to
our prayers. The ships you did not skirt by twenty miles reported initial contacts at ten to twelve miles, just like the *Chicago*.

"The boss is quite pleased with the results of these two tests, and
has directed that we make this mod a permanent part of the on-board
program. The necessary changes are no big deal, and our people at
Kunsan are making up the new circuit boards for installation when we
get there. Once these are in place, the symbols for all enemy GCI sites
will flash as long as you are within a twenty-mile radius."

Dumont was stuffing the flight data cards into his briefcase, when
Gates decided to pop the question.

"Colonel, everything we've checked out coming across the pond seems to be working o.k. However, we still haven't looked at the key system for getting us through unnoticed."

Dumont looked up quizzically, with a slightly pained expression that indicated his bubble had just burst. Things had been going too well, and the tone of Gates's request had the smell of three-day-old fish. Almost knowing he wasn't going to like the answer, he asked, "What's that, Bill?"

"The new Pictorial Format display needs a real shakedown in the Terrain Following mode. All this overwater flying hasn't told us too much about how the system will work over land. The simulator time at Lockheed was good, but like all simulators, it's not exactly like the real thing. Since fuel will be no problem on the next leg, what about a short dogleg over Korea on our way into Kunsan?"

Gates could see the wheels turning as Dumont thought for a moment before answering. "Kunsan's only a hundred miles from the southern coast. Do you think those few minutes over land would be worth it?"

"We believe it would. Ken and I were talking it over before you landed, and want to give it an initial try at Cheju Island. If things look good, we head northeast to hit the mainland just west of Pusan. Once inland, we turn back to the northwest and head straight for Kunsan."

Dumont took the flight charts from his briefcase and made some eyeball measurements of the distances involved. "Why detour all the way over to Pusan, when it's only a little farther from there to Kunsan than it is from the southern tip of the peninsula? The small extra distance doesn't seem to be worth all the effort. The air traffic in the southeast corner of Korea will be more congested than along the western coast, and it may take some doing at this late hour to get it all diverted."

"We thought of that, Colonel, but since we're practicing for the real thing, why not go in unannounced, and with no IFF? So far, the Stealth mod has worked pretty well, and the traffic density will be minimal at that time of the morning. The main reason for crossing Korea, rather than going up the coast, is to go over the mountains between Pusan and Kunsan. This is the type of checkout the Pictorial Format needs, and a run up the coast would not provide such a variety of terrain." Gates emphasized his point by showing Dumont the six-thousand-foot mountains on Cheju and the mainland.

It looked like the colonel was buying the plan, so he decided to add some more food for thought. He marked some quick distance measurements along the edge of a sheet of paper, laid it next to a longitude line on the chart, and said, "The dogleg we're talking about will only add a hundred and forty miles to the trip, which shouldn't take more than fifteen minutes. Even this short time would let us know if the system had any major problems." Gates paused a moment and then added, "Ken and I think this chance is too valuable to pass by, and it's definitely worth mentioning to General Cunningham."

Dumont realized that if they weren't given permission for the dogleg, they'd get over Kunsan, cancel their flight plan, and fly locally to check out the Pictorial Format system. "You're right," he finally admitted after running the idea through his mind one more time. "However, I expect some difficulty in getting the general to buy it. Since he's running the show, I think it would be a wise move to keep him advised of any deviation, no matter how small. I'm sure he'll eventually go along with it if we do our homework on this end. You two start working on the flight plan, figuring it with the dogleg and without it, so we'll have some hard numbers for him to compare. I'll get a hold of weather and see what they're calling for tomorrow, and also try to think up some deathless logic to convince the powers that be of the righteousness of our cause."

### Wahington, D.C.

At 11:00 P.M. Eastern time, CIA Director John Egbert was sitting in his office when he got a call from the agent trailing Sergeant Dunaway. He reported that Dunaway had left his apartment with a briefcase and was now traveling northwest on Massachusetts Avenue. The time had come to "neutralize" Sergeant Dunaway. Egbert immediately ordered other cars to parallel both sides of Dunaway's route, on Florida and Pennsylvania avenues, to keep the subject's car boxed in. Other cars were positioned farther along Massachusetts Avenue to take up the chase at various points along the way.

At the Thomas Circle, Dunaway turned southwest on Vermont Avenue. At once the car that had been north of him cut through numerous side streets and ended up on Rhode Island Avenue with lights flashing and siren wailing, rushing southwestward to keep the net tight. Dunaway only went two blocks on Vermont when he suddenly darted into a parking spot. The tail car radioed his position.

It only took eight more minutes for all the remaining units to arrive in the neighborhood and take up positions covering every possible approach to Dunaway's car. When everyone was in place, someone on the net mentioned that this whole thing was taking place fairly close to the Russian Embassy. The agent in charge of the entire opera-

tion told the units on both sides of the embassy to be on the lookout
for anyone entering or leaving the embassy grounds. His second in
command mentioned that it was odd for the Soviets to set up a drop
so close to the home office.

"Maybe with time so short, they couldn't establish something
more elaborate," his superior commented. "Or possibly they don't
believe Dunaway has anything worthwhile and decided on a plan that
could be called off at the last moment. Whatever the reason, they
won't have to go far for the information."

Their vigil lasted until just after midnight, when the team closest
to the suspect radioed that he had gotten out of his car with the briefcase, had rounded the corner to 15th Street, and was moving north.
About fifty yards farther, he stopped and was apparently waiting for
someone.

Another fifteen minutes passed, when a team close to a small rear
door of the embassy reported someone coming out of the embassy
grounds and walking in Dunaway's direction. Another team picked
him up as he passed the corner of 15th and L, where he carefully sur-
veyed the entire area and then headed south on 15th Street. He passed
Dunaway's position without giving any indication that he saw him
standing in the shadows of a tree. Opposite McPherson Square, he
crossed the street and headed back north, apparently satisfied that
Dunaway was alone.

This latest move was radioed to all units, along with the codeword indicating that the contact was about to be made and the pre-
briefed plan for preventing the transfer of information was to be
implemented. Egbert had been quite specific in his instructions for
this operation. He wanted Dunaway and whomever he was meeting to
be taken alive, since no one knew exactly just what information Dunaway was delivering. However, if things went awry and their capture
couldn't be assured, the backup plan was to kill them instantly.

One unit of Egbert's team was able to park in a "Handicapped
Only" spot on 15th Street before Dunaway had come around the corner to his rendezvous point. They were located about thirty yards
north of where Dunaway was now furtively pacing, while the KGB
man checked things out down toward McPherson Square. They had a
good view along the sidewalk toward Dunaway, and were kept advised
of the Russian's movements by another unit on I Street.

The two agents with tranquilizer guns fitted the night-vision
scopes in place and had their weapons at the ready as the Russian
crossed K Street and approached Dunaway's location. The cross hairs

of each scope were centered squarely on the chest of their individual targets as the two figures met, exchanged a few words, and passed the briefcase. The KGB man flicked it open, and using a small flashlight, riffled through the contents. He then closed the case, nodded at Dunaway, and withdrew an envelope from his inside jacket pocket. Before Dunaway could take the envelope, the muffled cough of the silenced tranquilizer guns ended the transaction. As the darts struck home, both men jerked spasmodically then collapsed on the pavement and lay still.

The area was immediately flooded by CIA agents, who quickly sealed off the entire block from pedestrians and traffic. Four agents carried the two inert figures to the nearby van, where they were blindfolded and handcuffed to the leg of a bench along one wall. A final check was made to ensure that no evidence of the operation was left lying about, and then the signal was given to clear the area.

Three minutes after Dunaway and the KGB agent had first made contact, 15th Street between K and L was deserted and quiet. In the van carrying the two spies, the team chief radioed Egbert that Dunaway's briefcase contained a long, descriptive narrative of all the particulars on PROJECT MONGOOSE. Egbert had been concerned about the security of the project. Now, as Gates and Brock made last-minute preparations for their mission, at least the threat posed by Dunaway had been safely and discretely intercepted.

### Anderson AFB, Guam

It took less than thirty minutes to pencil in the times and fuel from the latest winds. Jack Dumont made some notes on the margin of his map about the types of terrain and the heights of the mountains Gates and Brock would encounter on the dogleg.

He had received the go ahead from General Cunningham and could now tell the two pilots their idea to test out the Pictorial Format system was approved. Dumont returned from the communications room with a relieved look on his face. "Well it took some doing, but General Cunningham bought the entire plan. His office will alert the MONGOOSE team at Kunsan about the change of plans so they can have someone at the Air Defense Control Center keep things glued together, just in case they pick you up.

"We also talked about fuel on this trip, and decided that we can leave the centerline tank empty, but only if you agree. No big deal, but it might save us a little wear and tear on the brakes and tires. Either way, all tanks will be checked for proper feeding before you leave Kunsan. Which way do you want to play it?"

Gates and Brock looked at each other and shrugged their agreement to Dumont's plan, with Brock adding, "Only if the winds and weather stay as forecast. If things turn to worms, that extra gas might come in handy."

"I'll tell them to hold off on the centerline until I take a look at the weather tonight," Dumont replied. "If it's close, I'll have them filled before you arrive."

That evening, the word from the forecaster threw a small wrench into Dumont's confident plan that he had sold to General Cunningham. The en route weather was fine, but things were not too shiny over the Korean Peninsula. If the forecast held, they wouldn't have too much of a problem, but he had seen too many situations like this turn into a pumpkin in no time at all.

Dumont was tempted to call maintenance now and have them fill the centerlines. Then, considering the relatively short haul and the tailwind, he decided to wait until the crews finished their flight planning and knew their fuel reserves exactly.

Gates and Brock were at the hangar when Dumont arrived, and were going over the landmarks for their turn back toward Kunsan. The idea would be to hit the coast between Masan and Pusan, staying far enough from either to avoid any traffic. Brock looked up as Dumont approached and quipped, "Will the gods of Weather smile on us tonight?"

"I'm afraid not," Dumont answered. "Things aren't too bad until you're southwest of Japan, then it goes down for the remainder of the route." He handed them the forecast and continued, "It's not bad enough to scrub the dogleg, but ceilings are low and we'll have to keep a close eye on things. If they get worse and you can't stay VFR underneath, it might be wiser to forego the practice and fly at the minimum en route altitude. After you figure out your flight plan, we'll decide on filling the centerline tanks. The trucks are standing by, and it won't take long if you think you'll need it."

The latest winds gave them an ETE of three hours and thirty-six minutes. "That'll be easy after yesterday," Brock commented, "even with the bad weather thrown in. I don't think we'll need any fuel in the centerline. There's plenty of extra gas in case we have to use Osan or Suwon as an alternate."

Gates agreed, and even with the Chief of Staff's uneasiness about the diversion still in his mind, Dumont could see no reason for carrying the extra fuel. "Let's do it that way," he said. "I'll check back with weather in an hour, and if things have gone to pot, we'll top them off. I'll keep the refuelers standing by until you crank up." His caution flared up again and he added a caveat. "Keep in mind that the main idea is to get the birds in position for the strike, and be ready to go at the planned time."

"Sounds fair enough to me," Gates replied.

It was almost time to go, so the pilots zippered on their "go fast pants," gathered up their charts and other gear, and headed out to the airplanes. As they were leaving, Dumont said, "I'll run over to weather and get a last-minute update. Don't crank up 'til I get back."

They acknowledged with a thumbs up and went into the hangar where the aircraft were parked. Both jocks were strapped in and sweating uncomfortably by the time Dumont returned. He stopped at each fighter and shouted above the din of the power units that the weather was holding, and no changes were expected.

\* \* \*

CORONET RED was off on time, and things went as briefed for the first part of the flight, including a quick check of the Pictorial Format over some small islands southwest of Japan. Once past the Tokaras, the checkpoint south of Cheju was only forty-four minutes ahead.

Gates was reviewing what he had seen on the HUD during the pass over the islands when the course needle started hunting from side to side. When it hit the wingtip position, he banked smoothly around to a northeasterly heading. He rolled level and the pictorial representing the island of Cheju filled the Heads Up Display. The slopes of Cheju's sixty-three-hundred-foot mountain were clearly visible, and he marveled at how much easier it was to interpret this three-dimensional display than the standard F-24s. He headed for the mountain maintaining five hundred feet, changing course only enough to keep the green flight path ribbon centered on the apex of the display.

The broken deck of clouds above them was now a solid overcast with patches of lower scud and an occasional rain shower. It was back to total instrument flying because the scattered lights he could see on the island were too few and far between to give any depth or substance to the obstacles ahead.

Purely from habit when flying IFR, Gates rechecked that the Terrain Following Mode was programmed for five hundred feet and the radar altimeter was still set at four hundred feet, just as a backup.

Despite no indications of any malfunction, it was difficult not to think about the reality of the situation. Here he was hurtling straight for a mountain at five hundred knots, with only his faith in the information on the HUD between him and a large hole in the ground. His right hand encircled the stick grip ever so lightly just as a precaution.

Gates sneaked a glance outside the cockpit, if only to break his hypnotic stare at the artificial horizon, waiting for it to move. A little to the left there was a small cluster of lights—probably a fishing village on the coast. He quickly resumed his expectant glare at the images projected on the HUD, just in time to see them move downward slightly. The LANTIRN system had picked up the higher elevations of the beach area, and the computer predicted the reaction time necessary for the change and to still maintain five hundred feet terrain clearance.

Gates felt just a suggestion of G forces as the aircraft responded to the automatic control inputs, but this only lasted for an instant, as the more sharply rising ground farther inland was sensed by the system. The horizon bar kept moving down as the TFR commanded a steeper climb angle, until it registered about twenty-five degrees on the Heads Up Display.

Even though it was pitch black outside the cockpit, the Pictorial Format showed "blue" sky at the extreme right and left of the display, indicating that the airplane would be in the clear if it flew around the mountain, rather than over it. With the climb angle set, only small corrections were needed to maintain the command altitude, and now the flight path ribbon had some "daylight" between it and the crest of the hill, which helped a little psychologically.

As Gates neared the top of the mountain, the LANTIRN reacted to the momentary flattening of the ground at the peak. "Seeing" nothing because of the steep climb angle, the system sent pitch down commands to the flight control computer in order to maintain a constant 500-foot altitude.

The somewhat mild pushover needed to crest the very top of the hill lasted only for a second because the ground dropped away sharply on the far slope. Not caring about its human cargo, the airplane "flew the mission as briefed," as the nose came down abruptly to keep the flight path on schedule. The resulting negative G's lifted Gates out of his seat and hard against the lap belt. All loose items in the cockpit were afloat—maps, flashlight, goodie bag, and dirt from beneath the seat. Everything hung there, suspended in space, as the pushover maneuver continued down the northeastern side of the mountain, with Gates cursing himself for not having cinched down his lap belt. A strip map floated between his face and the instrument panel, and had to be batted away with a quick swipe of his left hand.

Finally, the major correction to maintain the correct altitude was completed, and the ride got a little easier as the airplane raced down the craggy slope toward the Korean Straight. As the autopilot eased the forward pressure on the stick, Gates thumped back down in the seat, and immediately made a grab for the loose end of the lap belt, giving it a healthy pull. Gates felt sheepish at being caught by such an oversight and made a mental note to stow everything before taking off the next day.

Flying the HUD through the ever-changing landscape now demanded his complete concentration. The Pictorial Format showed a horizon of rolling hills and valleys, making it easier to steer the flight path ribbon through the low areas. Gates was just getting used to maneuvering with this new display when the northeast coast of Cheju appeared on the combining glass, and faded off the bottom a few seconds later. Once over the water, he could relax a bit, as they roared through the Korean Straights toward Pusan, one hundred forty-five miles away.

Shortly, the small islands off the south coast of Korea were displayed on the HUD, but with no hilly areas, there was no challenge in overflying them. The bay west of Pusan took shape on the combining glass, and Gates ruddered in enough correction to center the flight ribbon between the shores. Crossing the coastline brought another "fly up" command, but not as severe as it had been at Cheju Island. The autopilot followed the elevation changes smoothly, as Gates dialed in the heading to Kunsan on the Horizontal Situation Indicator. Destination coordinates were punched into the computer, and when the needle pointed the way, Gates rolled into a left turn with forty-five degrees of bank.

"Turning to three zero zero," he called to Brock, who answered quickly, "Rog, tied!"

The terrain now became more rugged. Hills, mountains, and valleys were depicted in outline form, with darker shades of brown for those relatively close and tans for those in the distance. Rain showers were more frequent now, and the lower scud had thickened to a broken layer. Even with these conditions frequently reducing the visibility to zero, Gates found that he was becoming less inclined to bring outside references or the traditional blind flying instruments into his crosscheck. The HUD told him everything he needed to know about his airplane and the terrain it was flying over, without even a glance in the cockpit.

By the time they had reached Kunsan, he had complete confidence in the new system, and felt that this short practice session had been well worth the effort. It had certainly quelled any reservations he might have had about flying across the Asian continent relying solely on a new modification.

When the needle swung, telling him that they were over their destination, Gates turned the IFF back on, and the approach controller had them vectored to the GCA pickup point in no time. After turning off the active, they were led to the alert hangars at the approach end of runway 36 for parking.

### Kunsan Air Base, Korea

A swarm of maintenance men gathered around the airplane. Many of them wore plain, unmarked coveralls, indicating Dumont's shop had brought along some people from the Skunk Works. With or without writeups, the game plan was to give both planes a very thorough going over prior to mission time tomorrow night. Gates stepped out onto the ramp in front of the hangars, and his wingman joined him ten minutes later, reporting that his bird was Code 1, meaning it had no discrepancies. It felt good to take deep breaths of the cool night air—so refreshing after the rain-forest humidity of Guam.

Dumont's staff car wheeled up in a few minutes, and Gates started fielding the colonel's questions about the dogleg. After the two jocks described their ride through the hills, Dumont remarked, "I don't know what the Old Man will ask about the diversion, so you better come over to the Comm Center, in case he throws me a curve."

The Chief of Staff sounded quite relieved to learn that both birds were in position for the strike and would be ready to go on schedule. There had been no changes on the diplomatic scene, although the Secretary of State was still hopeful of some sort of a breakthrough. General Cunningham felt that there wasn't much chance of this happening, but told Dumont to check back with him three hours before takeoff for a final Go, No-Go decision.

After winding things up with the general, Dumont and the two pilots stopped by Base Weather on their way back to the tanker for dinner. The forecaster had good news, promising that local conditions would improve during the day, and skies would be clear with good visibility the next night.

While they were eating, Jack Dumont went over a few things that would be taking place that day. "While you guys are logging the Z's, our people will be clearing up a few things that have to be done before you launch. They'll paint out the star and bar insignia on the wings and fuselage of your aircraft and any other markings that would identify you with the USAF. The only thing we hope to gain by that is a little time due to the confusion factor. A lot of our allies have F-24s, and even the bad guys have fighters that are quite similar in design. If you're spotted, it won't take a mental giant to figure out what country you're from, given the state of international affairs. However, if we can screw them up, even for a minute, it's worth the time and paint involved.

"The new circuit boards are ready for the HUD, and things will work just like they did going over the carrier group. The radar guys have jury-rigged a piece of test equipment to simulate radar sites, so the whole thing can be checked out thoroughly.

"The armorers should be almost finished uploading the rest of your weapons. You'll still have the four AMRAAMs, four Sidewinders, and the gun that you brought from Burbank. You'll also have two Mark Eighty-Two High Drags with delayed fusing on the conformal wing mountings. Any one of the four bombs should trigger the isotope into decomposition, but since we're only going to get one shot, we figured a little insurance wouldn't hurt. My shop will be sending revised flight planning data later today that will take into account the weight and drag of the weapons, as well as dropping the external tanks.

"We'll run a complete power-on check of all systems, and peak each one as necessary. Refueling will be held off until the last possible moment, and probably won't be completed until just before you pre-flight so we can keep the fuel as cold as possible and thus be able to pack more in.

"The last item deals with your flying gear. We had you bring your winter flight suit and jacket because if you run into trouble, it will probably be after you hit the target and are egressing north. That area is inside the Arctic Circle, and if you have to punch out, you'll need all the cold-weather gear you can get. The ground temperatures up there are not extreme this time of year, but it's definitely not sunbathing weather.

"That's all I have now," Dumont continued. "I ran a no-wind check on the time to the target, and it comes out to three hours and forty-five minutes. Sunrise at Zhigansk is at zero five thirty hours, so this would give us a takeoff time of zero one four five. Once we get the real winds, we can adjust the time of departure so that you hit the target area at sunrise, or just a little after. We should allow some extra time for the weather briefing and going over the target layout one more time, so let's plan on briefing at 2200, and being down at the hangar by 2300. I'd recommend allowing enough time for a good meal before leaping off, since it's going to be a long day."

"Roger that," remarked Gates, thinking about the obvious inference from Dumont's statement—that if things didn't go exactly right, it might be their last meal for quite some time.

Gates and Brock were going into a situation that would be so fluid, and contain so many variables, that no premission briefing could cover all the possibilities. Their reaction to Soviet defensive measures would depend on the situation of the moment and their instincts. Each one's skills had been well honed by many years of experience, using tactics developed by countless engagements and refined by innumerable debriefings. Yet, despite their confidence, the specter of the unknown kept raising its ugly head, and their private thoughts repeatedly drifted to the scenarios they might face.

At 11:30 A.M., Dumont returned from a preliminary briefing by the Special Weather Detachment and gave the particulars to Gates and Brock. When at last the clock ticked off the noon hour, Dumont decided to call it a day.

The colonel envied the aircrews as they downed their STOP pills and would soon be sacked out for a solid eight hours of rest. The irregular hours and the strain of keeping things tied together during the past few weeks was beginning to catch up. A cloak of weariness hung about him that only the urgency of the mission kept from being overpowering. He knew he wouldn't need a STOP pill to fall asleep, but he also knew he'd have to be up in less than six hours to start the wheels in motion for the final phase of PROJECT MONGOOSE.

# *Chapter* **8**

*Kunsan Air Base, Korea*

The leaden, rain-heavy lower deck of clouds had lifted somewhat by the time Dumont made his way to the Communications Center that evening. However, the occasional sprinkles on the windshield served notice that the storm system had not yet run its course and the current letup was only a respite.

General Cunningham seemed depressed when he informed Dumont that not a lick of progress had been made in the diplomatic area. The Soviets were as intransigent as ever. Cunningham had met with the President and the Secretaries of State and Defense only a few hours earlier, and they were still trying to pursue a negotiated settlement. However, things did not look too promising and the mission was still a Go.

Dumont reported that since the prepping of the birds was going well, he assumed they would be ready on schedule. Cunningham's spirits seemed to lift at even this small bit of good news in an otherwise discouraging day. He told Dumont to call back an hour or so before takeoff, for a last-minute update.

The Special Weather Detachment people were taping their charts to the wall of the lounge when Dumont entered. The entire route was still dominated by an extensive and complex weather system that influenced nearly all of eastern Asia, particularly the northern areas. Using Weather's list of the low-level winds between each checkpoint, Dumont started to plug the numbers into the flight plan. Again it was a mixed bag, with speeds and directions varying quite a bit from one segment to another. However, the drill was necessary to establish the time and fuel over each checkpoint along the way, just in case the computer and navigation systems malfunctioned and the pilots had to rely on dead reckoning. Rather than make these guys go through a detailed presentation twice, Dumont decided to wait for the pilots' briefing and just utilize the strip weather maps.

"Hmmmm. Not bad, but it could be better," he mulled to himself while going over the charts. He had hoped for a solid overcast from the deck to forty thousand feet, with the exception of a sucker hole over the target to allow a visual weapons delivery, but the maps showed a broken to overcast layer at three thousand feet from the coast to central Manchuria. The visibilities beneath would be good, which meant the airplanes could be silhouetted against the bottom of the clouds around large, well-lit cities. And there were quite a few of those on the route for the first two hundred miles into China.

From there to the Soviet border, the number of population centers dropped considerably, and the weather offered even less help. The lower clouds would become scattered, and the upper layers would thin out to almost nothing. This large "open area" extended to within a hundred miles or less of the border, and the only break they would get during this stretch was the fact that there would not be much of a moon.

Farther north, things were more to his liking. The clouds became more layered, ceilings started to lower, and occasional rain showers would reduce the visibility considerably. When they got into the mountainous area inside the border, there would be periods of complete IFR at five hundred feet.

"This is more like it," he thought. "Tops high enough to provide lots of room for hiding, and bottoms low enough to let them stay below the radar." Where the track crossed the Lena River for the first time, the terrain moderated a little. The rugged mountains gave way to lower, more gently rolling hills, and with the decreased elevations came more layered sky conditions.

The multiple cloud decks stayed fairly constant all the way to the target, and Dumont was not too pleased about this. If, by some stroke of luck, the Soviets got wind of a threat to Zhigansk, interceptors would be deployed no less than two hundred to four hundred miles from the target, allowing them time for multiple attacks, in case the first fighters either missed or couldn't find their target. It also kept their forces close enough together to give them the flexibility to mass in the proper sector to counter the attack.

The basic premise in the MONGOOSE plan was that Soviet radar would be effectively nullified by the combination of Stealth and terrain masking. However, once suspicious of an attack, the Soviets would expect it at low altitude and would deploy groups of fighters in the clear areas between the lower cloud layers. If the F-24s were spotted by MiGs roaming these open spaces and the MiGs got inside the ten-mile "invisibility bubble," a serious threat could develop—particularly if they were discovered near the Lena River, which would give the Soviets better than three-quarters of an hour to work over the two F-24s. If they used a trailer aircraft, the run into the target could be a long day indeed. But the whole scenario depended on them getting and maintaining a visual on MONGOOSE Flight.

Dumont cursed this turn of events, and could only hope that the forecast of layered clouds was on the optimistic side.

Even more crucial than the weather south of the target were the conditions over Zhigansk itself, and the forecast called for the same layered clouds over the research site. This was what Dumont was hoping for, since the preferred delivery method would be visual, even if the target had to be acquired by LANTIRN. If the cloud layers did not permit an eyeballed release, the whole run could be made on the LANTIRN, but accuracy would probably suffer.

Weather conditions for the egress from the target were somewhat better. The layers of clouds still persisted, but they were thicker and the tops were higher. A footnote on the strip map indicated that ceilings along the western side of the Verkhoyanskiy Mountains would be right on the deck. "At last, a break for our side," he thought, knowing that this area would be critically important to the survival of MONGOOSE Flight. Deep in his heart, Dumont knew that if these guys got to the target and destroyed it, they would still need a sizable chunk of luck to make it out of Russia and to their tankers in one piece.

### The White House

White House Chief of Staff Tom Whitney went through his notes one more time before going to the Oval Office to give the President a "how goes it" briefing on MONGOOSE. The decision to go ahead with the plan had been an agonizing one. Even if everything went exactly as planned, this mission would place the millions of people in the United States and the Soviet Union closer to mutual annihilation than they had ever been since the dawn of the Atomic Age. Despite being an active participant in the discussions about MONGOOSE, Whitney was glad the ultimate decision wasn't his.

The President looked up eagerly as his Chief of Staff entered, and quickly pushed aside the papers he had been working on. "How are things going on the project, Tom?"

"So far, very good, Mr. President. Walt Martin just called to say that both aircraft have arrived at Kunsan in good condition. Only minor problems, which can be cleared up quickly while they're being prepared for the mission. Both pilots are in good shape and ready to go."

"How did we fare in the test with the Navy?"

"That was the big plus of the entire trip. The Stealth modification met or exceeded all of the Pentagon's expectations. Martin was very enthusiastic about the figures reported by the Navy, and said that one of his major concerns about the strike had now been eliminated. He predicted that if it works that well on the way into the target, it's doubtful that the Soviets will know that we're inside their borders until the laser facility is hit."

"I certainly hope he's right. Do we have any idea what the weather will be during the actual mission? General Woods gave me the impression that this would be a crucial factor in the success or failure of this project."

"The latest information from the Special Weather Detachment is that the route will most likely have extensive cloud cover. But they would not commit themselves on the height and the thickness of the overcast. As I understand the overall plan from General Woods, they are hoping for thick clouds down to very low levels. The weather people said that conditions were too unsettled in that area just now to be very specific. They should have a better handle on it in about eight hours."

"O.k., keep me advised on how that's going. Tom, ever since this thing kicked off, I've been having quite a few second thoughts about going through with it. But I have no intention of changing my mind unless we hear something very positive from Moscow, and Roy Butler sees no chance of that happening. Do we have any word on the Communist buildup in Europe?"

"No change there, Mr. President. Every one of our sources indicates that it's proceeding on schedule, and all units should be in place by the end of the month. NATO is moving their people into position to counter the threat as best they can, but our line is very, very thin. Since it looks like MONGOOSE will go off as planned, do you want me to cancel your appointments tomorrow while the strike is in progress?"

"No, I think it would be better to leave things as they are, if for no other reason than to present an air of normalcy. If there's another leak about the project somewhere and suddenly I'm out of circulation, the opposition may put two and two together. All the players on both sides are too edgy right now for someone to start making waves, no matter how small. We won't know how the mission went until they arrive at the refueling point, and by that time of day things will be fairly quiet around here.

"Naturally, if any news comes in during the day, I want to be informed immediately, no matter who I'm with. There's nothing on my calendar here that can't be interrupted. I'd like you to stay in contact with the Pentagon during the mission so that you can give me an update as things go along."

*Kunsan Air Base, Korea*

Gates and Brock finished their steak and eggs by nine-thirty, then reviewed the low-level winds and the Pentagon's fuel consumption figures.

Gates had a question. "What's with the new fuel flow figures? They're slightly different than the ones we've used on the last two missions."

"The guys at the shop took into account the armament that has been added, as well as the weight and drag changes that will occur when you drop the external tanks," Dumont replied. "Overall, we're coming out a little better when the tanks are dropped, even with the armament still aboard. They also figured on using full military power during the egress leg.

"If you're satisfied with the numbers, I'll have them enter the data into your computers. Meanwhile, this is Captain Waterman from the Special Weather Detachment, who will brief you on what to expect over the entire route. The significant weather for each leg will also be entered with the flight information."

After Waterman started his presentation, Dumont went to the communications room of the tanker to recheck the secure voice line. The weather briefing had finished when Dumont returned to the lounge, and the major from intelligence was waiting his turn. Introductions were made as he pinned up his maps over the weather charts.

"As far as we've been able to tell from diplomatic and radio intercept sources, the Chinese have not gotten involved in this latest international upset. Either the Soviets haven't told them about neutralizing

Star Wars, or the Chinese figure that any action we take will be against
the Soviet Union and not them. Things are relatively quiet in China,
with no increased alert status or movement of forces. Therefore,
unless you are spotted and identified visually or by radar, your passage
through Chinese airspace should be no problem. The chances of
being detected by military or paramilitary forces are quite slim because
of the Stealth modification, darkness, and the late hour. Casual sightings by civilians are not considered a threat because of the populace's
tendency to avoid involvement with the authorities on anything that
doesn't concern them directly.

"However, the Soviet Union is an altogether different ball game.
They are on an increased state of alert, and even though they hold the
upper hand strategically, they are prepared to react to anything we
attempt. If you are detected, you can expect that every resource at
their command will be used to defend both the ingress and egress
routes.

"Radar coverage along the southern border is good, and in most
cases, adjacent sites overlap. Once you're north of the Stanovoy
Mountains, the radars thin out a bit, but it is by no means a free ride to
the target. The cities of Aldan, Solyanka, Isit and Vilyuysk along your
route all have airports with traffic control radar in the vicinity, as does
Zhigansk. We also can't rule out the possibility of gap-filler radars in
between. The egress route is the same story in reverse—sparse radar
coverage until you are within two hundred miles of the coastline, and
then fairly solid. Once you get two hundred miles out to sea, the only
remaining site is on the New Siberian Islands.

"The biggest problem you'll be facing as far as radar coverage is
concerned will be from AWACS. They normally don't operate these
aircraft that far into the interior, but if they get spooked early enough,
it would be possible to get one into the area by the time you arrive.
Stealth will work against the AWACS radar the same as it does against
ground sites; however, since it would be cruising along with you, it
could get lucky and get inside a ten-mile radius of your position.

"Enemy fighters will be an even bigger problem. Along your
flight route, the Soviets have at least a dozen bases that are close
enough to scramble fighters for an intercept. In a situation such as
this, we expect that they would launch everything in commission if
they think they need it, and this would amount to roughly one hundred and eighty MiGs. Their only limiting factor would be the number
they could effectively control at any given time. By restricting close
control to leaders of four ship flights, they could introduce a large

number of interceptors into the problem. Also, other flights could be given an area to patrol on their own, with orders to engage anything they identify as hostile."

As the intelligence officer went on about the hordes of fighters that would be waiting for them, and continued with the scores of flak batteries and mobile SAM sites that could be moved in around the target, Gates began to experience his first misgivings about MONGOOSE. Two guys facing that number of fighters for the length of time they would be in Soviet airspace gave this flight all the appearances of a kamikaze mission. He could feel a knot tightening in the pit of his stomach and a trace of moisture forming on his palms. These sensations were not the result of any lack of confidence in his own ability but, the sheer numbers involved certainly tipped the odds in favor of the Soviets.

He realized that if he continued to dwell on this line of thought, his imagination would have him seeing a sky black with MiGs and flak thick enough to walk on. "Think positive," he told himself. "All the fighters in the world won't help if they can't find us."

The defensive systems in the F-24 provided very effective countermeasures against every weapon the Soviets could launch against them, except the gun, he reasoned. If a MiG did get within ten miles and got a good enough lockon to fire a radar missile, a flick of the ECM switch would help even the odds considerably. The system would analyze the enemy fighter's radar signal and, depending on the geometry of the attack, would activate circuitry for range gate stealers, angle deceivers, or chaff drops. These, used singly or in combination, would provide a more inviting, but false, group of targets for the missile to home in on. As a last resort, the system could also use barrage jamming in an attempt to saturate the enemy's radar scope with "noise," which would mask the target's exact location. However, this option had to be used sparingly since the Soviets had missiles that would guide on just such a transmitted jamming signal. There were also flares that could be dropped to help foil an attack with infrared guided missiles. And the layers of clouds would provide a good hiding place to prevent acquisition by an IR system.

The major from intelligence finished his gloomy litany of possibilities, and left the lounge to Dumont and the two pilots. The colonel had a lot of ground to cover, so he didn't waste a minute. "I just got a call from General Cunningham, and before we go over a few items peculiar to this flight, he wanted me to pass along some greetings. The President and the senior staff in Washington who have been working on PROJECT MONGOOSE all send you their prayers and best wishes for success. I'd like to add mine to theirs as well."

Dumont paused for just a second, and then touched on the procedures in case someone went down. "I know that SOPs and tradition stipulate that the surviving airplane should CAP the downed bird as long as fuel permits. However, on this mission we'll have to forgo that luxury. It is of paramount, repeat *paramount*, importance that the scientists at Eielson get a chance to analyze the data from the radiation detectors as soon as possible. Their findings will have a direct and immediate impact on national policy moves following the raid. It is essential that you get from the target to within radio range of the tanker as fast as possible and give your initial strike report.

"Then you will press on to Alaska at the best speed the tankers can make. This will mean refueling at airspeeds a little higher than you're used to, but this shouldn't cause too much of a problem. If it does, slow down to where things are manageable for the refueling, and then push it up for the times in between.

"A couple of things will be different tonight than on previous launches. The first will be that no clearance will be filed. The tower chief has been told that this mission has absolute priority, and one of our people will be there to make sure everything goes smoothly. The field will be officially closed for 'runway lighting repairs' from 2200 until after you're off, to prevent delays from transient traffic. Second, make no radio transmissions except those that are necessary between aircraft—and those will be on a secure channel. In case the Soviets are monitoring our frequencies, we don't want to give them anything to think about.

"When you're ready to take the active, blink your landing light and the tower will answer with a green light. At that time they will turn on the runway lights and clear out any traffic that may be in your departure route. No other signals to the tower will be necessary, and you are cleared to roll when ready. Make sure before taking the active that your transponder, navigation lights, and rotating beacon are all off. Check one another over, since this is an exception to normal procedures.

"Just before you get to the target, call that the radiation detection system is on. Make another reminder call about two hundred twenty-five miles from the refueling point, to turn your IFF on so the AWACS can pick you up. They will be monitoring your en route freq, and transmit vectors to join you up with the tankers. When you are close enough to make Eielson on internal fuel, plus an alternate if necessary, you'll be topped off and free to leave the tanker force. Press on at max cruise in order to get on the ground as soon as possible.

"There's one thing we haven't talked about yet, which may be unnecessary; however, we want to be sure you have no misunderstanding about it. That is the rules of engagement for this mission. The minute you cross the Chinese or Soviet border without clearance, particularly loaded with weapons, you've committed an act of war. Historically, their standard procedure has been to shoot first and ask questions later. Therefore, once you've crossed the Chinese border, you are cleared to fire on anything you consider a threat to the mission. This also includes the authority to fire first, if someone is blocking your way. In other words, do whatever you have to do to get to the target, destroy it, and get out. Any questions on the items we've just gone over?"

The two pilots looked at each other and then shook their heads. "I think we've got everything straight," Gates commented.

Dumont glanced at the wall clock and said, "It looks like it's gettin' to be about that time. I'm going to stick by the phone here in case the Pentagon has any last-minute words of wisdom. When you're off, I'll call in your departure time and then launch for Alaska. Make sure to take any personal gear out of your pockets, and recheck that you've only got your dog tags, Geneva Convention Card, Blood Chit, and E & E map in your flight suit. I'll bring your wallets and other stuff to Eielson."

Giving each pilot a warm handshake, he sent them off with, "Best of luck you guys, and give 'em hell! See you in Alaska!"

Gates and Brock were a trifle subdued, each mulling over his own thoughts as they piled into Dumont's staff car for the ride to the alert barns.

The refueling trucks were just leaving as they pulled up in front of the hangars, where the maintenance officer reported that both planes were loaded and ready to go. All apprehension about enemy fighters, flak, and weather disappeared as they began the preflight inspection and settled into the routine of the mission. Particular attention was paid to the fuse settings, arming wires, suspension of the five-hundred-pound Snakeyes snugged up to the undersurface of each wing. Gates smiled to himself as he noted that each iron bomb had been coated with the same Stealth material as the airplane. Dumont's people hadn't missed a trick!

After strapping into the cockpit, he asked the crew chief to check the next hangar to see if Brock was ready. The noncom was back in a

few moments with a "thumbs up" sign, so Gates motioned for the
hangar doors to be opened. The yawning doors at each end of the
barn, signaling the start of the most difficult flight of his career, also
triggered a tightening of the muscles in the bottom of his stomach.
The big game was about to kick off!

Startup and power checks went without a hitch, and both airplanes rolled out of the hangars almost side by side. Gates shut the
canopy immediately to get the air conditioning on line, and flicked the
landing light switch twice as he neared the approach end of runway
36. The response came instantly from the tower as the Aldis lamp
blinked like a distant green eye. The two blacked-out F-24s eased onto
the active like a pair of ghosts, illuminated only by the glare of the runway lights. The flight leader looked over his shoulder to check his
wingman for lights, and could just make out Brock's head nod signify-
ing that he was ready to go.

The knot was still in his gut as Gates stood on the brakes and
pushed the throttles to the military stop. The aircraft nosed over
slightly on the front oleo in response to the roaring thrust of the two
Pratt and Whitneys, as if eager to get airborne. A quick glance over the
instruments showed everything in the green. Toes off the brakes,
elapsed time button pushed, throttles around the detent to full afterburner, and MONGOOSE One was on his way.

It was probably his imagination, but the warm night and extra fifteen hundred pounds of weight seemed to extend the takeoff roll considerably. The wings finally got a good bite of the air, and the main
gears broke free of the runway.

Gates hit the gear switch to UP, and as the wheels tucked themselves into the wells, he felt the acceleration building more to his liking. He rolled out of his left turn to a heading of three zero four
degrees as the altimeter hit five hundred feet, then trimmed out the
climb and backed off the throttles to cruise R.P.M. The auto flight control system engaged smoothly and the data for the first checkpoint
was called up from the computer. The turn point was a few degrees
port at one hundred eighty miles. Gates went left twenty degrees to
get a good cut back to track, and Brock called, "MONGOOSE Two,
tied."

"One, Rog!" was the only reply needed to let his wingman know
the radios in both birds were o.k.

The weather was turning out just as forecast, with a deck of
clouds at three thousand feet and at least ten miles visibility underneath. Over the Yellow Sea, it was once again like flying through ink,

with only the occasional lights of a fishing boat far to the starboard. There was nothing on the HUD out to the pickup limits of the LAN-TIRN, except the solid horizon line. They reached the turn point on schedule, and Gates wheeled around to a heading of north while rechecking the fuel panel by feeling the switches for each tank set, to make sure they were in the proper position.

The second checkpoint was just north of Fengch'eng, so he called up a graphic of that area on the auxiliary screen. The course line showed him passing just west of Antung and Sinuiju near the mouth of the Yalu River. Historic places, he thought, as these names recalled battles he had read about between the MiGs and the Sabre Jets over MiG Alley nearly forty-five years ago.

Gates moved the elevation scan control of the radar up a few degrees so that the beam would search level and high. No returns appeared on the scope after three or four sweeps, confirming the intelligence report of little or no traffic over the coast. A distant glow from the base of the clouds at his one o'clock position marked the location of the two cities on the Yalu, and soon it was possible to make out scattered lights from villages along the shore.

He sensed a definite increase in the "pucker factor" as the HUD displayed an image of the approaching Chinese coastline, prompting a recheck of the armament panel to make sure it was set up to fire the AMRAAMs. The switches were correctly positioned, so he hit the Weapons Status button on the computer panel. The primary display screen immediately showed a graphic of the entire weapons system, indicating that each missile station was loaded, and a Ready light was on next to the one Gates had selected to fire first. He then checked IR missiles and the gun, and after getting a Ready on each, he switched the system back to AMRAAMs. The flight control switch was put in the Combat position so that the Decoupled mode was available in case of a hassle. He was now set for all comers, and the only thing needed to fire the weapons was a flick of the Armament Master Switch, a squeeze of the trigger, and a reason.

Details on the coast became more distinct, so Gates angled toward the largest dark area to minimize being silhouetted. He could feel the flight controls starting to respond to the increasing elevation inputs from the LANTIRN, and the rate of climb indicator began moving upward slightly. The surf line disappeared under his wings, and the rock-steady overwater flight was replaced by the gently undulating path dictated by the changing terrain below.

Gates's eyes were glued to the radar scope, carefully checking any return that even looked like it might be an airplane. Every so often he glanced outside to make sure he was avoiding the more brightly lit areas, followed by a quick check of the course deviation needle to see if he was wandering too far off track. "So far, so good!" he thought to himself, as both the radar screen and the sensor system showed no threats from the air or ground in any direction.

The HUD did show a yellow X on the extreme right of the display, which Gates figured was a radar site more interested in the traffic around Antung, or northeastward along the Yalu. The eerie feeling of flying over enemy territory on a mission that could initiate a global conflict grew even more intense within him.

A few minutes later the lights of Fengch'eng appeared just a shade to the starboard, so he nudged the fighter ten degrees port to give the town a wide berth. After correcting back to track, the inertial system indicated he was over the second checkpoint. Jotting down the time and fuel figures, he noted that they were right on the money. Since he hadn't heard from his wingman for quite a while, a fuel check would be in order.

"MONGOOSE Two, what state?"

A few seconds later Brock replied, "I'm about seventy-five pounds under par."

"Rog. I'm just about on speed."

Despite the fact that things seemed to be going well up to this point, Gates was under no illusion that the rest of the mission would follow suit. He probed the sky in front of his aircraft relentlessly with the radar, checking out each return thoroughly. On one high search pattern, he did pick up a definite target.

"MONGOOSE Two, bogey thirty port at seventy-five."

"Contact there," came Brock's matter-of-fact reply.

Gates locked the radar on the target to analyze the track, and in a few seconds the readout came on the scope: Altitude 25,000 feet, speed 480 knots, course 240 degrees.

"Most likely a commercial transport on a feeder run, judging from the speed and altitude," he said half aloud. Nevertheless, he quickly broke lock and returned to the Search mode, just in case it was a military plane with gear that could detect a radar lockon. He also wanted full-system capability to search for other strays that were closer to his altitude.

Glancing at the navigation graphic, he decided that the lights just becoming visible up ahead must be Pench'i. The flight plan called for him to pass ten miles east of the city, but his correction to avoid the last town had put it dead ahead. Gates banked farther to the port to keep him clear of Pench'i, as well as the next city thirty miles farther down the road. This deviation would take him closer to the metropolis of Shenyang, which had a civil airport, but he still felt that he could skirt the field by at least twenty miles.

His sensors had already picked up the radar at Shenyang, but the yellow X was forty-five degrees port and moving slowly to a greater angle off. Once they got by this major city and deeper into the interior, it would be easier to stay on course, since the terrain became more rugged and the population centers more widely scattered.

The on-course needle was just centering, and MONGOOSE One was adding a little left aileron to roll out on track, when he caught some movement out of the corner of his left eye. Jerking his head around, he stared in disbelief at the approaching bulk of an airliner in his ten o'clock position at the same altitude. He was so close that he could see the muted glow of the cockpit lights behind the windscreen. Reflexively, he slammed the stick to the full right and back in his gut, and stood on the right rudder pedal to increase his turning rate. Pulling as hard as he could, Gates laid over six G's on the airplane instantly, while leaning over in his seat and straining his muscles in the M-1 maneuver to counter the vision-dimming G forces.

The instant he started his evasive action, Brock's frantic call boomed in his headset. "Break right! Bogey nine o'clock close in!" Steeling himself for the explosive crush of a midair, Gates was too terrified to answer. All he could do was hold the plane in a max performance turn, and hope that he had reacted soon enough.

Although in reality it only took a split second for the F-24 to flash across the nose of the airliner, it seemed like an eternity in the cockpit as he worked desperately to avoid certain disaster. A few more split seconds passed before he dared to think that the two aircraft had missed each other. Gates's heart was pounding like a trip hammer, and his entire body had broken out in a cold sweat, as the massive jolt of adrenaline worked through his system.

He quickly whipped the bird back to a wing-level position, and frantically looked in every quadrant for the airliner. Only darkness met his eyes, since the two aircraft were now miles apart, each feeling lucky to be there after so close a brush with death.

Sucking in deep draughts of cool oxygen to calm the aftereffects of his near miss, Gates tried to reconstruct the "moment of stark terror" often quoted by wags in the definition of flying. He knew there was an airport at Shenyang, but what would a transport be doing at such a low altitude that far from the field? Whatever the answer, it didn't alter the fact that the airliner was there, and he had very nearly bought the farm.

His violent evasive action carried him east of track, so Gates rolled in a correction to the left. While checking the cockpit to set up for the next leg, he noticed that the radar antenna was still tilted up to scan above his altitude. This was the reason the airliner had gotten that close—it was flying so low that it was beneath his search pattern. Had his antenna been looking just a littler lower, he would have gotten a contact in time to avoid taking such drastic evasive action.

Another thought crossed his mind that troubled him even more than the transport being at such a low altitude. Unless they were too concerned with their own avoidance maneuver, the crew most certainly got a good look at him as he streaked by, belly up to their cockpit. Was he in view long enough for them to identify the airplane as not being one of theirs? Would they report the near miss to the control agency, who would be immediately suspicious since they were not aware of any other traffic in the area? A pang of frustration went though him as he bemoaned, "Here we are, only five hundred miles into the mission, and our cover gets blown by a set of circumstances that defied all odds."

"MONGOOSE Two, this is One. I don't know where that guy came from, but it was the closest call I've ever had! When did you get an initial contact on him?"

"First time I saw him he was right next to you. He must have been down in the weeds and too far abeam for you to get a paint. Can't figure why he'd be so low. Don't think he was in trouble since he was still climbing after you passed until he went off the side of the scope."

"I wonder if the crew will report nearly being hit by a fighter? It wouldn't take the military long to find out it wasn't one of theirs."

"I'd say the odds are fifty-fifty. That jock is probably no different than any other throttle bender in the world. My guess is that he was at such low altitude because he screwed up his departure from Shenyang, or else he was buzzing his girlfriend's house. I doubt he'd want to call attention to the fact that he was tooling along at less than five hundred feet with no declared emergency. Another thing, even if that guy was supposed to be at low altitude, it isn't likely that he would criticize the air force. He'd be sticking his head in a noose."

Brock's assessment of the situation comforted Gates somewhat. The probability of things happening just that way was as good as the chance that the crew would report the near miss.

"I hope you're right, but from now on, I think I'd better keep the bottom of my search pattern a little below our altitude, and let you take care of the higher traffic."

"Roger that."

Gates was alone with his troubled thoughts for the next half hour or so. The terrain avoidance system was functioning smoothly, and the cities were so few and far between that only small deviations from track were required to stay clear of their lights. He was just rolling out on course after swinging to the east of Ch'ich'ihaerh, when he noticed an odd-shaped return on the radar. Ever since his close call with the airliner, he was checking out everything that he couldn't positively identify as ground clutter. This target appeared as a straight line angling in from the southwest toward his line of flight. Too big for an airplane and too straight for a river, and nothing from the sensors to indicate hostile intent. He hit the computer for a graphic of this area, and there was the answer—a segment of the Great Wall of China. The map also showed a long stretch of semimountainous and sparsely populated terrain just north of the Wall.

This was just what he needed because the EMPTY light for the external wing tanks had been flickering on and off for the past five minutes. Finally the light came on steady, and the fuel counter for the internal tank system started decreasing. Rocking and yawing the aircraft slightly did not slosh any more trapped fuel into the feedline, so Gates turned the wing tanks off and the centerline tank on.

Brock's call interrupted his mulling over a place to drop the tanks, "MONGOOSE Two, wing tanks empty, centerline on."

"Roger. Lead the same, and centerline on. It probably would be best to drop the tanks just after crossing the road at the end of the Great Wall. The area northeast of there is supposed to be more mountainous, so I'm going to crank in twenty degrees to the right for the drop."

"Sounds good. I'll do the same."

In a few seconds, Gates could make out the end of the Wall on the HUD, with the river running past it at right angles. The road slowly took shape on the display about five miles farther north. He banked to the right long enough to get the heading change he wanted, and rolled wings level.

The area in front of him was as dark as the inside of an eight ball—no towns, villages, or other signs of population. The only lights were widely scattered pinpoints that most likely were isolated farm houses. Gates reached down and switched the armament panel to the external wing stations, and snapped the master switch to the ARM position. The image of the river slid off the bottom of the HUD, followed by the road. He waited a few seconds until the last farmhouse light had disappeared beneath him, and pressed the button on the side of the stickgrip. A dull "thunk" was all he felt as the charges fired to push the tanks away from the underside of each wing. He called "Tanks away" and reselected radar missiles after checking that the status lights for the wing stations were out, indicating that the tanks had released.

His wingman answered, "Roger, coming up on my drop shortly," and in a few moments, "Tanks away!"

By the time Gates was heading north again, he noticed that the airspeed had crept up to five hundred fifteen knots. Without the weight and drag of the tanks, the airplane was flying a little more on the step, so he eased the throttles back a couple of percent to stay on the flight plan. A checkpoint was passed, and after jotting down the information, he noticed heavy ground returns being picked up on the extreme left sweep of the radar. He coded the request for the next graphic into the computer, and it confirmed that the radar was seeing the eastern foothills of the Greater Khingan Mountains. Even more ominous, it showed that the next checkpoint was the Soviet border.

# Chapter 9

*Over the Soviet Union*

The DME clicked down to 100 miles to the Russian border, and the yellow X's started to appear on the HUD. These would be Chinese GCI sites whose controllers would be more interested in tracks originating in the Soviet Union than in internal traffic. "Still no problem," Gates thought. "These radars aren't close together, so there shouldn't be too much difficulty in staying beyond the twenty-mile limit."

The terrain-following radar was generating a roller coaster ride as they neared the junction of the Greater and Lesser Khingan Mountain ranges. MONGOOSE One was sticking to the valley between these lines of hills, by watching the ground returns painted by the aircraft's radar. He steered right or left to equalize the amount of return on each side of the scope, using this as a broad-gauge measure to stay between the two ridge lines. The fine-tuning was done by the LANTIRN system after he had picked the optimum path through the converging foothills.

The HUD began displaying a large river, which, after comparison with the graphic, he knew was the Amur. Gates did pick up some airborne targets about fifty miles east of course, but after checking them out, decided they were a couple of redeye flights going to the airports about a hundred miles to the east. The sensors were now detecting two early-warning radars, but they were too far away to be of concern. The Amur rushed by, and Gates could feel the tension building even more, now that they were over Russian soil.

Forty miles ahead was the city of Skovorodino, which also had an airport on the northern side. After his narrow escape at Shenyang,

Gates wanted to avoid this area by a good margin, and checked it over carefully with the radar, both high and low. A deviation east of track looked like the best bet, so he headed for what looked like a shallow valley in his two o'clock position.

He was just rounding some low hills on his left to start up the valley, when it suddenly appeared. His heart froze as he stared at the HUD in disbelief. A little to the left of center, near the top of the combining glass was a flashing yellow X. Continuing straight ahead was out of the question since this would give them maximum tracking time. The only solution was to create as much lateral separation to the east as he could, and do it as rapidly as possible.

Even as these thoughts were racing through his mind, Gates wracked the F-24 over in a hard right turn, while slamming both throttles to full military power. In the same split second, he frantically jabbed the mike button and yelled. "Two, go hard right. GCI site at ten o'clock."

"Toop," came Brock's clipped reply, reflecting the hard onset of G's as he also tried to avoid the searching radar beam. However, Gates's warning came too late as Brock's display suddenly showed a flashing X before he had completed forty-five degrees of turn.

MONGOOSE One knew that the hills forming the eastern side of the valley lay just ahead, and their masking effect would be lost as they crested the peaks in their frantic dash from the radar site. He also realized that the minimum recommended altitude for the terrain-following system was five hundred feet at their normal speed of five hundred knots. The airspeed needle was nudging five seventy-five and the yellow X was still flashing, so Gates decided to gamble and push the system over its limit.

"Takin' it down to three hundred," he called to Brock, as he set the lower parameters. Not too sure of what to expect, he kept a light grip on the stick, with one finger resting on the disengage switch. If things got too hairy, he would take over and fly the plane manually. Then he'd have to climb well above the five-hundred-foot mark to ensure adequate ground clearance, and at that altitude, the GCI site would have no problem tracking them.

His winter flying gear was becoming oppressively hot, and anxiety had him sweating profusely. The ride down at three hundred feet was extremely rough, mainly because of the increased airspeed. The aircraft jerked from one attitude to another in response to the TFR inputs, as the G meter oscillated wildly between the plus and minus sides of the dial. Gates was glad his seat belt and harness were tight, since he was being bounced around the cockpit like a Ping-Pong ball.

Despite their gut-wrenching sprint from the radar, the flashing X remained on the HUD for an agonizingly long time. It took forever to drift slowly to the left, and then to the bottom of the combining glass. Before reaching the lower edge of the display, the flashing quit, but Gates decided to continue eastward for another fifteen seconds as insurance. The hills on the far side of the valley now became a factor, since they appeared on the HUD about fifteen miles away. He was reluctant to risk a turn as the seconds ticked off, but he did back off on the throttles to the normal cruise setting.

"Turning on course and going up to five hundred feet," he called to Brock, while rolling into a steep left turn and gingerly climbing back to the planned altitude.

Neither pilot spoke as they both realized the gravity of what had happened during the past three or four minutes. If the Soviets had their act together, they had plenty of time to check out these pop-up tracks thoroughly. They also had a lot of time to investigate the unknowns by scrambling interceptors, since the target was better than an hour and a half away. Gates rationalized that, as far as their options were concerned, it was academic whether the Soviets had picked them up or not. At this point in the game, they could only press on to the target and hope for the best.

At least the weather was helping to dispel some of the gloom generated by the events of the last five minutes. As the ground started to rise toward the mile-high Stanovoy Mountains, ceilings began to lower and the layered clouds above MONGOOSE Flight were thickening up.

*Kirovskiy, U.S.S.R.*

Sergeant Boris Postnikov sat staring at the surveillance scope, and to all outward appearances was diligently scanning the airspace for traffic. However, Postnikov's mind was miles away from the scope— thirty-five miles to be exact, in the city of Skovorodino. A few weeks earlier he had met a girl who had captivated him completely, and just as things were progressing nicely, the entire unit was put on alert and restricted to the site.

The commanding officer, Major Snetkov, gave no explanation other than the increased readiness being ordered by higher headquarters, and all air traffic was to be monitored closely. All this was not unfamiliar, and Postnikov seriously doubted that even the major knew what all the commotion was about. A remote radar site, thousands of

miles from the major happenings along the western border would certainly be kept in the dark about anything important, unless it concerned them directly. His only consolation was that other radar units
in their sector were under the same restrictions. The shift was only
half over, and he was already numb with boredom from watching the
ever-circling trace.

Even though his eyelids were leaden, Postnikov dare not show
any signs of inattention. The lieutenant in charge watched each man
relentlessly, and things would go hard for anyone he suspected of day-
dreaming. Although the airspace around Kirovskiy was quiet as a
grave, he feigned interest by adjusting and readjusting the scope controls, and sector-scanning certain areas.

Although he was only half looking, the sudden appearance of
what seemed like ground returns just south of the station snapped him
to full alertness. There had never been clutter in that spot before, and
from force of habit he marked the position of the dimming image with
a grease pencil. The trace dragged slowly around, and when it passed
the one-hundred-sixty-degree line, the return appeared again, but this
time it had moved. Automatically, he locked the tracking tag on the target, and called the coordinates in to the plotter and the identification
section. The latter had no traffic scheduled for another three hours, so
the plotters drew the track on the Plexiglas board in orange:
Unknown!

The lieutenant bolted from his chair when the initial plot was circled in orange, shouting to the crosstell position to check with the
sites on either side to see if they had picked up this track. With the
lieutenant now looking over his shoulder, Postnikov continued working the target, which by this time was heading away from the station in
an easterly direction, and moving at better than five hundred knots. As
it crossed the ten-mile circle, the blip started to break up, looking
again like the initial pickup a few moments ago. While puzzling over
this, the sergeant saw an identical return pop up south of the station, a
mile or so to the east of his first grease pencil mark. After a couple of
sweeps, this second target firmed up like the first, and was definitely
recognizable as an aircraft return. This track was also curving to the
east, and roughly paralleling the other. Then, as suddenly as they
appeared, the tracks were gone, with Postnikov's last dot on the scope
at the twelve-mile mark.

The pair of Russians stared at the display, not believing what they
had seen. The two small crescents of dots ended abruptly in an area
where their low-level coverage had always been good.

Postnikov expanded the picture and sector-scanned the area where the targets disappeared, in hopes that the magnification might enhance the faded images. The scope remained blank, and the lieutenant ordered the height finder to sweep the eastern sector in hopes that its narrower beam could focus more energy on the targets and regain contact. He was starting to get nervous about what these mystery tracks might mean. With the entire command on alert, something big was obviously in the wind, and now he had to explain the unexplainable to his superiors.

Knowing full well that there would be lots of questions, the shift chief and Sergeant Postnikov reviewed all that they had seen, and what actions were taken. Both were satisfied that the proper procedures had been followed, but the lieutenant had a sinking feeling that none of this would placate his commander and those above. Nevertheless, Major Snetkov had to be informed, so he reluctantly dialed his superior's quarters.

Thinking aloud, Sergeant Postnikov commented idly that he had never seen targets disappear so quickly when they were that close to the station, unless they had crashed or had a midair. Totally frustrated, the lieutenant was ready to grasp at straws, even though the way the returns faded from the radar was not typical of a sudden crash. He quickly called the district police in a small town close to where the targets were lost.

After a prolonged ringing, a sleepy magistrate answered in a tone that left no doubt as to his displeasure at being awakened. Desperation prompted the lieutenant into exceeding his authority and ordering the magistrate to check the surrounding area for any signs of a crashed aircraft. He stilled the official's protests by adding that this was a matter of national security, and he needed an answer within the hour—sooner if possible!

Major Snetkov was clearly worried after being briefed on the situation. He knew no more than the crew about the reason for the increased readiness condition, but realized that the Division Headquarters at Khabarovsk must be notified. As expected, Division was not overly enthusiastic about the sparse information he provided; nonetheless, they dutifully relayed the report to Central Headquarters in Moscow.

The gloomy mood at Kirovskiy did not improve as the replies to the lieutenant's inquiries started filtering back. None of the adjacent radar sites reported picking up any track in the area in question, nor did the height-finder section have any luck in reacquiring the targets.

The Fighter Control Center confirmed that no interceptor activity was scheduled within two hundred miles of Skovorodino that night, and they had no other missions airborne for the last four hours.

The crash/midair theory was also dashed when the magistrate finally called back. He had contacted numerous settlements throughout the area, including two forest-fire lookout towers, and no one reported seeing any fires or hearing any explosions. However, he and his deputies were leaving immediately for a personal search of the countryside and would radio back anything of interest.

## Moscow

The War Room in the Kremlin was having another slow night, even with the military on alert. The novelty of the situation had worn off after the first three or four days, and now the only thing out of the ordinary was the presence of a brigadier general as shift commander. The Situation Board showed no unusual activity by the United States or any of its allies, with the only thing of note being the addition of a dozen fighters, two tankers, and an AWACS to the Alaskan area. Such a move was not unexpected, since the relations between the two world powers had gone downhill during the last month or so.

Brigadier General Aleksandr Gulayev stifled a yawn as he puzzled over the AWACS. The Americans normally didn't deploy this kind of aircraft to Alaska, since radar coverage was good throughout the state, except along the Aleutian Chain. "Too many unknowns to solve this one," he thought, "especially when it seems like we're not being told the whole story." All the bigwigs were staying in the Kremlin, and the standing order was to call General Colonel Kulikov immediately if anything unusual occurred.

The unknown track from Kirovskiy was just being posted on the Situation Board, when the command line from Khabarovsk rang. The control tech answered, and quickly handed it to Gulayev with the comment that it was the division commander.

"General Gulayev, this is Colonel Gororov. You should be getting the report of the unknown that we just received from Kirovskiy."

"Yes, it's just going up on the board now. Do you have any additional information concerning it?" While he was talking, Gulayev was gesturing to the control tech to call Marshal Volzhin and General Kulikov.

"I'm not sure, Comrade General, but it is a little irregular, so I thought I'd pass it along. Our communications section was monitoring Chinese radio frequencies as usual, when an operator picked up a conversation between two of their commercial aircraft. One, who had departed from Shenyang earlier, told the other, who was heading in that direction, to watch out for low-level fighter activity near the airport. The first pilot said he nearly had a midair collision with what he thought was a fighter aircraft. We queried the Chinese Control Center at Haerhpin about this, but as usual they were very circumspect and gave us no information one way or the other."

"Still exhibiting their normal cooperation, I see. What time did this incident take place, Colonel?"

"We don't know, Comrade General, since the pilot never mentioned it. However, his scheduled departure from Shenyang was zero two three three local, and he landed at Haokang on time, so our estimate is that it must have occurred a few minutes after takeoff."

"Yes, that sounds reasonable. Do you have anything to add to this report?"

"No, sir. I will call you at once if we learn anything new."

Gulayev thanked him and was just hanging up the phone when General Kulikov sat down next to him and Marshal Volzhin was approaching the dais, still in his bathrobe. Both officers listened intently as Gulayev went over every detail of the unknown track that faded and the airline captain's remarks about his near miss.

Volzhin looked at Kulikov expectantly, "Well, Aleksey, what do you make of all this?"

Kulikov stared at the Situation Board, frantically trying to piece these fragments of information into a plausible scenario. Volzhin had briefed him on the new laser weapon, so he knew what pressures the Marshal must be under from the Central Committee.

Finally something started to gel in his mind and he got up quickly, saying, "Comrade Marshal, would you please accompany me to the Map Room? I have a theory I'd like to discuss with you." Realizing that if he was right, time was of the essence, Kulikov hurried through the door behind the dais without waiting for his superior to answer.

Volzhin knew that his chief of air defense was an extremely capable and thorough individual, so he shrugged at Gulayev, saying, "If anything new comes up, let us know immediately."

Entering the Map Room, Volzhin commented, "Aleksey, I hope this theory of yours provides us with some answers!" Kulikov was already at the wall map, marking locations and measuring distances. "So do I, Comrade Marshal, because if I am correct, we have a grave problem on our hands. May I proceed?" he asked while shutting the door to ensure their privacy.

"By all means," Volzhin answered as he pulled his chair closer to the map.

"Let us assume, Comrade Marshal, that the Americans have decided not to accept General Secretary Petrov's offer. Once this decision was made, they must have devised an alternative plan, which would probably take one of two forms. The first would be that their refusal would buy them more time, and if a negotiated settlement did not materialize, their intention would be to capitulate. This course of action, however, does not follow traditional American policy in such matters. Being reluctant to initiate a nuclear missile exchange, a more likely hypothesis is that they decided on a desperate attempt to destroy the laser weapon. Between their intelligence activities and surveillance satellites, I do not imagine it was a difficult task to determine the origin of the beam."

Going to the map, he emphasized his remarks with, "This is point one: Zhigansk! Now consider the track that faded at Kirovskiy—here!" making another mark on the map. "Then, our only other piece of information is the sighting of an unknown fighter down here at Shenyang. Now, if we connect all three points, realizing that the last two are approximations, and extend the line south, we end up near the Korean peninsula, where there are numerous American air bases.

"This may sound preposterous, but it is my guess that a small force of American fighters are en route to strike our facility at Zhigansk. I know the evidence is flimsy, but the consequences of any misjudgments on our part would be disastrous. I recommend we take action at once, and then, if all this turns out to be a false alarm, we can only be accused of being overly prudent."

Volzhin stared grimly at the line on the map, still not convinced that Kulikov was right. "I cannot subscribe entirely to your theory, Aleksey. Our intelligence people are not aware of any American fighter that could make such a flight at low level. Could this be a suicide mission? Also, was not the track picked up at Kirovskiy heading east?"

"It is true that we do not know of any such fighter, nor do we know if it is a suicide mission," Kulikov replied, becoming a little irritated at his superior's reluctance to take action when time was so precious. "The aircraft may be ones we already know about that have been modified with extra fuel tanks for this particular strike. Although suicide missions are traditionally abhorrent to the Americans, we cannot rule them out, given the dire straits in which they find themselves. As to the eastward heading at Kirovskiy, I believe that was only temporary. Remember that the contact was lost less than fifteen miles from departed from Shenyang earlier, told the other, who was heading in that direction, to watch out for low-level fighter activity near the airport. The first pilot said he nearly had a midair collision with what he thought was a fighter aircraft. We queried the Chinese Control Center at Haerhpin about this, but as usual they were very circumspect and gave us no information one way or the other."

"Still exhibiting their normal cooperation, I see. What time did this incident take place, Colonel?"

"We don't know, Comrade General, since the pilot never mentioned it. However, his scheduled departure from Shenyang was zero two three three local, and he landed at Haokang on time, so our estimate is that it must have occurred a few minutes after takeoff."

"Yes, that sounds reasonable. Do you have anything to add to this report?"

"No, sir. I will call you at once if we learn anything new."

Gulayev thanked him and was just hanging up the phone when General Kulikov sat down next to him and Marshal Volzhin was approaching the dais, still in his bathrobe. Both officers listened intently as Gulayev went over every detail of the unknown track that faded and the airline captain's remarks about his near miss.

Volzhin looked at Kulikov expectantly, "Well, Aleksey, what do you make of all this?"

Kulikov stared at the Situation Board, frantically trying to piece these fragments of information into a plausible scenario. Volzhin had briefed him on the new laser weapon, so he knew what pressures the Marshal must be under from the Central Committee.

Finally something started to gel in his mind and he got up quickly, saying, "Comrade Marshal, would you please accompany me to the Map Room? I have a theory I'd like to discuss with you." Realizing that if he was right, time was of the essence, Kulikov hurried through the door behind the dais without waiting for his superior to answer.

Volzhin knew that his chief of air defense was an extremely capable and thorough individual, so he shrugged at Gulayev, saying, "If anything new comes up, let us know immediately."

Entering the Map Room, Volzhin commented, "Aleksey, I hope this theory of yours provides us with some answers!" Kulikov was already at the wall map, marking locations and measuring distances. "So do I, Comrade Marshal, because if I am correct, we have a grave problem on our hands. May I proceed?" he asked while shutting the door to ensure their privacy.

commanding officer. He will pass to the commander the following direct order in my name: 'I want all, repeat *all*, available personnel to start work immediately on sandbagging the laser weapon, and any other components that are susceptible to damage by shock or blast effect. This work will take precedence over all other activity, and will proceed at top speed until the weapon is protected. As soon as this task is finished, they will set up air defense positions around the facility, and stand by with their weapons until further notice!' "

Kulikov went to the door, motioned the staff officer in, and quickly showed him what they suspected and what must be done. Gulayev was speechless. He jotted down a few quick notes for the call to Zhigansk while Kulikov cautioned him, "Marshal Volzhin and I will be in the Map Room and want to be informed immediately if any interceptor makes contact with the Unknown. Be sure to pass on to the interceptors that the intruders must be shot down as quickly as possible."

Gulayev acknowledged with a quick "Yes, sir," and hurried to the control dais to set the plan in motion.

"I think it would be wise if I called the General Secretary to let him know what we are doing. In case he asks, are there any follow-on actions you plan to take?"

"Yes there are! When the four alert aircraft are airborne, another four should take off as soon as they can be manned. This will allow us to cover a search area twice as large. In the meantime, all other fighters will be brought up to a Cockpit Alert status to be used as needed. The planes that are airborne will recover at airfields to the north, such as Vilyuysk or Sangar, for refueling and any later action that may be required. I believe we should keep at least eight MiGs patrolling the route until the Americans are destroyed—more if it looks like they will be needed. The patrol flights will be moved north along the route until they must land for fuel. This should occur in the area of the Linde River.

"There are no other interceptor bases closer than Batagay here, and Olenek over here. A similar force of eight or more should be scrambled from each of these bases. If the five-hundred-knot figure is correct, the Americans are scheduled to reach Zhigansk at about zero five thirty their time; therefore, these fighters should be airborne no later than zero five zero five in order to be in position. One group will proceed to a point about one hundred miles south of Zhigansk to pick up the patrol duties from the recovering flights. The other will go directly to Zhigansk and form a line of defense just south of the facility. If the Americans do reach the target, I assume they will try to escape to the north. The airplanes from Batagay and Olenek will pursue and recover at Tiksi or Buolkalakh, here on the coast. Should more interceptors be needed, they will be scrambled from those two bases.

"Comrade Marshal, it is my feeling that the Americans must be shot down regardless of the cost. Obviously, catching them before they reach the target is our primary objective, but even if they get through and attack our facility, they must be pursued relentlessly. Their leaders will have no way of knowing whether or not the mission was successful unless these aircraft reach some point up here in the Arctic Ocean and transmit their results to a relay aircraft or submarine."

Volzhin's eyes narrowed as he followed Kulikov through his scenario, making mental notes of his own questions, and trying to foresee those of the General Secretary. He was impressed by his subordinate's rapid analysis of what needed to be done.

"Very good, Aleksey. It appears that you have considered the problem from all angles. My only question is: Do we have any radar sites along the route the Americans will take? And if these aircraft are Stealth-equipped, will any radar be effective?"

"There are none north of Aldan, Comrade Marshal, except for the terminal control facilities here at Isit, Vilyuysk, and Zhigansk. These may be of value as surveillance sites only, since there are no interceptor control teams there. I will have Gulayev alert them to report any unknown traffic to the military site at Aldan. Beyond that, there are no radars until you reach the coastal bases of Tiksi and Buolkalakh.

"Since our coverage is so spotty from Aldan northward, my recommendation would be to launch an AWACS to work with the fighters patrolling the route. The status board shows one is available at Yakutsk, but it would require your orders to use it, since they are not totally under my command. The aircraft is on Alert status, so it shouldn't take long to get it in the air. I urge you to order the AWACS aloft as soon as possible because Yakutsk is more than thirty minutes flying time from the suspected track.

"With respect to our ability to pick up a Stealth aircraft, I really cannot answer that. I don't believe the Americans have developed this technology to the point where the aircraft is totally invisible. As our research has shown, the Stealth protection breaks down when the airplane is very close to a radar site. I think the evidence on hand supports this premise, since Kirovskiy did have contact with these targets for a short time. It's a long shot, but our best chance is to get the AWACS close enough to the Americans to pick them up, and then parallel their course until they are destroyed."

Volzhin's response was immediate, "Have Gulayev call Yakutsk to get the AWACS into the air immediately, and also have him establish a communications link so that we can talk directly to the plane."

Kulikov hurried out the door to the nearest bank of phones and called Yakutsk himself. Using Volzhin's name to speed things up, he received confirmation that the AWACS would be taxiing shortly. In the meantime, Volzhin had called General Secretary Petrov, who responded ominously that he would be down at the War Room in a few minutes. Petrov's presence would only add pressure to a lot of tough decisions, based on very little information, that must be made shortly. Volzhin had hoped these matters would be left to the military, but apparently that was not to be.

After Kulikov finished his call, the tracks representing the MiGs scrambled from Aldan appeared on the board. He noted with satisfaction that the controller vectored them northward, and split these flights into four pairs. Each would be searching a clear area between cloud layers, on alternate sides of the suspected track. So that Petrov could visualize the situation more readily, he had the plotting section draw a line from Kirovskiy through Zhigansk, and out to the Laptev Sea. Another few minutes went by, and a white arrow pointing westward appeared at Yakutsk: The AWACS was on its way, and should be in the area of the track in about twenty-five minutes.

*MONGOOSE Flight*

The highest point of their route rushed beneath Gates's left wing, as the F-24 topped the Stanovoy Range and started down the northern slopes. Seeing over seven thousand feet on the altimeter brought a smile to his face under the tight-fitting oxygen mask. Numbers that high had not been registered since they had left Burbank. He then brought up the next graphic, which included Aldan and its interceptor base, just to the north.

"Two, it's my guess that if they picked us up after we passed Skovorodino, we'll probably have a reception committee out of Aldan waiting up ahead."

"That's the way I've got it figured, too. I'm all set up except for the Arm switch."

"Same here. This weather looks like it's thickening up, and since there are no GCI sites in this area except Aldan, I think we'd be better off in the soup. They might know we're here, but I doubt they know exactly where. I imagine any search effort would have to stay VFR for maximum effectiveness, even though they won't be able to see much in the dark. Sing out if you pick up anything. Let's take it up another three or four hundred feet into the lower deck. No sense in making it easy for them.''

"Roger that," came Brock's confident reply. However, both pilots knew that with dawn less than an hour away, the MiGs would have a much better chance for a visual.

They passed the next checkpoint and Gates was entering the fuel and time figures on the card when something on the radar scope caught his eye. Immediately, his thumb was on the El Scan control, moving the antenna up and down slightly for the next two or three sweeps.

"Two, I've got multiple contacts port and starboard at seventy-five miles. Looks like they're stacked at different altitudes—just like we figured! They appear to be running east and west.''

"Rog. I'm getting a few contacts too! Must be MiGs, 'cause I'm gettin' an intermittent AI light on the RHAW gear.''

The bird leveled out at nine hundred feet after Gates set the new minimum altitude into the terrain-following system, and the total darkness inside the clouds was just what he wanted. The blips on the scope became a little more distinct as the range decreased, and he could now see eight separate targets.

"I count eight of them, Two, and from the way they're spaced on either side of the scope, it looks like they've got our track figured out pretty closely.''

"Rog! I've got the same. Think we should take out a few just to even the odds a little?''

Gates pondered the question a few moments before answering. "If we fire the AMRAAMs now, the Soviets will definitely know MONGOOSE was here; however, they must be fairly certain that we're in the neighborhood anyway, or they wouldn't have all this firepower airborne at such an oddball hour of the night.'' He was reluctant to confirm their suspicions, but knocking one or two down would mean that many fewer eyes and radars to pick them up.

Another thought crossed his mind that prompted caution. If they had interceptors this far south of the target, it was a good bet there would be even more around Zhigansk, and it might be wise to save a few shots for the main event. However, if these guys up ahead got lucky there might not be a main event, and if MONGOOSE bagged a couple now, the confusion factor produced would be well worth the effort. Getting their attention early in the game also might make the survivors a little more cautious. The tiger in him won out as he answered Brock.

"Yeah, that sounds like a good idea. I'll slide out to the left and take that group, while you move to the right far enough for your missiles to clear me and work on the foursome on that side. Let's give them two shots each so we can save something for later on."

"Roger that. Moving starboard now."

"Call when you're ready so we can fire together!"

Gates rolled a little left, and in quick succession locked the radar onto the leader's aircraft in each of the two elements. He quickly rechecked that radar missiles were selected, and the weapons display showed Ready for each of the four AMRAAMs. Then he flicked the Master Switch to the Arm position and noted that the Ready lights were flashing, indicating that the missiles had received the necessary launch parameters.

"Two's ready!" came Brock's call.

"Roger, fire—NOW!" Gates answered as he squeezed the trigger, paused, and squeezed again. The blackness inside the clouds exploded with light as a missile roared out, first from under the left wing, and then from the right. He immediately broke the lockon so that the targets would have minimum warning of the attack from their RHAW gear.

Traveling at better than Mach three, the AMRAAMs only took seventy seconds to reach their targets fifty miles away, as Gates peered intently at the scope to see if his shots struck home. The split seconds ticked by agonizingly, until finally two blips faded from the screen. He was just about to let out a victory yell when a vivid strobe of electronic jamming bloomed the entire right half of the scope into glowing luminescence. The signal lasted for about ten seconds, blotting out all returns on the starboard side. After the jamming stopped, Gates could see only three targets in that sector.

"Looks like you got one, Two," he called to Brock.

"Yeah, but the guy in the second target must be pretty sharp. Hit his jammer and probably did a whifferdill at just the right time to knock the second missile off track. Nice goin' on your two!"

"Well, now they know we're for real. I hope by the time they get reorganized, we'll be north of this first bunch. I'm not picking up any contacts farther out."

"No, it looks clear to me, too, but I'm sure we'll get some reaction to their losing three fighters." Things were quiet for almost thirty seconds, and then Brock came on the air again. "I think they're getting their act together. The three on the right are swinging around to the north, while the pair on the left are coming south. They're trying the old sandwich game."

"Seems that way, but the guys on the left are a little far out. If they don't angle toward us in the next few seconds, they'll be off our beam, and out of the fight." Gates watched the scope for a few more sweeps, and the targets on the port side didn't change course until they disappeared off the screen. "I think they're out of it. No way they could still make a one eighty and catch us. Let me know when they go off your scope."

Almost a minute went by before Brock called, "Lost them off to the left, still heading south, but they did light up my RHAW once or twice. They probably got a couple of contacts, but not good enough to keep a lockon."

"Oh! Oh!" Gates warned. "Looks like they passed those contacts to the group on the right; they're turning in toward us. Better arm 'em up just in case!"

Gates checked his armament selection and was reaching for the Master Switch, when a loud buzzing from the RHAW gear brought him up with a start. The MiGs were closing extremely fast now, and the strobe near the red image on the HUD had just started to flash, indicating they were locked on to him. His hand leaped to the ECM switch just as the buzz rose to a higher pitch, and the strobe was flashing quicker, telling him that a missile had been launched. He hit the switch to Multiple Target Generator, and kicked the plane over in a hard slicing dive to the right.

Instantly he was out of the clouds, and luckily caught sight of a couple of ground lights that gave him a quick reference. The altimeter jumped through five hundred feet, and the red warning light hit him in the eye like a visual scream. Reefing the stick back into his gut while ruddering hard to the left, he leveled out the F-24 a little under three hundred feet. Gates had a deathgrip on the stick and kept the Disengage switch pressed, forcing him to fly manually with only the Pictorial Format as a reference for terrain clearance. He knew this was extremely risky, since there was no way he could react to the display in time to avoid a sudden increase in ground elevation. Survival was the stronger instinct, however, and it was imperative that he stay right on the deck to force the missile to look for him among as many ground returns as possible. These numerous targets, in combination with those generated by his ECM system, would hopefully confuse the AA9 during its terminal-guidance phase.

Staring through the HUD, he saw a distant pinpoint of light a little above him, growing brighter and brighter. His whole body tensed as if anticipating a heavy blow to the gut, while he steered directly toward the onrushing missile, in order to present as small a radar target as possible. He felt himself cringing involuntarily in the seat, trying to make himself as little as he could in the face of the missile's probing radar beam. Like a huge tracer bullet, the Russian projectile roared over his canopy, and a split second later detonated well behind his aircraft. A flood of relief swept through his body as he snapped the ECM switch to Off, and checked that the scope was clear of all targets. The MiGs must be well behind them by now, considering the rate at which they were closing.

"That Russian jock must be pretty sharp to get a contact on a quartering front setup at low level, and still have enough tracking time to get a missile off," he said half aloud to himself. "Thank God for those false targets. That was too damn close!" Still no indication of the interceptors on the radar or the HUD, so he eased up toward the cloud deck.

"Going back IFR, Two. Just had a real close one. They hosed one off on their way through, but I lucked out and dodged the silver bullet. See anything on your radar?"

"Yeah, I saw it go off between us. One of them locked onto me for a moment, but I zapped him with the ECM and broke it. By that time, he was too close and went behind us with the others. I don't see a thing on my scope. Following you up."

*Kremlin War Room*

The shock of losing three airplanes at the first crossing of swords unnerved Kulikov no small amount, but outwardly he remained calm. Volzhin and General Secretary Petrov sat together farther down the control dais, talking in lowered tones and occasionally casting a glance toward him.

Things were not going well. He had done everything he could under the circumstances; however, you can't shoot down what you can't find. When he scrambled the fighters from Aldan, he knew the chances of finding a blacked-out Stealth aircraft at low level in the dark were extremely slim. But, if he had done nothing, the lack of radar sites along the route would have guaranteed the Americans unhindered access to the target. This was unthinkable and, although the loss of the three fighters was regrettable, it proved the Americans were inside Soviet borders, and were certainly making an attack on Zhigansk.

The time of the shootdown also validated his schedule of where he thought the Americans would be. The arrows on the Situation Board showed that the interceptors from Aldan had been turned back to the north and were pursuing the pilots of the now-declared Hostiles. By the time the controllers determined that the MiGs had passed their quarry and turned them around, they were a considerable distance behind the enemy aircraft. Such a lead would be tough to overcome.

He leaned over to Gulayev and said brusquely, "Call the site controlling the fighters and find out their speed, then get a weather report from the flight leader."

Gulayev knew the interceptors were going as fast as they could, but in view of the current mood of his superior, he answered with a quick "Yes, sir," as he picked up the phone. It only took a couple of minutes to get the information. "The aircraft are flying at full power, Comrade General; however, they still have no contact on the Americans. Weather conditions are deteriorating, with fewer clear areas between cloud layers, and they are in solid weather about a third of the time."

"Tell them to bring the interceptors up to the latest estimate of the American's position and then resume the search pattern in a northerly direction at five hundred knots!"

Gulayev passed on the order as Kulikov eyed the latest sequence from Zhigansk: 1,200 feet broken, 2,600 feet broken, 6,000 feet overcast and five miles visibility. "Not too bad," he thought, "but he'd prefer clear and fifteen so that his fighters could make a visual attack.

He cursed the weather under his breath, and after looking at the position of the AWACS, also cursed the relative slowness of this last trump card he could play. It was only halfway to the position he wanted it, but like so many other facets of this burgeoning nightmare, there wasn't too much he could do but wait. The airborne order had been sent to Olenek and Batagay, and these fighters would be off the ground in less than a minute.

Turning to Gulayev, he said, "Get in contact with those interceptors just scrambled, and have them proceed at maximum power to their assigned search areas. The AWACS will contact them once it is in position!"

Kulikov glanced nervously at Petrov and Volzhin just in time to see the latter beckon for him to join them.

"Well, General, our situation is not too encouraging. What do you plan to do about it?" The question was presented in such a way that Kulikov knew the General Secretary was expecting him to say that the Americans would be disposed of before reaching Zhigansk.

"I agree, Comrade General Secretary. We have not fared well thus far. The only reason we did not detect the Americans on radar is that they must have developed their Stealth technology to a degree we had not expected."

"Does this mean," Petrov interrupted, "that these aircraft will fly across the entire country without being found and destroyed?"

"I do not think so, Comrade General Secretary. This masking device apparently has its limitations, since the site at Kirovskiy did pick them up at close range for a short time. I believe that if they pass within fifteen miles of a station, they can be detected; however, north of Aldan we have no control sites except those on the northern coast.

"We are confident that the American fighters are very close to the tip of that red arrow on the plotting board. Interceptors from Aldan are in the same general area, and are crisscrossing the suspected track in hopes of getting close enough to find them on radar. If this occurs, they will of course launch an attack. Should this not be successful because of weather or countermeasures, the interceptor will be employed as a trailer aircraft. It will stay behind the Americans and maintain radar contact. Other interceptors will be vectored into the trailer, and once they have contact on the hostiles, they will initiate multiple attacks. I believe that bringing many radars to bear on the enemy at the same time will overload their countermeasures system and allow some of our weapons to be successful. Unfortunately, darkness and weather necessitates an all-radar search for the Americans, since it would be impossible to find them visually under these conditions.

"Radar is the key to our success. Therefore, I have ordered an AWACS aircraft from Yakutsk to fill in the void north of Aldan. They will S along the hostile track and try to get inside the fifteen-mile detection radius. The AWACS will also vector interceptors to the trailer aircraft, if that option becomes available. The airplanes currently airborne will continue searching until they reach the absolute minimum fuel needed to recover at the nearest airfield. If one of them does get a contact and is used as a trailer, he will maintain that position until he is relieved by another aircraft or his fuel is totally exhausted."

Kulikov detected an imperceptible arching of the General Secretary's eyebrow, but he continued. "Fighters were scrambled from Olenek and Batagay, and are en route to relieve those from Aldan. This should occur in the vicinity of the Linde River, and these interceptors will pursue the Americans northward and land at bases in that area. Other fighters from these same bases will then take up the battle."

Petrov's face hardened at these words, and his voice lost a little of its composure. "Kulikov, your job is to ensure that these aircraft do *not* reach their target!"

"Comrade General Secretary, let me explain our problem," Kulikov began weakly, intending to point out the difficulties of finding a Stealth aircraft at night in the weather. However, Petrov interrupted him with an annoyed wave of the hand.

"I do not want explanations, General. I want results! See to it!" The discussion ended as Petrov angrily turned his back on the Air Defense Commander and resumed his conversation with Volzhin.

Kulikov returned to the control dais. Introducing more fighters into the problem was not the answer. Having such a large number of aircraft operating in a relatively small area would complicate control and maneuver procedures to the point where they would not be effective. Yet he must do something, so he directed Gulayev to double the scramble orders to Olenek and Batagay, and to bring eight fighters up to Cockpit Alert at both Buolkalakh and Tiksi. The brigadier complied mutely, trying to keep a low profile in the face of the gathering storm in the War Room.

MONGOOSE *Flight*

Gates knew the MiGs that had just passed them would turn around and give chase, and undoubtedly would be doing more than five hundred knots. He wanted to firewall the throttles, but fuel considerations and the time of first light over the target stayed his hand. They still had a long way to go after hitting Zhigansk, and during the bomb run they'd need some illumination for positive target identification.

"Any signs of those guys that just went by?" he called to Brock.

"I think they've caught up to us. I've been getting some intermittent red silhouettes on the HUD, but everything has been in the Search mode. No lockon attempts as yet."

"O.k.! Let's make sure we stay IFR to keep from getting tagged with an IR missile, and keep the ECM on in case they get within fifteen miles. They're liable to be anywhere near us, so if we pop into the clear, take a quick look around before going back into the clouds. How you doing on fuel?''

''Right on the money at the last checkpoint, and the ECM system is on! Wait a minute! I think we've got company close in at my six! This guy's been sniffing around back there for two or three minutes, and I think he's beginning to smell a rat. He's spotlighted me a couple of times, but still no lockon. He started out dead astern, but just went out to about five o'clock—probably to get a better aspect angle.''

''Try easing starboard a little to kill that angle, and keep an eye in your mirrors.''

Brock's little finger rested against the flare-dispensing switch on the throttle grip, in case the MiG pilot tried an IR attack. This would jettison a flare behind the aircraft that would offer a much brighter and more inviting source of infrared energy than the F-24's shielded tailpipe. Hopefully, the oncoming Acrid would home on the flare while the real target was in a maximum G turn to escape the missile's field of view.

Brock knew the enemy pilot was sure he was on to something and was undoubtedly calling in others to help out. The MiG's radar put out less power than a GCI site, and would have to be a lot closer than the magic ten miles to achieve a good, solid lockon. His jammer was effective enough to deny a lockon until the interceptor was inside missile launch range, but he wasn't sure it could handle multiple fighters to the same extent. He didn't want to use the barrage jammer, since this would confirm the trailer's suspicions and also allow him to use the Home-On-Jam feature of his weapons.

While preoccupied with his options in this situation, his gaze shifted to the fuel counter and compared the figure with his flight data card. ''Be able to drop the centerline tank pretty soon,'' he thought to himself, when suddenly a flash of apprehension shot through his entire body. Looking outside, he couldn't believe it! He had flown out of the clouds and hadn't realized it for a few seconds. He started to ease gently back on the stick, while nervously scanning the rear view mirrors.

''My God! There it is,'' he almost yelled as the right-hand mirror showed a tiny point of light growing larger by the instant, and the IR sensor flashed a warning strobe on the HUD. The MiG had been waiting below the clouds, and when Brock dropped out of the deck above him, the Acrid missile had a clear look at the F-24's tailpipes. The pilot was sharp, reacting immediately to the growl in his earphones, by hosing off two IR missiles at the target that had frustrated him for so long.

Reflexive action took over as Brock jabbed at the flare switch twice, and reefed the stick back into his gut, while feeding in right aileron. At the same time, he twisted the throttle grip hard to use maximum vertical translation. The F-24 shot upward in a hard climbing roll to the right, and the sudden application of better than nine G's immobilized Brock in his seat. He fought against the onset of gray-out by leaning over and straining every muscle against the two-thousand-pound invisible force that pulled at his body. He knew he had to look back and check for the missile, yet the G load made it feel like his head was going to snap off and fall into his lap. His neck muscles screamed in protest as he moved his head out of line with his backbone, and looked quickly over his shoulder. The instant before he entered the cloud deck, he saw that the Acrids had swallowed the bait and were heading for the flares.

Despite his relief, he suddenly realized that he was inverted in the clouds at low altitude. However, by the time he started his recovery procedure, he had already reached the top of his roll, and was now slicing down the opposite side. Brock didn't want to break out in the clear again since the MiG might be still back there waiting, so he quickly began to roll wings level, and held in the back pressure. But, he was just seconds late, and found himself skimming along the bottom of the cloud layer as he rolled level. His mind had already sent the message to his hand to haul back on the stick, when a light at his nine-thirty position caught his eye. He looked again, and stared in disbelief as he glimpsed another light close to the first.

"I can't believe it!" he said in amazement. "That's the MiG out there, and the dummy has his nav lights on." Even as the incredulity of the situation raced through his mind, he was acting to seize the opportunity. His thumb nudged the speed brake switch on the throttle grip to slow the bird down. Then he hit radar to Standby to keep the MiG's RHAW gear from giving him away and moved the armament selector switch to IR Missiles.

Brock stayed in the bottom of the cloud layer to make it difficult for the Russian pilot to spot him, should he happen to look this way. Thanks to the MiG's running lights, he could still keep the airplane in sight, while staying partially hidden by the clouds. The open speed brakes were now beginning to make a difference, as the range between the F-24 and the enemy fighter started to increase. Brock closed the brakes so as not to drop too far behind, and began easing his bird slowly to the left until he had the MiG in his eleven o'clock position. While sliding astern of the Russian, he glanced quickly at the

Weapons Status screen to confirm a Ready light for the IR missiles.
The Armament Master Switch went to ARM as he dropped down below
the MiG, to give his weapons a better look angle at the enemy's tailpipe. Target range was nearly right, so he bumped the throttles forward to synchronize speeds with the MiG.

"This is almost too easy," he thought, since years of training had
stressed the importance of always looking out for the enemy's
wingman, especially when he appears to be such a pigeon. There was
nothing on the HUD to indicate the sensors had picked up anything,
and the rearview mirrors showed total blackness behind him. Brock
positioned the cross hairs of his visor sight in the center of the MiG's
fuselage and squeezed the acquisition switch. Instantly, a loud, steady
growl filled his earphones, telling him the missiles were looking right
at the hot section of the MiG's engines and were tracking it properly. A
quick squeeze of the trigger sent a Sidewinder arcing off the rail, its
fiery exhaust tracing a slight climbing turn to the left. Knowing that he
would need a lot of firepower later on, Brock launched only one
round, but kept the other missiles locked on the target and his forefinger resting on the trigger.

The missile ran true, and suddenly the night was shattered by a
huge fireball with black overtones. The warhead detonated in the
engine compartment, and caused an instantaneous disintegration of
the turbine and compressor sections. The blades on these components, spinning at better than ten thousand revolutions per minute,
tore through the fuel bladders surrounding the engine bay and shred-
ded the outer skin of the MiG like so much tissue paper. The flame
from the burner cans followed, and instantly the exploding fighter
was engulfed in a sea of fire.

Brock viewed the kill with a slight air of detachment. "That poor
son of a bitch never knew what hit him. Probably had his head buried
in the scope trying to find me again."

The glare from the stricken MiG was subsiding into streams of
fire, cascading from the larger pieces of falling wreckage, as MON-
GOOSE Two climbed to relative safety in the lowest cloud layer. His
immediate problem was to find Gates, since just before the attack he
was riding a little under ten miles behind lead. He switched his radar
back to Operate, but the Stealth mod was now working against him, as
the scope showed no signs of Gates's aircraft. After resetting the armament panel to fire AMRAAMs, he turned the UHF selector switch to
DF.

"Lead, this is Two! Scratch one trailer. He got close enough to hose off an Acrid, but I saw it in time and dropped some flares before pulling up into the clouds. Came back underneath a few seconds later, and there he was, in my nine-thirty position with his lights on yet! That whifferdill put me better than ten miles behind you. No joy on the scope; give me a short count."

Gates congratulated him with a "Nice shootin'," followed by a count up to five and back to one.

While lead was transmitting, Brock's DF needle pointed steadily fifteen degrees to the port. The wingman quickly swung to the left, added some power, and in a few minutes a faint return appeared on the screen and Brock called, "Tied on!"

Now that everything was back to normal, he tried analyzing what happened during the last three or four minutes to give him such an easy kill. The only scenario that made sense would be one where the MiG pilot had a faint contact on radar, but couldn't get a good lockon because of the Stealth mod. He knew he was in a tail chase and had IR missiles selected as the best weapon for an ECM environment. However, since Brock was in the clouds, the Russian's missiles weren't picking up a definite point source of infrared energy. He was probably sitting there trying to figure things out, while making sure he stayed behind the only target he had, even though it was faint. Then, all of a sudden, the F-24 pops out of the clouds, and his IR missiles lock on immediately. Not wishing to screw up the first break that's come his way, he squeezes off a couple of Acrids while cobbing the throttles to close for a reattack. Brock's hard climbing roll to keep the missiles in sight really amounted to a High G Barrel Roll. This gyration effectively reduced his vector velocity, while the MiG was increasing his through throttle action.

Brock smiled to himself, recognizing the classic, textbook example of the counter to a stern attack, when the opponent is closing rapidly. The High G Barrel Roll reduces an aircraft's velocity along its flight path, without an appreciable loss of airspeed. The attacking aircraft with its high rate of closure can't slow down quickly enough to keep from squirting out in front of his target, and suddenly the roles are reversed. As Brock came out of the clouds on the down side of his roll, the MiG's increasing speed carried him past the F-24's beam, and that was all she wrote! As to why the Russian pilot had his nav lights on, Brock could only conclude that with all the other interceptors around, they wanted to be sure of seeing each other.

As Brock fought back the first twinges of weariness by stretching against the tight seat belt and harness, thoughts of Angela flashed though his mind. He had left Las Vegas just over a week ago, but missed her already and was counting the hours until he would be back with her again. His estimate was that it would be at least another three or four days, providing the Pentagon didn't overdo the debriefing. But for now, the problems at hand required all his attention, so these pleasant reveries would have to wait.

The fuel light that was flickering before the excitement started was now glowing steadily, so Brock gave his leader a call. "Lead, my centerline tank just went dry, and this looks like as good an area as any to get rid of it."

"Roger that! I was just about to give you a call. I'm punching mine off now." Gates selected the centerline station, armed the system, and pressed the bomb release button on the stickgrip. He felt a slight jar through the airframe as the tank under the belly was blown downward and away from the aircraft. The fighter was now clean except for the two five hundred pounders in their conformal mountings, and seemed to spring ahead with new life.

After Gates set his weapons system back to missiles, a cross check between the flight-path graphic and the radar screen confirmed that the river up ahead was the Vilyuy. When the next graphic flashed on the screen, he felt an involuntary tightening in his gut. The picture told it all: Zhigansk dead ahead. Time to target: twenty minutes!

### Kremlin War Room

The news of a fighter being shot down southwest of Batagay was something Kulikov hadn't expected. Even though the pilot reported getting only a faint contact, he should have maintained his position until other fighters could be brought in to assist him. All they knew was his last transmission, "I have a contact, and am launching an attack." This wasn't much to go on, and definitely less information than Volzhin needed.

Petrov was now visibly angry with the way things were going. He was pacing back and forth behind Kulikov.

Mercifully, the AWACS was now in position, paralleling the suspected track, and the first flight from Batagay was under its control. The AWACS rolled out a little ahead of where the Air Defense Commander thought the Americans were, and it immediately reported a contact.

His elation at finally having the breaks go his way nearly brought a shout from Kulikov, but wariness tempered his enthusiasm. Glancing at the clock, he noted that it was 0515. With time so short, he must not fail to capitalize on this fortunate turn of events. Turning to Gulayev, he ordered sharply, "Have the controllers bring the fighters in behind the contact at maximum possible speed and to close with the enemy, no matter what the obstacles! Work them in trail, and vector each fighter to the point where they get a contact and can launch their weapons. If the American's jamming prevent launching armament, continue vectoring on a collision course until the blips merge. If they get a visual on the enemy, they will destroy them with cannon fire, or as a last resort, they will ram them, repeat *ram*! These targets must be destroyed immediately!"

Gulayev quickly relayed Kulikov's order verbatim to the AWACS controllers. The latter acknowledged the order, but said they were losing ground on the contact due to its higher speed, and they were already operating at their engine and airspeed limits. However, they had now picked up a second contact ten miles behind the first.

Kulikov exploded out of his chair and shouted at Gulayev. "To hell with their limits! They will not, repeat *not*, lose those contacts! Tell them to use the water injection system continuously if need be, but they will not let the Americans get out of range. Inform them that these orders come directly from the Kremlin!"

Kulikov knew that continued use of this technique would put a considerable strain on the engines, but at this point he had no choice. He took a quick look over his shoulder and Petrov was still there, but apparently did not disapprove of his actions.

Seconds ticked by, and finally a pilot reported getting close enough for a missile launch, but the American countermeasures had been too effective and lured the missile onto a false target. The aircrew also mentioned that the weather had thickened considerably, and despite pressing on after firing his weapon, he had been unable to obtain a visual. Kulikov wondered silently if his order to ram had been the cause of any "deterioration" of the visibility.

Multiple reports of interceptors launching armament were now coming in, as the controllers drove their fighters in, first for an attack on the rear target and then a quick repositioning on the first.

Gulayev broke in with what he thought was some good news to ease the tensions. "AWACS reports that the fighters from Olenek are on station just south of Zhigansk, and are cruising in a figure-eight pattern across the projected track."

"Good!" Kulikov replied. "Tell them to maintain visual conditions at multiple levels if possible, and attack instantly if they sight the Americans. Let them know that they are expected to use ramming techniques as a last resort. Get an acknowledgment from the AWACS on that!''

Gulayev nodded, and after a brief conversation, turned to Kulikov and said, "AWACS acknowledges the order, Comrade General." Now, all they could do was wait.

# Chapter 10

The last ten minutes had been a nightmare for both Gates and Brock. The Soviets made continual attacks from the stern, yet thanks to their ECM gear, none ended in lockons that allowed a radar missile to guide on anything but bogus targets. The Pictorial Format Display showed an enemy fighter in their rear hemisphere almost constantly—one would make an attack, couldn't find them, and be broken off, only to be followed by another.

Gates finally doped out something that had been disturbing him from the time they crossed the Vilyuy River. Shortly thereafter, a yellow X appeared on the HUD and within a few minutes, started to flash. This was worrisome enough, but what really puzzled him was that the X didn't move, or only moved slightly on the combining glass. All other displays were normal, which ruled out a malfunction of the system, and then it dawned on him. A GCI site that stayed with them could only mean an AWACS.

He called Brock to bounce this idea off him, and his wingman concurred that this was the most likely explanation. AWACS had not been emphasized in their briefings, although it was known that the Soviets had this type of aircraft. Apparently, intelligence didn't consider them a potential threat. The fact that they had one in this area, and got it so close to them on such short notice, did little to cheer up either MONGOOSE pilot.

Soon after the flashing X appeared on the HUD, the fighter attacks began. The Soviets had learned that frontal and beam attacks against the F-24's jamming system simply would not work. Their only chance of success was to use a trailer and hope that interceptors vectored on him could get a contact and launch armament. The bottom of the HUD now showed two or three red silhouettes nearly all the time, with the RHAW gear confirming their attempts to lock on. Occasionally, a glowing light would streak by in the clouds, as a MiG pilot fired a missile at what he thought was a real target.

"Thank God for that jammer, or we'd be dead meat by now," thought Gates. Suddenly, a slow-moving light caught his eye off to the left. Jerking his head around, he just had time to see navigation lights disappearing in the darkness at his ten-thirty position. It was one of the interceptors, pressing in to overpower the jammer and get a good lockon. But, before he could react the ghostly shape was swallowed by the thick clouds, which were now lightening up with the approaching dawn.

Gates now realized that they had another problem. These turkeys were driving through the minimum target range to get a visual. Another thought crossed his mind that sent a chill down his backbone. The Russians might be desperate enough to try ramming techniques.

"Two, I just had a MiG pass off my left wing. He never saw me in the murk, and I only got a glimpse of his lights before he disappeared. They're having problems locking on and might be trying to ram us."

"Yeah, I had one go over me about thirty seconds ago. I think you're right on the ramming—they sure aren't observing any minimum break-off ranges."

"I suspect that once it gets lighter, one of these guys is going to get a visual in time to make a gun attack. For what it's worth, I'm going to try the Chameleon lights. As long as we stay in the clouds, they might make our outline less distinct."

"Good idea! Mine are coming on now."

Gates's DME showed a hundred miles to the target when he started getting some contacts on the radar. As he was changing the elevation scan to sharpen up the paints, Brock called.

"Contact on a flight of four between us and the target. Looks like there's a couple on each side of track."

"Roger—got 'em. I think we'd better take them out now. I'll take the two on the left. Arm 'em up hot!"

"Rog! Sliding out to the right for launch."

Gates's radar was tracking both targets, and after rechecking for Ready lights, he squeezed the trigger twice. The AMRAAMs leaped off their rails with a fiery roar, each pursuing its target more than fifty miles ahead.

These Soviet fliers were a little more alert than their ill-fated companions who got tagged back around Aldan. The missiles were in flight for only a few seconds, when Gates started to pick up signs of enemy countermeasures. Seconds ticked by as the AMRAAMs sped toward the MiGs, who were now maneuvering wildly in an attempt to avoid both the missiles and each other. Gates never heard the pair of explosions that ripped through the layered cloud decks, but smiled with satisfaction at seeing two fewer blips on the radar scope.

"Looks like we only batted five hundred on that one," came Brock's call.

"Yeah, they hit us right away with the jammers, but I guess it's better than a sharp stick in the eye. You'd better start closing up to about eight miles for the pop-up. My radiation detector is on."

"Rog, mine's on. Closin' up now. This might get a little tricky if these jokers keep trying to slip in between us to get a shot off at you."

"You're right, but I think we'll just have to let them play around until we get rid of the bombs."

*　*　*

Gates switched the LANTIRN over to Ground Attack and brought up a graphic of the target complex on the auxiliary screen. A drawing of the research facility appeared. It was the same size and from the same perspective as he would see it on the HUD at maximum range. The computer would now monitor the DME and automatically expand the picture as he continued inbound, providing a real time reference into the target. Planning on a solid overcast at Zhigansk, he set up the weapons delivery panel for a fully automated pop-up attack. Theoretically, all he would have to do in this mode was to press the bomb button and hold it for a computer-generated release signal. However, Gates intended to use the auto system only as a backup. If the weather permitted a visual delivery, that would be the way he would go.

The navigation system showed him dead on course, with the Initial Point from which the pop-up attack commenced only forty miles ahead. With a quickness born of innumerable practice bombing runs, Gates ran through the final checklist for dropping iron bombs: Sight set for air-to-ground, mils set for the correct depression of the sight reticle, delivery mode Auto, both bomb stations selected and lights on, release sequence Bombs Ripple, fusing set to nose and tail, armament master On.

The knot in Gates's stomach tightened perceptibly as he raced

toward the IP at better than eight miles a minute. Despite his flying
gloves, he felt the increased dampness of his palms and a tense prickly
feeling spreading over his body as the miles clicked off the DME. He
was sure his heart was pumping pure adrenaline by now, but the calm
precision of a professional fighter pilot was in total control. His right
hand lightly circled the stick grip, which continued moving slightly in
response to the commands of the autopilot. The throttles were held
more firmly by his left hand, ready to jam them into afterburner or utilize the Vertical Translation mode should they get bounced. His eyes
were riveted on the radar, waiting for the image of the target complex
to separate from the large return coming from the city itself.

As well as being able to see his surroundings better with the
approach of daylight, Gates noticed that he was catching occasional
glimpses of the ground. "A good sign," he thought, even if a break in
the weather over the target would certainly mean more MiGs. The
auto system was good, but old fighter pilot traditions die hard, and he
felt sure that a visual attack would result in better accuracy.

Quickly checking the radar screen, he noted another flight of
interceptors approaching from the northwest, but they were still too
far out to pose an immediate threat. They couldn't do much about
them anyway, since only AMRAAMs would be suitable for a long-range
front-quarter attack. The two remaining aircraft from the flight they
just hit still patrolled either side of the route to the target.

The locations of these two interceptors were particularly worrisome to Gates, with one at ten o'clock and the other at two. Both
were shown in red on the HUD, indicating that they were in a position
to launch an attack if they got a visual. "If these clouds are still layered, one of those guys is probably above this deck I'm in, and the
other below it. Chances are that I'll only have to slip by one of them."

The radar screen was now clearly painting the entire target complex and the surrounding area. He could make out the Lena River paralleling his course, and the town of Uolba to the south of Zhigansk.
Directly north was the target city itself, the airfield showing up clearly
ten miles to the northwest.

As Gates passed the Initial Point twenty miles south of the target,
the radar picture of the test facility was just starting to break up into
returns representing individual buildings in the complex. After a few
more sweeps, the X-shaped structure of the new laboratory was
clearly discernible, located a little to the right of center.

Gates quickly positioned the horizontal and vertical cursors on
the radar screen, directly over the middle of the building and hit the

Track button. From that point on, the cursors would stay over the target, providing range and azimuth information to the bombing computer. The latter fed in a bit of right aileron and rudder to center the target on the scope, and as the range decreased, the definition of the building sharpened even more.

The larger picture of the structure showed Gates that his initial positioning of the cursors had been just a little off. He corrected this rapidly by manually slewing the cursors back to the center of the target. The update was completed none too soon because, when he returned the system to Auto-Track, the vertical steering bar on the HSI flipped upward to a full-scale deflection. The autopilot applied smooth back pressure, building to a momentary four G's, which brought the needle back to the center of the instrument. While climbing, he could feel the little jabs of rudder required by the system to keep the course needle in the middle.

He perceived an easing off of the back pressure to stabilize the pop-up climb, when suddenly the plane was in a clear area between the cloud layers, and at the same instant, his heart nearly stopped. Barreling in from two o'clock was a MiG, who spotted him the second he was out of the clouds and was pressing in for a gun attack. Gates slammed the throttles wide open as he wrenched the bird into a nine-G turn toward the enemy fighter, while kicking in hard right rudder to accelerate the turn rate. He knew his only hope of escape lay in getting back into the cloud bank and heading straight at the MiG until they passed each other.

"Two, you've got the lead. I got bounced in the pop-up. Breakin' right. Will come in behind you for the run! The bogey on the right is just above this layer!"

"Two, Rog," came Brock's clipped reply.

Despite the violent control inputs, the F-24 seemed to take forever to rotate through forty-five degrees of turn while rolling nearly inverted to head back into the clouds. The enemy pilot was certainly surprised to see such a golden opportunity appear directly in front of him, but was by no means flustered. He banked sharply to pull the required lead on the diving American fighter, and before Gates reached the clouds, the 30mm tracers were arcing over the canopy.

The MiG pilot would surely correct his aim with the next burst, and Gates needed some answers fast. The only thing that could save his bacon now was a higher rate of turn, so he twisted the throttle grip to use the Vertical Translation mode. The added G's nearly blacked him out, even though it already felt like the G suit was cutting him in half. The Russian put in his correction, but the unorthodox jump out of the predicted flight path caught him unawares. The streaks of orange fire were closer than before, but Gates felt no hits on the airframe. Mercifully, he was swallowed by the clouds before the MiG driver could make that one final correction.

The maneuver inside the clouds to get right side up was just as violent as his initial break, and it had to be. He had rolled almost to the inverted position, and was in a thirty-degree dive when he hit the cloud tops, and most of the recovery was done on instruments. Hard top rudder and full left aileron while keeping the G load on flipped the airplane over, but the altimeter continued to unwind.

The F-24 screamed through the bottom of the deck before he could get the airspeed down and point the nose at the horizon again. Gates stayed in a steep right turn to a heading of south, and held it until the image representing Brock's aircraft disappeared from the right edge of the HUD. With his wingman passing off the starboard beam, Gates could now start a turn back toward the target and fall in trail with Brock. He got up into the weather before another MiG could pick him up, and it only took a small correction after rolling out to get back on track.

By the time Gates reacquired the target on radar, the DME showed four miles to the pullup point. Just then, MONGOOSE Two called "Rollin' in hot!" Apparently the MiG that had bounced him did not get turned around in time to get a visual on Brock. Gates quickly rechecked the armament switches, and everything was still set up properly for the bombing run. The HUD now showed the second flight of interceptors as possible threats, but they seemed to be converging on Brock's aircraft.

"Can't do too much about them until I'm off target," Gates thought as he concentrated on the image of the research complex displayed on the HUD.

"Two away!" came his wingman's call, indicating he had dropped his weapons. "Target area clear below two thousand. I've got some MiGs closing!"

"Roger that! I'm in my pull-up now," was Gates's reply.

The MiGs spotted Brock just as he released his bombs, and expected him to head north and climb toward the cloud deck. The flight leader maneuvered his element accordingly, while telling number three and four to cover his tail during the attack. The wing element went wide and fell back as directed; however, the leader suddenly realized that the American fighter was not climbing, but had started a low-level turn around the target. He would have been in great position if the F-24 had climbed, but now had to kick the nose over through a large arc to get it pointed at the enemy's tailpipe.

Crushed in his seat by the seven-G load on the plane and now sweating profusely from the strain and the excitement of the moment, Brock could see the Russian's strategy unfolding. The leader still had a good bit of turn to finish before he became a real threat, but the wing element would pose a problem once he started his dash back into the clouds.

Struggling against the enormous force on his body, he selected IR Missiles, and got an immediate Ready indication. Despite all his problems, he sneaked a quick look at the radiation detector, but it was still not illuminated. Survival again became paramount, as he centered the visor sight on the lead MiG in the wing element and squeezed the acquisition switch. A sharp growl sounded in his headset, so he pressed the trigger and watched a Sidewinder smoke out and turn the number three MiG into a ball of flame. The number four man was so startled at seeing his leader explode, and banked so hard avoiding the debris, that Brock knew that he was effectively out of the fight—at least for the present.

Brock's turn around the target was just about complete, but still no radiation light came on. Glancing at the structure housing the laser weapon, he saw that he had put the bombs just where he wanted them. The entire southern half of the building was destroyed. The walls and the roof had been blown away, revealing the shambles that the two five hundred pounders had made of the interior.

"Lead, I'm just finishing my turn around the target and have a pair of MiGs on my tail. I took out the southern part of the target, but I have not, repeat NOT, gotten a radiation light! You might want to move your aim point a little to the north. I'm headin' for the clouds!"

"Roger that! One's rollin' in now!"

At the apex of his pop-up climb, Gates was still in the weather, but the radar screen showed him right on track as he started down from thirty-five hundred feet. Dive angle ten degrees, airspeed coming up to five hundred knots—everything looked good as he moved his thumb over the bomb release button on the side of the stickgrip. When the altimeter wound through two thousand feet, he was suddenly in the clear, and the target complex was just over the radome and a little to the left. Gates ruddered in a correction to center it on the HUD, while looking over the damage done by Two's bombs. The near side of the structure was completely demolished as Brock had said, with smoke still rising from a few fires inside.

Gates twisted the throttle grip to use just a tad of vertical translation to move the airplane perpendicular to its flight path, without changing the dive angle. The maneuver instantly moved the pipper closer to the base of the building. As the dive progressed, the pipper moved forward normally, and at the pickle altitude of 1,000 feet, it was centered on the undamaged rear portion of the target. He felt the bombs leave as he pressed the button, and immediately started a recovery from the dive, combined with a hard jink to the right.

When he broke out of the clouds on the bomb run, he noticed a pair of MiGs at his ten-thirty position. They were headed his way, but did not actually spot him until he was pulling off the target. Seeing the F-24 make a hard right turn, the Russians countered with a shallow cutoff turn to the left.

Gates saw them take the bait and knew they'd be firing momentarily. He only held the jink for an instant, and then slammed the stick to the front left corner of the cockpit, while jamming in full left rudder. Without the high G forces of the jink, the unloaded F-24 instantly flipped from a ninety-degree bank to the right to a ninety-degree bank to the left. Then, full back stick, throttles firewalled, and the Vertical Translation mode engaged. The sudden changes of heading and the alternate high G, zero G, high G loading in the time it takes to blink threw Gates about the cockpit like a rag doll. Without the restraint harness and helmet, he would have been knocked out by the force with which his head banged off the canopy. Anticipating that the Russians would launch the IR-guided Acrids, he hit the flare button twice just before starting his jink to the left.

Gates now had the turn around the target complex established, and knew his bombs would detonate any second. The sight picture at release had been good: pipper right in the middle of the back half of the building, wings level, with dive angle and airspeed right on the money, pickle button pressed at the exact altitude! Glancing toward the ground he could see soldiers shooting at him with AK-47s from hastily dug foxholes around the facility. He added a little top rudder to change his flight path just enough to throw off their lead calculations, and then a second or so later bottom-ruddered the bird back downward again. There were two holes in the flat roof where his bombs had gone through, and their positions left no doubt that he had "shacked the target."

Suddenly the entire center of the building erupted in a cloud of smoke laced with flame. Gates held the arc of his turn steady and stared alternately between the radiation detector light and the destruction under the cloud of smoke ballooning above the facility. Things became a little clearer inside the building, and he could see numerous small fires flaring up and the occasional secondary explosions they caused. The rest of the interior was a jumble of broken machinery, twisted and shattered beams from the ceiling and walls, and electric lines arcing blue sparks as they dangled beneath the ragged edges of what remained of the roof.

Gates tried another jink using the rudders to throw off the gunners below. While he was scanning the large amount of destruction within the target, a glow from inside the cockpit caught his eye. The radiation light was on!

MONGOOSE was a success up to this point at least, and now all they had to do was fight the Russian Air Force for the next eight hundred miles or so. No time to dwell on that now, though, since the two fighters he had faked out with the jink were now countering his hard turn in their direction.

The two MiGs were indeed surprised by Gates's sudden turn to the left. What looked like an easy kill was now pretty much a standoff, with the American fighter heading in their direction, rather than away from them. Their missiles were just coming off the rails when the F-24 reversed, and the flares now provided a more inviting target than the tailpipe that had rotated out of their field of view.

The Russian flight commander watched in frustration as the missiles veered toward the flares and finally exploded harmlessly on the ground. The abruptness with which the American aircraft had literally "swapped ends" made him realize that the MiG's traditionally superior turning ability had more than met its match. Already the American was crossing under him, staying low as he arced around the target. When the F-24 streaked by, he had no choice but to start a hard diving turn after it, or else he would soon be in the American's gunsight. Struggling against the G's in the high buffet turn, he wondered why the enemy pilot hadn't raised his nose and used the gun as their paths crossed a few instants ago. It would have been a high-deflection shot with little chance of success, but if their roles had been reversed, he would at least have given it a try—just for the psychological effect.

When he finally completed enough of his turn to reacquire the American visually, he knew that he was out of the fight. The F-24 had rolled out of its turn around the target on a northerly heading, and was climbing rapidly for the clouds. He tried horsing the MiG through

the remainder of its turn to get a missile off before the American disappeared, but his airplane only responded with the severe bucking of a
high-speed stall. This forced him to ease off a little to keep from de-
parting the controllability envelope.

Gates knew the Russians would throw every available fighter at
them, and with the research facility destroyed their motivation for a
kill at any price would be that much higher. The urgency of his predicament made him check, for what seemed like the tenth time, that both
throttles were locked hard against the military stops. He needed one
hundred percent power from now on, since speed and cloud cover
were the key factors in keeping them alive.

Once Gates rolled out of the turn around the target, he pushed
the nose over slightly to keep it in a zero-G condition. Even during
that extended high-G turn, he was able to maintain a good airspeed,
but now with no G forces to contend with, the plane shot ahead like a
scalded dog. The zero-G maneuver made this acceleration even faster,
since it canceled out the weight of the aircraft and allowed every bit of
thrust to be converted into airspeed.

With all the enemy fighters surrounding them, Gates realized that
he better let his wingman know the results of his run, just in case one
of the MiGs got lucky.

"MONGOOSE Two, this is Lead. My radiation light is on. Repeat,
radiation light is on!"

"Roger, Lead, I copy. Your light is on. I'm back in the clouds, but
there's bogeys all around. Sure hope this cloud cover holds."

"Two, that AWACS has probably got our course figured out pretty
well, so just to throw a little crap into their game, I'm going to head
toward that mountain range to the east, and get as low as I can and still
stay in the weather."

"Sounds like a good idea. It might throw them off the trail long
enough to give us a breather."

Gates's Machmeter hesitated at .98 momentarily, and then
jumped to 1.02. He was still in the clear, but the MiGs following him
had not completed enough of their turn to give their missiles a look at
his tailpipe.

Suddenly a pair of bogeys in close formation flashed out of the
clouds in his two o'clock position, heading northwest across his nose.
"Those guys behind me must have called for help," Gates thought,
hitting the acquisition switch while keeping the visor sight on the lead
Russian. The instant the missiles "saw" the target, he squeezed one
off, and then started his escape maneuver. Moderate back pressure on

the stick caused the supersonic F-24 to skyrocket upward into the base of the clouds.

He only allowed himself a small sigh of relief as the weather closed in around him. "Now, at least, they'd have to beat the jammer and the Stealth mod to get at me." After rolling out of his turn around the target, he stayed on a northerly heading during his acceleration and climb into the clouds. He wanted to give the MiGs some indication that his egress route was straight north.

As soon as he was in the murk and the terrain-following system was set, he punched a request into the computer for the graphic showing the area just beyond Zhigansk. Down the middle of the screen was the Lena River and just to the east were the rising foothills of the Verkhoyanskiy Range. Taking over manual control with the momentary interrupt switch, he laid the bird over in a hard right turn to zero three zero degrees.

His plan was to hold this heading until he was twenty miles from the ridgeline, and then turn back to the north and parallel the hills until reaching the Laptev Sea. Once he was headed north again, he would gradually ease the bird starboard to get close to the rising slopes and hopefully prevent any attack from that side. Gates knew this grand strategy wouldn't fool the Russians for long, but if he could get off the AWACS's radar for only a few minutes, some of their fighters would be out of position when they found him again.

Five minutes after his turn, the peaks of the Verkhoyanskiy's were painting clearly on the radar, prompting a thirty-degree turn to the left. Ceilings might be lower this close to the mountains, so he started stepping the airplane down in small increments. By getting below the ridgeline and staying close to the western slopes, he was betting the Russians would be reluctant to press their attacks to such a low altitude. This was their backyard they were flying in, and they would know that the clouds now had rocks embedded in them. The Russian interceptors didn't have terrain-following radar, so it took a real gutsy or foolhardy pilot to chase a supersonic target in the weather at less than a thousand feet above the trees.

Gates's dogleg toward the mountains did cause some momentary confusion aboard the AWACS. The contacts on the Americans were lost; however, just before they faded, a sharp-eyed controller noticed that they had moved slightly toward the east. He quickly relayed this to the cockpit, and the pilot swung the aircraft toward the northeast. The Airborne Battle Commander rightly surmised that the enemy fighters were heading for the protection of the Verkhoyanskiy's, and alerted the pilot to be ready for a turn back to the north at any moment.

The pilot muttered an obscenity in reply, since all this maneuvering was only adding to his already considerable troubles. The engines had been at maximum power well beyond the recommended time limits, and the flight engineer was reporting exhaust gas temperatures on each engine well into the danger area. He warned that the nacelles were not designed to provide adequate cooling air for continuous operation at these power settings. To bolster his argument he added that the oil pressure gauges were showing intermittent fluctuations, probably caused by a viscosity breakdown due to the excessive temperatures.

The pilot replied testily that his own instruments showed the same readings, but the orders were clear: Do not lose contact with the enemy fighters.

Along with the potential for a seizure in any of the engines momentarily, the pilot also began to experience control problems. Flying at maximum power and using water injection almost constantly caused the Machmeter to creep just beyond the red line. The slight airframe buzz that developed as the maximum airspeed was approached increased dramatically on the other side of the limiting Mach number. Now, the entire airplane was shaking with a high-frequency vibration. It felt like they were flying through moderate turbulence, except that the jolts were following a quick-tempoed, rhythmic pattern.

Rivulets of sweat trickled down the pilot's face as he struggled with the aircraft in a region of flight totally unfamiliar to him. The plane responded skittishly to his inputs—overreacting to a light touch in some instances and sluggishly answering a heavy hand in others. Airloads not planned on by the designers buffeted the control surfaces and wreaked havoc with the laminar flow over the high-lift wing.

The flight crew and radar controllers were visibly apprehensive at this strange phenomenon, and glanced uneasily at each other and the groaning aluminum shell around them. Only the iron-willed glare of the Battle Commander, backed up by their orders from Moscow, kept the radar people frozen in their seats. The flight crew were more knowledgeable of the inherent dangers of their situation, and each stayed at his position, ready to execute the emergency procedures they knew would be needed any minute.

### Kremlin War Room

When the report came in that the Americans had destroyed the laser beam weapon, a pall of gloom and desperation settled over the control dais. Petrov sat off to one side shooting acrimonious glances of blame at Volzhin and Kulikov. In the General Secretary's eyes, no amount of excuses would alter the fact that a pair of American fighters crossed two-thirds of their country, destroyed their best chance for worldwide military domination since the second World War, and were now escaping unharmed.

The General Secretary was used to dealing in hard figures. He could not understand why a force this size, made up of interceptors whose capabilities had been touted to the heavens, couldn't easily handle a mere two enemy aircraft.

Although he tried not to show it, Kulikov felt the prevalent air of despondency most keenly. He was politically astute enough to know that for a failure of this magnitude his fate would become a pawn in the continual power struggle between rival factions in the Kremlin, and the best he could hope for was to spend his remaining years in the Gulag. The apparent ease with which the American fighters penetrated their entire air defense system only sharpened his resolve for a revenge kill.

He, too, saw the enemy's dash toward the mountains as a predictable maneuver, and assumed that they would continue northward along the western slopes. The plotters were told to draw the new estimated track, parallel to the first but displaced seventy-five miles to the east. When they were finished, he noted that this new track passed very close to Tiksi, one of the bases where his last-ditch fighters were located. This fact made no particular impression on Kulikov as he glanced down the latest weather sequences posted on the board, until he reached the entry for Tiksi. They were reporting clear and fifteen miles visibility, while other stations had the layered and overcast clouds that were prevalent over all of central Siberia.

This might be the break he was looking for. His general plan up 'til now was to scramble the fighters at Tiksi and Buolkalakh after the Americans were north of Govorovo. This break in the weather, even though it was localized around Tiksi, gave him the opportunity for massing the interceptors for a final visual attack against the Americans.

Turning to Gulayev, he told him to scramble all available fighters from Buolkalakh and use them to intercept the Americans in the area of Govorovo. Every interceptor at Tiksi would be scrambled in five minutes to patrol the clear area when the enemy passed through.

The first twinges of desperation started to cloud Kulikov's normally precise thinking. Although he knew there was only an outside chance that they would arrive in time to do any good, he ordered every operational fighter scrambled from Kazack'ye. That base was 180 miles east of Tiksi, and its airplanes would proceed north and land at Zemlya Bunge on the New Siberian Islands. There they would be refueled immediately after landing, and then relaunched to the west in hopes of intercepting the Americans over the Laptev Sea.

Even as Gulayev was transmitting the instructions to Kazack'ye, Kulikov knew that the odds of finding the enemy under these circumstances were so low that the entire action would be labeled as folly. However, foolish or not, this was the only card he had left to play, so he let Gulayev continue.

Another nagging problem that added to his worries was the predicament of the AWACS. The airplane was being pushed beyond its limits, and a structural or engine failure was a definite possibility. Although the AWACS had successfully countered the enemy's dogleg to the east and regained contact, the data it was transmitting to the control center included some disturbing information. Inbound to the target, the Americans maintained five hundred knots, and even though it was a strain, the AWACS had been able to keep up with them. Airspeed data on the fleeing enemy now indicated they were supersonic, and even if the AWACS were able to continue, it would soon lose radar contact because of the marked speed differential.

The next transmission from the AWACS said they had just run out of water injection fluid. They tried to conserve it by using it intermittently, but the tank was now empty and they had lost contact with the enemy.

Although the AWACS had fallen considerably behind the F-24s, Kulikov ordered them to continue on a northerly heading, in case they could be of some help in the Tiksi area.

It wasn't long before the Status Board showed all interceptors airborne and white arrows appeared on the plotting board showing the various flights en route to their assigned areas. Turning to Gulayev, Kulikov told him to call Zemlya Bunge and order all available fuel trucks and crews standing by to turn around the inbound aircraft immediately upon landing. He also wanted all other maintenance personnel at the flight line to help minimize the ground time of the fighters. Shaking his finger at the brigadier for emphasis, he said there should be no aborts at Zemlya Bunge. Unless the airplane had a *seri-*

*ous* problem, he wanted it in the air! Minor discrepancies would *not* be acceptable reasons for failing to get off the ground!

While Gulayev was on the line to Zemlya Bunge, Kulikov called the weather section and told them he wanted to be notified instantly of any change in conditions around Tiksi. The forecaster assured him that Tiksi would remain wide open for at least the next hour or so, but if any change did occur, he would call. Having been misled by forecasters in the past, the Chief of Air Defense told him to keep a line open to Tiksi and to monitor it continuously, until he was ordered otherwise.

All the wheels were in motion that could have any effect on the outcome of this operation, since no other AWACS were close enough to do any immediate good. The weather reports from the New Siberian Islands were not much different from the prevailing conditions everywhere. Layered conditions predominated, but the forecaster thought the clear areas between cloud decks would be larger farther north.

The lull in the action allowed Kulikov to consider for the first time the question of where the Americans were going. Surely they didn't have enough fuel to go across the pole to Thule, and trying to make Alaska seemed just as improbable. Norway and Sweden were not likely prospects either because of the distance. Did the Americans intend to fly north until their fuel was exhausted and then eject? Were they banking on finding an ice-free area in the Arctic where they could be picked up by submarine?

This line of reasoning seemed feasible, so he ordered the naval situation in the Arctic area to be displayed on the plotting board. When no enemy vessels showed up north of the New Siberian Islands, he told the surveillance section to double-check. Their answer wasn't what he wanted to hear. Because of the extensive weather system in that area, the surveillance satellites had been sending negative reports for the past day and a half. However, there had been no contacts reported on their prior passes when the weather was good.

Kulikov cursed vehemently under his breath. Were it not for these clouds, he was sure his interceptors would have downed the enemy fighters. The curious circle around the target by each airplane still had him puzzled. This tactic involved considerable risk, and did not follow standard ground-attack procedures, so they must have been gathering photographic evidence of the target's destruction. Reviewing the information, Kulikov was forced to discard his theory of a submarine pickup. There had to be another way!

His new line of reasoning was built on the premise that the aircraft must be saved, to bring back proof that the target was destroyed. The only answer there would be tankers. He realized from the plotting board that tankers from either Greenland or Alaska could fly to a rendezvous point in the Arctic, while staying well beyond the range of Soviet radars. Yet, the board showed no flights from either of those areas, which was understandable since the Americans would not tip their hand by flying through the Soviet radar net.

Although it was a long shot, Kulikov dialed the number for the Message Traffic Surveillance Section. After identifying himself, he inquired about any unusual radio traffic from Alaska or Greenland. Leafing through his message intercepts, the captain reported that the Greenland area was normal, and there was only a slight increase in pickups from Alaska. Kulikov asked for more details with respect to time and content. The traffic officer read the summarized report, which identified the messages as air-to-air transmissions of what seemed like a sizable group of airplanes joining in formation.

The Air Defense Commander muttered a vehement, "That's it!" and rushed to the handset connected to the NCO in charge of the surveillance section.

"Sergeant, check your logs for any contacts north of the Chukchi Sea area around four hours ago."

"No contacts anywhere along the northeast coast for the last sixteen hours, General, except for the American's routine electronic intelligence-gathering flight. This we tracked throughout its entire route until it was well inside Alaska returning to base."

The lack of positive information did not sway Kulikov's belief that his tanker theory was correct. What few pieces there were all fit, and the events of the last few hours made him desperate enough to put credence in any evidence.

The large amount of radio transmissions intercepted most probably indicated that not only tankers were being launched, but also a fighter escort. This made sense because at most it would only require two tankers with perhaps a third as an airborne spare, to handle the pair of mission fighters. However, he didn't believe the Americans would ever send so vulnerable a force on a mission of such importance; therefore, the extra airplanes must be the fighter cover, and perhaps additional tankers as well. Once the mission fighters were refueled, this task force would most likely head for the northern coast of Alaska, and then turn south for recovery. Although this would not be the most direct route home, it would certainly keep them well out of any land-based radar coverage, and also at the range limits of fighters based along the northern coast.

Looking again at the Status Board, Kulikov noticed that interceptors were available at numerous bases along this northern perimeter: Chokurdakh, Pevek, and My Schmidt. "More than enough aircraft to give the Americans a good run for their money," he mused. "But the problem will be to find them."

"Gulayev," he snapped, "give me a display that shows the position of all our AWACS aircraft from the Laptev Sea to the Bering Strait!" The brigadier was on the phone instantly, and in a few moments the symbols flashed on the board.

"Perfect, just perfect," Kulikov muttered to himself, as the bases at Srednekolymsk, Nizhniye Kresty, and Uelen all reported operational radar aircraft. He motioned to Gulayev, and said brusquely, "Call Srednekolymsk and Nizhniye Kresty and have them get those airplanes in the air right away. They will head northward and establish an orbit just to the east of De Long Island. After that, notify the other AWACS unit that I want the crews in the aircraft, ready for an immediate launch. Next, have all interceptors along the northern coast brought up to a Five-Minute Alert status. I also want a weather briefing on the Arctic Ocean from the New Siberian Islands eastward to the northern coast of Alaska."

The scenario evolving in Kulikov's mind had one drawback that was troubling him considerably. If he were the American commander of this task force, he would take every precaution to avoid being intercepted by Soviet fighters. The best way to achieve this would be to return to Alaska on a course that would keep them as far from the northern coastline as practical. Undoubtedly, the Americans would do everything they could to make the detection and interception of their force as difficult as possible. What bothered him the most was the distance from land that the air battle would take place. Even with external tanks installed, the interception point would be at or beyond the maximum radius of action of these aircraft. The high power settings required for combat would certainly eliminate any fuel reserves they might have.

No matter how he combined the facts, the answer was always the same: without tankers, every fighter launched was on a one-way suicide mission. Even if sufficient tankers were available, would all the MiGs be equipped with an in-flight refueling system? He damned the myopic planning that had denied this essential modification to their fighter fleet for such a long time. The project had finally started a few years ago, and was proceeding much more slowly than expected. The last figures he recalled showed that less than two-thirds of the interceptors had been modified to date. Also, the bulk of the modified aircraft were assigned to the primary threat area in the west.

Kulikov hesitated at the thought of sending every third pilot to an almost certain death in the frigid Arctic wastes, regardless of how they performed during the air battle. There were plenty of fighters available for the mission, but he had a sinking premonition that tankers would not be too plentiful in northeastern Siberia. He turned to Gulayev, "Get the availability and location of all tankers in northeast Siberia up on the board!"

As the edge-lit Plexiglas started to show the various tanker bases, Kulikov's worst fears were realized. Only four aircraft were anywhere close enough to the probable battle area to be used in time. The ones farther away could not be brought to a forward base, turned around, and relaunched in time to do any good. He shrugged his shoulders in frustration at having to work with such shortcomings. It wasn't any consolation that no one, not even his glowering critics at the end of the dais, ever expected the Americans to get this far.

"What is going on, Kulikov?" Volzhin asked. "Do you have any new information on the escaping Americans?"

The Air Defense Commander could not help noticing the slightly increased emphasis on the word *escaping*, since subtlety was not Volzhin's strong suit. "No, Comrade Marshal, nothing new since the last report when the AWACS lost contact with the enemy."

"Well then, Kulikov, what is your plan now?" asked Volzhin.

Kulikov's brashness under the circumstances took Petrov and Volzhin by surprise, as he started to sketch out the details of his last ditch plan. "Comrade General Secretary, Marshal Volzhin, as I mentioned before, all indications point to the fact that the Americans intend to get those fighters and the evidence they carry back under their control." Then, looking directly at Petrov to make sure his point went home, he continued, "I believe the American President needs this information before he undertakes any negotiations with you, Comrade General Secretary. Apparently, the airplanes are equipped with cameras or some other recording device to prove that the target was destroyed. Since they do not have enough fuel to reach their bases in Greenland or Alaska, they must intend to utilize midair refueling. We have indications of an unusual amount of aerial activity in Alaska; therefore, I have formulated my plans on the premise that the Americans will recover the mission aircraft there.

"It appears that the tanker force will have an escort of fighters, and their course to the rendezvous will keep them beyond the coverage of our coastal radars. I expect the refueling point will be somewhere north of the New Siberian Islands. I also think, and I must admit that this is a guess, that the radar-masking technology employed on the two fighters that attacked Zhigansk is not in widespread use in operational units. If such were the case, I'm sure we would have more information on this new development. Therefore, since the task force will most likely be detectable by our radars, the problem is reduced to locating the tanker force and dispatching interceptors to destroy it."

Kulikov noticed questions starting to surface on the faces of his two superiors, but he continued quickly before they had a chance to interrupt. "However, this is easier said than done, since we only have a very general estimate of where and when the refueling will take place. The Americans were still heading north when the AWACS lost contact, and using their last known airspeed, it will take another hour for them to reach the area north of the New Siberian Islands.

"We have AWACS available at Srednekolymsk and Nizhniye Kresty, and I have ordered them launched. The timing will be close, but the first should arrive at a position east of the New Siberian Islands about the time the Americans are refueling their strike fighters. The second AWACS will be positioned three hundred miles farther east, and will assume control from the first as the Americans enter its area of coverage. Once contact is made, interceptors will be scrambled first from Chokurdakh and then from the other, more eastern bases along the northern coastline. The two AWACS will control these aircraft during repeated attacks on the American force as it heads eastward. There is another AWACS located at Uelen on the Bering Strait, which will be used if the enemy gets that far.

"The weather is considerably better in this area than it is over land, which should increase our chances for success. Also in our favor is the fact that the speed of this entire force is limited to that of the tankers. This results in two positive aspects: first, they will not be able to use their speed to fly out of radar coverage, and secondly, their exposure to our defenses will be considerably longer. All in all, I would say that if our assumptions are anywhere near correct, our chances are very, very good."

Kulikov could see that, although his plan had apparently impressed Petrov and Volzhin, he had by no stretch of the imagination dispelled the skepticism generated by the events of the last few hours.

Volzhin replied with an undisguised tone of distrust, "Aren't the distances you are talking about north of our coastline well in excess of the operational radius of our interceptors?''

Kulikov answered immediately. ''Yes, Comrade Marshal, I anticipate that the Americans will be a good bit beyond the radius of action of our fighters, but not beyond their maximum range. Unfortunately, there are only four tankers along the northern coast that are available for this operation. These aircraft have been placed on Alert status, and are awaiting for airborne orders.

''Obviously, these few tankers are not sufficient to refuel all the aircraft we will launch from the northeastern bases. The best we can do is to ration the fuel among the planes, and hope that it will allow them to make landfall.

''Regrettably, we are faced with another problem in connection with these interceptors. I do not have exact figures as yet, but I estimate that at least one-third of the MiGs at these bases are not equipped with the in-flight refueling modification. If any of these aircraft engage the enemy force, they will run out of fuel when they are well out over the water and be forced to eject. I also anticipate that many of those who are capable of refueling will abandon their aircraft because of the limited amount of fuel available from the tankers.''

Kulikov paused and looked straight at Volzhin before continuing. ''Since it is a very good possibility that numerous aircrews will eject over a widespread area, well beyond land-based helicopter range, we will need assistance from the Navy. Comrade Marshal, I am requesting your permission to order every available ship along the northeast coast out to sea immediately, to help with the rescue effort.''

Normally Volzhin would have preferred having much more concrete evidence before authorizing such a move, but he was enough of a realist to know that time was of the essence. In addition, when Kulikov made the request, Petrov turned toward him with a look signaling that he expected an affirmative reply. Yet, the disaster at Zhigansk still rankled Volzhin.

''I agree that we must not waste a minute in getting those ships in motion,'' he answered, ''so have Gulayev give the required orders in my name. However, I am not convinced of the soundness of your plan, primarily because of the tenuous information on which it is based and the considerable losses incurred if it is approved. I also have some questions on what will be done between now and the time we attack this hypothetical American force.''

''Of course, Comrade Marshal,'' Kulikov replied, ''but let me tell Gulayev what must be done, before I explain the issues you have questioned." With that he hurried to Gulayev's position and ordered, "Have all ships of destroyer size and larger, in ports from the New Siberian Islands to the Bering Strait, weigh anchor immediately. They will proceed at flank speed due north for two hundred miles, and wait for further orders as to their final position. This order includes all submarines in the same area."

Returning to Petrov and Volzhin, he began, "Admittedly, there is a good amount of guesswork behind this course of action, but given the meager facts available, it is the only logical scenario we can follow. If the Americans plan to recover at Thule, there is nothing we can do. However, if Alaska is their destination, I believe we can disrupt their aims considerably. I do not intend to scramble the interceptors until we have located the refueling task force. If our AWACS does not find the enemy, we can recall the fleet, but until that time, having them in position is a prudent move. If the information carried by the American fighters is so valuable to Washington, we cannot spare any effort to deny them such an advantage."

Pausing to let this point register, he noticed a slight flicker of approval cross Petrov's face. "Of more immediate importance is our tactics for the next hour or so. The latest weather reports show a large area of clear weather around Tiksi, and if the Americans maintain their last known heading, they will pass directly through it. Also, the forecaster thought there would be some improvement in the layered conditions over the Laptev Sea, which will better our chances for visual attacks. I have scrambled all available interceptors from Buolkalakh and Tiksi to take advantage of these breaks in the weather. These airplanes will be positioned to cover the clear area completely and commence visual attacks as soon as the Americans are sighted.

"By the time the enemy reaches the coastline north of Tiksi, these interceptors will be too low on fuel to pursue much farther," he added. "For this reason I have deployed all operational aircraft from Kazack'ye, north to Zemlya Bunge on the New Siberian Islands. There they will be refueled in minimum time and take off immediately to form a blocking force west of the islands where we predict the Americans should pass. However, once more the weather plays a dominant role, and we must rely on a chance visual or radar detection of the enemy fighters. Ground-based radar will be little or no help in that area, and there is no AWACS close enough to get there in time. Comrade General Secretary, Comrade Marshal, we have played, or will shortly play, almost every card in our hand, and the eventual outcome now rests with the aircrews involved."

Kulikov stood quietly while his arguments were being digested by his superiors.

Volzhin motioned him over with a wave of his hand, and curtly told him to go ahead with his plan. The look in his eyes and the clenched set of his jaw imparted an air of finality to these orders, and left Kulikov with the definite impression that the Americans must be shot down. Apparently, his explanations of how the enemy fighters got through their defensive network had made no impression on his superiors. The bottom line was that the Americans had frustrated the efforts of the entire system and destroyed a target of immense strategic importance. This was the damning evidence that smoldered inside Petrov and Volzhin, and which despite any successes in the next few hours, would never be forgotten or forgiven.

# *Chapter* ■■

*MONGOOSE Flight*

Gates inched his bird down to successively lower levels, looking for the optimum mix between flying at low altitude, staying IFR, and keeping within the parameters of the terrain-following radar. Flying supersonic this low made for an exceptionally choppy ride. Instead of the gentle undulating flight experienced at normal cruise speeds, he was now banged around the cockpit, as the automatic flight controls responded to the rapidly changing landscape below. Although it was a rough ride, he knew the lower he was, the better his chances of avoiding an attack by the MiG still dogging his tail.

Gates was unaware of just how close the MiG was. All at once the Gun Ranging Radar light on the RHAW panel came on, and the HUD flashed a strobe pointing to his five-thirty position. At the same instant, tracers began to streak by his right wing. In a reflex action, Gates rolled the F-24 into a hard left break, holding the maximum G's available at this high airspeed. Once in the thicker clouds, he paused for a few seconds and then reversed his turn back to the north. Taking a couple of deep breaths to calm his racing pulse, he noticed that the image of the trailing MiG had moved to his seven-thirty position, but showed no warning strobes. The Russian had apparently turned left to follow him, but lost his visual when the clouds thickened. However, the MiG was still being picked up by the sensors, meaning that the Russian figured Gates would probably resume course, so he, too, had turned to the north.

The graphic of their present position showed that they were approaching the town of Sakhandzha, on the Besyuke River. ''Once we're past that river, it's only a hundred miles to the coastline," he mused half aloud.

Although the Laptev Sea marked the beginning of the last crucial leg, he didn't believe that things would be any easier over the water. The Soviets would have every available plane in the act by then, and their only hope was to stay hidden in the bad weather. Another factor that would help once they reached open water was the ever-increasing distance back to the MiGs' recovery bases. Although not a sure bet, Gates felt that some of the pursuing pilots might lose their zeal for the chase, once they realized that punching out over the Arctic Ocean was a given.

He didn't have too long to ponder this because the radar showed he now had much more immediate problems. The scope was painting numerous enemy targets, arrayed roughly in a line across their flight path, and extending to either side of the antenna scan. He sampled a couple with lockons, and the readouts for target speed confirmed that they were fighters. He raised and lowered the radar search pattern, but the picture remained essentially the same: enemy fighters above and below their altitude.

Returning to normal scan, Gates noticed something odd about the arrangement of the airplanes waiting ahead. There were no contacts closer than eighty miles, and none farther than a hundred and thirty miles away. "Why were they just staying in that area instead of being committed to an attack? The AWACS could have dead-reckoned them into our general area, even though it had lost contact after we pushed the speed up."

Gates was mulling over the curious groupings of the enemy formations, when suddenly the chilling implications of the scope picture dawned on him. "Those guys out there are VFR!" he said aloud in amazement, and as the thought sunk in, he felt a tingle of apprehension go through his entire body. The specter of a whole gaggle of MiGs waiting to bounce them the instant they broke into the clear was unsettling, to say the least. If that open area extended for any distance, it would give the Soviets ample time to work them over in visual conditions. Should this be the case, their odds of reaching the tanker were poor to nil.

"Lead, this is Two. I've got what looks like half the Red Air Force about sixty miles ahead. They seem to be spread across a fairly shallow area, and it's my guess that they're milling around in a big sucker hole, waiting for us to run through it."

"Yeah! I'm picking up the same thing, and I think you're right.

No sense in doing them any favors by staying in trail. Crack your throttles just a tad so I can ease up to a line-abreast position—might come in handy for some mutual support. I'll be comin' up on your left."

"Roger, backing off on the power now. Sure wish we had some AMRAAMs left."

After a moment or so, Gates saw the green image on the HUD start moving downward, so he banked a little to the left to set up some lateral displacement. He rechecked the armament selector on IR Missiles and the master switch in the Armed position. The HUD now indicated that he was almost abeam his wingman, so he thumbed the mike to call Brock.

"I'm off your left wing now. Push it back up!"

"Roger that! From the looks of the scope, we'll be right in the middle of them in about forty miles. Don't think we'd make any money trying an end run, since they're spread out pretty far. Our best chance would be to break through the center of that line, and try to make it to the clouds on the other side—if there are any! Maybe we'll even create some confusion when they try converging both sides against our track through the middle. That closest flight ten port at thirty miles looks like it's crossing left to right. We'll probably be passing right behind them, and if they get a tally, it would be easy for them to drop into our six. Think we ought to take them out first?"

"Yeah! Good idea! I'm painting them just a little high, so we might be in their blind area when we roll in behind them. I'll take the one on the left."

It was only a minute after Gates and Brock set their game plan when the two F-24s burst out of the clouds into a sun-drenched arena, stretching for quite a distance on either side. The barren, snow-covered slopes of the Verkhoyanskiys lay just to the right, while across the sparsely treed tundra to the left was the Lena River valley. Unaccustomed to the bright sunlight, Gates snapped the tinted visor down even as he was rolling to the right to stay in position off Brock's wing. The MiGs were spotted at two o'clock and just a little high, so MONGOOSE Two banked hard in behind them to give his Sidewinder a better look angle, and squeezed the trigger once. Gates had acquired his target while still in the turn, and his missile lagged behind Brock's only by a millisecond.

The twin fireballs from the stricken fighters immediately caught the eye of every Soviet pilot in the area, and as each flight leader got a visual, the formations wheeled down in pursuit of the highballing Americans. However, coordination between these flights became almost impossible when Gates and Brock switched on their communications jammers that blocked out transmissions between aircraft. Now that the enemy had a visual on MONGOOSE Flight, these devices could be used to disrupt their attack.

The confusion only lasted a short time, since the Soviet flight commanders quickly hand-signaled their wingmen over to scrambled frequencies that were not bothered by the jammers. But, even this momentary interruption caused some to lose their one fleeting opportunity to get in a good shot.

After rolling northward following the quick kill, Gates was rapidly scanning the large number of distant specks that were growing bigger every second. Judging from the bogeys he could see, it looked like an equal number coming in from both sides of their formation. In the distance, he could just make out another wall of clouds that hopefully indicated the other side of this open area.

"From the looks of things, Two, I think we ought to make a run for those clouds at twelve o'clock. Burners now!"

"Two, Rog! I don't think we can stay together much longer. We've got bogeys comin' in from ten and two o'clock, so it looks like it's time for a split."

"Roger that! Break now!"

The fighters rolled into ninety-degree banks in opposite directions and held them for forty-five degrees of turn, so as to face the approaching enemy flights head-on.

Gates stayed low to minimize the chance of anyone getting in his six o'clock low blind spot, and headed straight at the closing MiGs. A quick glance at the radar scope showed that a turn to the north would not be a good idea, once this first flight of MiGs had passed. Behind, and farther to the north of the attacking flight, were numerous blips, all positioned to block any move in that direction. He saw that if he tried a dash northward, they could quickly fall in behind him and launch IR missiles.

The Soviets were surprised by the boldness of the maneuver, since they expected the Americans to maintain flight integrity and both turn to one side or the other. If this happened, the flight turned away from could easily drop in behind the F-24s for the kill.

The split, coupled with a closing rate that approached fifteen hundred knots, unsettled the Soviet pilots just long enough to negate the effectiveness of their attack. Frustrated at seeing the advantage slip away by this simple maneuver, they fired a pair of missiles in a desperate attempt to salvage the pass. Gates saw the smoke trails racing out in front of the MiGs and realized that those two jocks were firing for effect, and not for a kill. In such a head-on pass, the Soviets would have their armament systems set up for radar-guided missiles, and he was confident that the jammer could handle anything in that category.

The two smoke trails passed harmlessly overhead, never deviating from a straight-line course. Gates smiled at this, knowing that his opponents were not as sharp as they should be. They fired inside minimum launch range, which meant that the missiles were in the boost phase when they passed his aircraft. As such, they were still ballistic since the guidance system would not take control until the rocket motor had burned out. "A break for our side," he thought as the MiGs started to take on definite size and shape, after closing to within two miles.

Gates knew that the second the two flights passed, standard tactics called for an immediate turn in one direction or the other. He figured that the Soviet flight leader would expect him to turn north, so he decided to give him a little bait to nibble on. Just before the MiGs barreled past, he rolled the bird into a vertical bank to the right, but kept a little forward pressure on the stick to keep the plane from actually turning to the north. Seeing what they had anticipated, the opposition responded with their own turn to the north as the proper counter.

The instant the MiGs went by his beam, Gates kicked hard left rudder and banged the stick full over to the left and back in his gut, at the same time twisting the Vertical Translation control to the maximum position. The F-24 flipped over into a steep bank to the left, and almost seemed to swap ends as the elevators and canards took effect at once.

The explosive onset of the G's caused his "go fast pants" to tighten with a numbing grip, as he leaned forward and strained every abdominal muscle to keep the blood from pooling in his lower extremities. This M-1 maneuver helped a little, but still his vision grayed and tunneled as he kept the airplane at the maximum angle of attack for better than one hundred eighty degrees of turn. The fighter bucked and heaved as he worked through the turn, the pitch rising to an audible level as the shudders of the disturbed air wracked the entire airframe, before he finally released the back pressure.

Rolling out in a general northeasterly direction, Gates spotted the pair of MiGs he had just passed. They were still in their left turn but hadn't pulled it as tight as they might have, probably to prevent going belly up to the flight attacking Brock. The enemy birds were in his ten o'clock high position, since they had elected to Chandelle after the head-on pass, rather than stay in a level turn. "Another dumb move," thought Gates, since the silhouette of the MiGs against the sky made them easy to relocate after the turn.

Since the two flights had turned in opposite directions after passing, the Soviets were now just out of range, so Gates left the burners on while pushing forward on the stick and starting a left turn to stay behind them. The combination of the zero-G maneuver and full afterburner made the F-24 accelerate rapidly, and by increasing his cutoff angle he was quickly inside missile launch range. He had to hurry because the MiGs would soon be at the top of their arc, turning their tailpipes away as they started down after him. He concentrated on the moves he needed to make: burners out, keep the turn going, visor sight centered on the leader, missile acquisition, and squeeze the trigger.

As soon as the Sidewinder was off the rail, Gates rolled hard to the right and dumped the nose into a slicing dive to the deck, continuing his dash to the cloud cover ahead. Leveling out at two hundred feet, he looked over his left shoulder and saw the flaming wreckage of the Soviet flight leader at the end of a long plume of black smoke that was just about to touch the ground. Glancing quickly to his right, he could barely make out a lot of fighter activity, a few missile smoke trails, and a large dissipating black smudge, indicating a kill.

Gates had no time to ponder whether it was his wingman because the flights that were originally blocking his turn to the north were now boring in from his ten-thirty position. He could do nothing but once again turn hard into the attack and stay low to make it difficult for the enemy to keep their visual against the variegated background of the tundra.

The four MiGs were now spread out, with one pair in his eleven o'clock position and the other at one. This tactic would allow them to sandwich him if he turned to engage one element or the other. The jammer was still keeping their radar missiles from being a factor, since a few errant rounds went by quite wide of the mark.

Gates knew he could not afford another turn to the south because he had to reach the cloud deck as quickly as possible. As long as he stayed in the clear area, it would only be a matter of time before all the MiGs got their act together and coordinated an attack for the final kill. Since north was the name of the game, he pointed his plane straight at the element lead at one o'clock, and made it look like he intended to ram. The idea was to preoccupy the enemy with what they had to do to avoid a midair, rather than allow them to concentrate on getting a shot off.

The Soviet flight leader didn't realize what was happening initially, but when the F-24's position on his windshield didn't change, he knew that he had to take evasive action. He and his wingman tried some shots with the gun, but the high crossing angle and excessive closing rate threw their aim way off. At the very last instant, the Soviet flight leader broke frantically to the left, as the American jet hurtled by only a few yards away. His turn was so abrupt, and so lacking in any consideration for his wingman, that the latter fell hopelessly out of position. By the time they got reorganized and had their Mach back up, the fight would be too far away for them to be a factor.

Just as the MiGs went by, Gates reefed the aircraft around in another gut-wrenching turn to the left, intending to roll out north and continue his race for the sanctuary of the clouds. When he eased off the back pressure during his rollout, he saw the lead element of the flight he had just passed. They were a little east of where he thought they might be, having been forced to make a wide turn because of the evasive action by numbers three and four. Gates couldn't roll out north because the MiGs would easily slip into his six, so he laid the G's back on and S'd into the rear hemisphere of the enemy fighters.

The combination of the Chameleon lights and the snowy background must have made the F-24 hard to pick up because the MiGs made no move to counter the attack. They continued in a moderate left turn, each varying his angle of bank frequently to check below and outside their turn for the elusive American.

As Gates settled in behind the enemy flight and adjusted his bank to match theirs, one of them must have caught a sun flash off the F-24's wing or canopy. They broke hard left, but the reaction was a trifle late. MONGOOSE One acquired the target while rolling in behind the Soviet element. Gates squeezed the trigger and the Sidewinder had no trouble outmaneuvering the desperate turn of the Red flight leader. The missile struck the starboard wing root, sending the MiG into a spinning roll to the right. As Gates came out of his turn and zero G'd down to treetop level, a fire blossomed on the MiG's side, followed by an explosion that blew the MiG's entire wing off. The rate of roll accelerated and the aircraft started to tumble, finally plunging to a fiery end on the tundra below.

Gates thought his heart must now be pumping pure adrenaline, streams of perspiration were trickling down his forehead and into his eyes. He had no time to raise the visor and give them a quick wipe, so all he could do was blink away the stinging distortion to his vision.

The wall of clouds didn't look too far away when he noticed a gaggle of enemy fighters in his three o'clock position, all chasing a wildly twisting F-24. His wingman was in dire need of help. Brock was right on the deck, S'ing back and forth with high-G turns to keep the MiGs from getting off a shot. Gates slapped the throttles into full afterburner and bent the airplane around in a hard turn to cut off some of the pursuing Soviets.

The enemy flight commanders had not handled their situation of advantage properly. In their eagerness to shoot down the American, they had allowed far too many fighters to join in the chase. Because Brock was swinging back and forth as he worked toward the cloud deck, the MiGs got out of sync with his rapid reversals. As each tried to maneuver for position, he was thwarted by another plane slashing in front of him, or by having to take evasive action to miss someone with target fixation. As long as Brock continued his S turns, the Soviets would keep getting in each other's way, but sooner or later they would figure out their problem and make the necessary corrections.

Gates streamed along just above a landscape nearly devoid of trees, and hoped that his exhaust plume didn't stir up a telltale billow of snow. The MiGs were so intent on chasing Brock and avoiding each other, they didn't notice as Gates moved into gun range. He yanked the power back to full military to prevent an overshoot and noticed that the wingman in the element ahead was flying a fairly tight fighting-wing position. His leader's violent maneuvering forced him to spend most of his time behind and below his lead's aircraft. Gates switched the armament selector to Guns, and uncaged the sight reticle on the HUD while calling Brock. "Keep that turn going for a couple of seconds and I'll scrape one of these guys off your tail!"

"Make it quick! They're really getting me hemmed in!" The tone of Brock's voice indicated the strain he was under, as the Soviets gradually narrowed his options.

Brock held his turn and dropped the last of his flares during these few vulnerable instants. This longer turn gave the enemy wingman the break he needed, and he started to slide to his left to get back into position off his leader's port wing.

"Looks like two-fers night," Gates thought as he banked to settle the pipper on the center of the lead MiG's fuselage. He held it there to stabilize the tracking solution, and just as the wingman was in trail with his leader, he pressed the trigger for a full two-second burst. The six-barreled Gatling Gun came alive with a sustained roar, as it spewed forth a veritable solid stream of armor-piercing incendiary and high-explosive incendiary projectiles.

Knowing that Brock's situation would deteriorate the longer he held the turn, Gates called, "Reverse!" just as he saw his cannon fire strike home. The entire midsection of the enemy airplane was instantly engulfed in a myriad of silver flashes as the 20mm slugs found their mark. The MiG shuddered as if poleaxed, both from the impact of the hail of lead and from the disintegrating havoc it was creating internally. A split second later, it exploded in an immense fireball. The wingman's shock at his leader's destruction only lasted for another split second, since he was too close to react. He flew into the fiery cloud of exploding debris, and came tumbling out the other side, fatally stricken by pieces of the leader's airplane.

Gates had just pulled off the target and was frantically looking over the entire battle area to see how they could best extricate themselves, when he heard the call he had been dreading. "Lead, took a bad hit! Out of control! Punchin' out!" and then silence.

Far to his right he could see the F-24 arching skyward, streaming smoke and flame as Brock struggled for altitude to increase his chances for a successful ejection. There was nothing he could do for his wingman now, so once more Gates zero G'd toward the cloud deck a few miles ahead.

Apparently all Soviet eyes were focused on the death throes of their long-denied victim, and they failed to notice Gates's dash into the clouds. In all his flying career, IFR never felt so good as he took his first deep breath in what seemed like years, while turning off the comm jammer. No sooner than he had gotten into the clouds when the yelping sound of a beeper came over Guard Channel. He immediately hit the Mark and Bearing buttons on the computer to record his present position and the bearing to the beeper signal. The beeper meant that Brock had gotten out of the airplane and his chute had worked. The signal didn't last long, which was another good sign, and it meant that Brock had turned it off to prevent the Soviets from homing in on the signal to pinpoint his position on the ground. Knowing that his wingman had gotten out o.k. and was functioning well enough to turn off the beeper took a large weight off Gates's mind.

The radar showed that he was now out over the water, so he decided to ease the bird down to the bottom of the cloud deck. He put the airplane back on auto since no enemy fighters appeared on the HUD, and set the altitude at five hundred feet. The system took him down smoothly until he broke into the clear a thousand feet above a gray, wind-whipped sea. He quickly readjusted the altitude to fifteen hundred feet, where he had been in some pretty solid weather.

The exertions of the last quarter hour, and the entire mission, all seemed to register at once. His flight gear was soaked with sweat, and his body felt utterly drained. Total exhaustion folded over him in waves, and he had to fight an overwhelming urge to close his eyes, if only for a moment.

He had to get his wits about him immediately and counter the mind-numbing fatigue that was setting in. After unhooking one side of the oxygen mask, he washed down a GO pill with a long swig of water from the plastic bottle carried in his leg pocket. It took a few minutes for the Dexedrine to work, but he began to feel a bit more alert and equal to the task at hand.

The ammunition counter for the gun indicated there was a little more than half his supply remaining. Only enough for a couple of short bursts, and that was it. Then, his only defenses would be speed and his skill in maneuvering. The sensor system wasn't registering anything approaching from the rear, so Gates figured their next try would be with fighters from the New Siberian Islands.

During this momentary respite, the impact of Brock's loss flooded back into his thoughts. Fighter pilots tend to be somewhat indifferent about a comrade being shot down, since it is one of the accepted dangers in their profession. Their feelings spring from a realization of the fortunes of combat, and the need to avoid dwelling on such mission-distracting thoughts. Yet, he had lost a friend who had fought valiantly and would be sorely missed. If he ever got out of this mess, one of his first tasks would be to visit Brock's parents in Trenton and try to explain the unexplainable. But, the classification of this mission and the uncertainties of Brock's exact status would make this an extremely difficult chore.

He hadn't thought about fuel for quite some time, and a glance at the totalizer nearly froze his heart. The flight plan allowed for some combat time; however, the instrument showed that they had stayed too long at the fair. The extra burner time and additional maneuvering had eaten up nearly all the planned reserves. "The rendezvous and hookup with the tanker will have to go without a hitch, even if the MiGs don't find me," he thought. "And if they do . . . ." The last premise he left hanging, knowing full well what the implications would be. He could only hope the weather would hold because, without AWACS or GCI, the interceptors would have to be very lucky to stumble across one aircraft in such a large chunk of airspace. Still nothing on the HUD, so he turned off the jammer to prevent its multiple targets from drawing any interest to his location.

Gates throttled back just below full military in an effort to conserve whatever fuel he could without appreciably slowing down his run for the tanker. The airspeed dropped to six hundred fifty knots, which compromised between what he needed to foil the interceptors and conserve fuel.

A hundred miles from the coastline, the GO pill finally worked its magic. His alertness returned none too soon because he started to pick up numerous targets on his starboard side. Switching to Right Scan, he raised and lowered the beam to check all altitudes. It was the same as before, with flights of MiGs deployed at varying altitudes and heading westward to form a blocking force. Gates rechecked the armament selector on Guns, and that he was armed hot.

Studying the blips on the radar screen, he noticed that the MiGs were more strung out than the interceptors they had battled in the clear area. "Probably because they were near the maximum range from the GCI site on the New Siberian Islands," he reasoned, "and control was getting a little spotty." Another encouraging sign was that the total number was considerably less than before, which meant fewer eyes to spot him, and less to contend with if they got lucky.

Some of the bogeys were far enough west to rule out going around the left side of their force. Another worrisome factor was that he began encountering more and more areas of thin clouds, where the in-flight visibility was not too bad. It wasn't wide open, but it was good enough in some areas for a sharp-eyed MiG driver to jump his tail.

Gates ran another check of the targets with the El Scan, and their altitudes looked about the same as before. One pair was painting just a little higher than his altitude, and if things didn't change, they would be fairly close when their flight paths crossed. The enemy fighters were going from right to left, and the geometry of the setup looked like the classic ninety-degree beam intercept. Now his concern was to keep the Soviets from suspecting that an American fighter was anywhere around. He ran the El Scan full down so that the MiG's RHAW gear didn't pick up his radar beam. With all the fighters in the area, he knew the MiGs were getting a lot of intermittent buzzing from their sensors, but he didn't want to draw their attention by illuminating the target constantly.

As he neared their position, he raised the antenna quickly to get

one or two paints and then lowered it again. Doing this every fifteen
seconds or so allowed him to keep tabs on the flight of MiGs without
alerting them to his presence.

When the slant range to the MiGs was fifty miles, the weather was
definitely not in his favor. The clouds had again thinned appreciably,
and it looked like more of the same up ahead. Eyeballing the intercept
geometry once more, he knew that staying on course to sneak past
this pair of MiGs would put him within ten miles of their radar. They
still didn't know Gates was there, and he had to do something quickly
to capitalize on that advantage. Also, because of his fuel status, he
couldn't plan on an extended engagement with a lot of burner time.

After another quick peek at the enemy using the El Scan, Gates
made up his mind and rolled over in a steep turn to the right to position the MiG flight dead ahead. He allowed himself one sweep of the
radar to verify that the Soviets were in his twelve o'clock position. His
plan was to convert the beam intercept he was on to a 90−20 stern
attack.

His right turn started the conversion that would result in his rolling out behind the target, about twenty degrees off their tail. He
stopped the turn after forty-five degrees and from then on played the
bank angle to keep the MiGs twenty to thirty degrees port, utilizing
momentary looks with the radar.

While heading northeast, he got a quick contact on another flight
farther to the east, who were following the same route as the pair he
was stalking. With the improving visibility, this second element ruined
any chances of sneaking behind the first pair of Soviets and then
pressing on to the north.

Gates realized that his attack on the flight ahead must be quick
and effective to preclude the leader from calling the trailing flight to
help out. Throttling back to keep the closing rate under control, he
rolled out on a westerly heading, which put the bogeys twenty
degrees to starboard. Raising the antenna once more, he saw that the
range was now six miles, and it appeared that the enemy flight was in a
line-abreast formation, a more flexible tactical formation. The scope
picture didn't allow him to determine which one was the leader, so
Gates decided to attack the southernmost MiG first, then make a
quick, slashing run at the other plane, and hopefully generate enough
confusion to make a break for the north.

Gates lowered his antenna again and hoped that the flight to the
east wouldn't decide to join this element for at least another few minutes. One final look before the attack showed his range was now two

miles, so he started to ease upward while continuing to close on the
targets. He hadn't gone up a thousand feet when he broke into the
clear and spotted the MiGs in his one o'clock position, slightly high.
He made a quick recheck for sight uncaged, guns selected and armed
hot, after which he pushed up the throttles to bore in for the kill.

The Soviets' lookout doctrine was a little shabby, since they never
picked him up coming in from their seven o'clock low. A half mile
from the enemy flight he figured that the wingman would be his first
target, since he was riding slightly behind the other MiG's beam. Gates
had hoped to hit the leader first and thus eliminate the most experienced man at the outset, but there was no time or fuel to change the
game plan now.

The closing rate was picking up rapidly as he reversed his turn
and slid into the groove behind the MiG. The cross hairs of the visor
sight were centered on the cockpit area. He pressed the acquisition
switch and, when the sight reticle indicated a range lockon, he
slammed the throttles to the military stop. A practiced hand on the
stick quickly settled the pipper on the enemy's midsection, as the
range bar on the combining glass shrank down to indicate optimum
firing range.

Just as he was squeezing the trigger, the flight leader must have
screamed the warning to "Break left!" The wingman's airplane was
about halfway into the break when Gates's short burst struck. His
frantic reaction saved him from a quick and merciful death, but probably doomed him to a slower and more painful demise in the icy waters
below. The sudden break moved the bullet impact point, but not far
enough. The splash of cannon fire erupted on the MiG's right wing,
sending large pieces of skin and structure flying off, while making a
sieve out of the internal wing tank. A cloud of vaporizing fuel
streamed behind the stricken MiG, whose aileron controls must now
be jammed, since the aircraft stayed in a near vertical bank, as it slowly
nosed over into its last plunge.

Gates had no time to follow the wingman since he was definitely
out of the fight, and his leader was in a hard turn into Gates, who
reversed his turn toward the oncoming MiG. Both aircraft were now
approaching each other head on, with the MiG spraying cannon fire
all over in an attempt to unnerve his opponent. Gates couldn't afford
this luxury, since the indicator showed only enough ammo left for a
short burst.

Just before their flight paths crossed, he hauled back on the stick
while rolling into a vertical bank to the right. As soon as the MiG

flashed by his canopy starting his roll to the right, Gates eased off the bank by a stiff application of left rudder and fed in maximum vertical translation. All the while he kept the stick in his gut to keep the G load pegged at nine.

With no armament and not very much fuel, the F-24 responded beautifully, arcing above the plane of the MiG's turn, while reducing the lateral separation between the two fighters. With a full load of fuel and missiles aboard, the Soviet pilot was forced to fight in a more horizontal plane, so as not to dissipate his energy level too quickly. The MiG's traditionally great turning ability would normally be a definite advantage in this type of scissors maneuver, and after a couple of crossovers it would be eating its opponent's socks. Not so on this occasion, however. Gates saw the MiG pilot look back over his shoulder, noting that the American had gone high, and realized that he was in a quandary.

The usual counter to the high-speed yo-yo that Gates had tried would be to unload and dive for separation. But the F-24 was still a little ahead of the MiG's beam, its pilot realized, and the standard counter would achieve nothing but to give his opponent his six o'clock position. Unaware of the effectiveness of the Decoupled Mode, he still felt he could outturn the American and it would only take another crossover or so to get behind him.

Gates was inverted in his yo-yo above the MiG when their paths crossed for the second time. He noticed the Soviet was trying to horse the plane around, since it was bucking occasionally and getting a little wing tuck now and then, as the pilot momentarily overloaded it while flying along the feather edge of the controllability curve. Surprised at not seeing the MiG perform the expected counter to the high-speed yo-yo, Gates thought, "This guy's no slouch. Looks like he's going to stay in the scissors, rather than diving away."

The MiG had now reversed his turn and only dropped the nose a little to keep up his Mach. The two aircraft were canopy to canopy again, with Gates above the MiG in a forty-five degree inverted bank. His plan to continue his roll in behind the Soviet was now down the tubes, since the two birds were just about to cross over again, still pretty much line abreast.

As the MiG pilot pulled harder to start working toward Gates's six, he finally ran out of energy maneuverability. The MiG shuddered violently, forcing the pilot to realize he was crossing the boundary into uncontrolled flight and leaving him no option but to ease off on the G's and dump the nose.

Seeing the MiG head downward, Gates didn't want him to achieve a separation that would prolong the fight. His chance to gain the advantage was fleeting, but he saw it and reacted accordingly. Neutralizing the ailerons, he held full aft stick and again used the Vertical Translation to whip the nose down into an almost instantaneous split S. Pointing straight down, he fed in left rudder to roll the bird around its axis, in order to keep the enemy in sight. Again his light weight was the decisive factor, and the F-24 accelerated quickly under the zero-G situation.

The Soviet's Mach had bled off considerably during the scissors, and it took him longer to build it back up to fighting speed. This slight delay was all that Gates needed to close the gap behind the diving MiG and move in to maximum gun range.

The Soviet pilot rolled frantically to keep his opponent in sight, and seeing how rapidly the American was gaining, knew he had to start a turn immediately or it would be all over. He did not have sufficient airspeed to maneuver the MiG at its maximum potential, so he played the G load carefully to keep from sliding back into the stall area. As soon as Gates saw the MiG starting to rotate out of the dive, he knew he had him.

The Soviet wasn't bending it around as hard as he should, so it was no problem to cut inside his turn with help from the Decoupled Mode. The F-24's tighter turn brought him inside gun range quickly and, after using a bit of rudder to match his wings with the MiG's, he eased in more back stick to settle the pipper on the Soviet's forward fuselage area. Through the gunsight reticle, he could see the enemy pilot looking back at a picture that every fighter jock dreads most. The American was camped in his six-thirty position and would certainly open fire at any instant. His only choice was to start a last-ditch maneuver right now, or he would be a dead man.

Gates knew he had the advantage and he also knew that the MiG driver was aware of his predicament. Thus, he anticipated that his opponent would try some type of violent maneuver to shake him off his tail. Based on their attitudes, he figured this guy would try a high-G rudder roll over the top, so he let the pipper ride just a little high as the range closed. Since he would only have time for one shot, he held his fire for a few more heartbeats in order to close to the optimum range.

The MiG was growing large in the reticle as Gates's finger tightened on the trigger, and just before it was fully depressed, the Soviet pilot made his move. Gates's prediction was right. Suddenly the MiG's

nose started to rise in an arc to the right. The entire airplane seemed to
stop in midair and fill the combining glass with its plan view as the
maneuver took effect.

Gates mashed down the trigger and held it, knowing that he
would overshoot the target quickly. The small amount of lead he had
put in paid off, as the high-G roll rotated the MiG back into his gunsight just as the first rounds arrived. The majority of the burst caught
the MiG amidships, raking the cockpit and the engine compartment
with a lethal hail of lead, steel, and fire.

The extreme rate of closure generated by the Soviet's last-ditch
maneuver forced Gates to bang the stick to the left forward corner and
kick hard bottom rudder to avoid ramming his opponent. He held this
for the second or so it took to clear the mortally wounded MiG, and
then reversed his turn to the north.

A quick visual scan showed no other enemy aircraft in sight, so
Gates dove for a protecting cloud deck a few thousand feet below.
While throttling back to a more economical power setting he checked
the fuel gauge, and his heart sank. Even before calculating things
exactly, he knew he had a big problem. The power required to maintain an edge during the last engagement had eaten up what meager
reserves he was counting on, and then some. Hoping that the real
numbers might be more encouraging, he queried the computer for his
present position and the distance to the refueling point. After entering
the amount of fuel remaining, the news was still bad. It was obvious
he could no longer afford the luxury of staying at low altitude, but had
to cruise-climb much higher to take advantage of the decreased fuel
flow that altitude would make possible.

The radar scope was still painting two flights of patrolling MiGs
about forty miles ahead, and at least ten thousand feet above his altitude. Even though he desperately needed to climb to conserve fuel,
his only chance of escape lay in heading for the deck and trying to
sneak by underneath them. After a very anxious five minutes at 300
feet, the fuel gauge was telling him in no uncertain terms that he had
to make his move, and make it now.

With so little fuel left, Gates was reluctant to add power, but knew
that slowing down too much in the climb would only make things easier for the Soviets. He bumped the throttles up a couple of percent,
trimmed in some back stick, and the F-24 climbed like a homesick
angel because of its low gross weight. The rate of climb needle was
pegged as the bird shot upward, and in less than a minute he popped
into the clear area. There, in sunlight filtered only by some thin clouds

above him, he felt conspicuously exposed to every Soviet eye in the area. Twisting around as far as he could, Gates looked back over both shoulders to give his six o'clock a thorough visual scan. There was nothing in sight to the rear, so he searched the area ahead with radar for any other patrolling MiGs. Again no contacts, and for the first time in what seemed like ages, he felt a twinge of cautious optimism.

It didn't last long, though, as suddenly the HUD started flashing intermittent strobes pointing behind him. The MiGs he had just flown under apparently caught a sun flash off his airplane and were in hot pursuit to investigate. Gates knew he was close to ten miles in front of them, but was positive they were in full afterburner to close the range as quickly as possible. The random strobing on the HUD meant they had no firm contact, and showed them grouped fairly close together almost dead astern. All he could do was steer to keep them directly behind him, in order to minimize his radar cross section.

There wouldn't be much help from cloud cover, as the only layers above him were some broken decks that looked a little thin. The lowest one wasn't too far above his present altitude, so Gates trimmed in more backpressure in order to get through it quickly, and make it tougher for them to get an IR contact. The INS indicated less than two hundred miles to the refueling point, so he decided to start calling the tanker. The first couple of tries got no answer, which he expected because of the distance involved. Passing twenty-five thousand feet, he went through a broken deck and was still climbing toward another that looked to be at thirty grand. The MiGs were still sniffing around for a solid contact, but the lessening activity on the HUD proved that the Stealth mod had them buffaloed. The fact that they were still there caused some concern because it meant that they, too, were climbing.

"MONGOOSE Flight, this is MONGOOSE Control. Do you read? Over!" It wasn't very loud, but it was definitely there, and Gates's spirits soared.

"Roger, Control, this is MONGOOSE One, transmitting ROSEBUD, repeat ROSEBUD. Do you copy?"

"Roger, MONGOOSE, copy ROSEBUD. Will relay. Squawk six three two five. We're only reading you about three by!"

He quickly dialed in the transponder code and flicked the switch to ON, replying, "Understand, squawking six three two five. Be advised MONGOOSE Two shot down. Stand by for coordinates."

"Standing by, One, and we have contact at one hundred miles."

Gates recalled the data from the computer and read the fix to the controller, who acknowledged and repeated the numbers back to Gates.

"Control, this is One. I am extremely low on fuel. Head south from your position and push it up. Am unable to make original rendez-vous. I've also got some MiGs behind me somewhere, so bring along the escort."

"Roger, One. Tanker is turning south now at full blower. He's twelve o'clock at one hundred. When you get closer, we'll turn the tanker east, and roll you in behind him. What's your state?"

"I'm in hurtsville! Fuel low-level lights on both sides are starting to flicker. It's going to be real tight!"

"Roger that! Tanker's level at Angels three five, and will be indica-ting three two zero knots at hookup. We're painting the bogeys behind you. They're six o'clock at thirteen miles. We only see four, so we're sending half the escort to engage. BLUE Flight is eleven thirty your position at seventy-five."

"Roger, Control! Contact there. Also have a contact twelve o'clock at eighty—should be the tanker. Judy on the tanker, but keep coming with the vectors, since I can't afford to miss him."

Gates made sure that the radar was in the Visual Identification Mode, to bring him in directly behind the tanker and a little off to the right. He quickly set up the fuel panel for an air-to-air hookup and tried to ignore the fuel low-level lights, which were now on steadily. As he rocked the wings and yawed the bird gently to milk any trapped fuel out of the empty tanks, BLUE Flight opened fire. Dirty white smoke trails from four missiles appeared at ten thirty, and raced past a mile or two off his left wing. He tried adjusting his rearview mirror to see if they scored, but just then MONGOOSE Control called.

"One, this is Control. Tanker twelve o'clock at twenty miles, starting his turn to the east now. Go starboard to zero four five degrees. Tanker should be forty port at ten miles when you roll out. Looks like we scraped those MiGs off your tail. BLUE Flight reports two kills, one of the bogeys is heading for home, and they're engaging the other one now."

"Roger that. Steady zero four five. Still have a Judy on the tanker." Even though his overtake was higher than desired, he only reduced the throttles a couple of percent. If an overshoot started to develop, he could control it with speed brakes, and he didn't want the joinup to degenerate into a long tail chase by slowing down too early.

"Tanker's steady on zero nine zero. He should be ten port at five miles."

"Got him there, and have a tally ho!"

"Roger, One. You're clear to contact MONGOOSE Three on this frequency. Boomer standing by."

Gates kept his speed up as he sliced in behind the tanker and saw the bright red paint on the tail. The fuel gauge for the tank that fed both engines was starting to touch the zero mark. About a mile astern of the tanker, he started reducing the power slowly to keep the fuel from sloshing forward in the tank to any great extent. The last thing he needed now was to uncover the feed line and get a flameout due to a momentary interruption.

He continued to slow the closing rate as he slid in astern of the tanker and just a little below its altitude. Gates had never been in such a critical situation fuel-wise, and he could feel a hot, prickly sensation go over his whole body as the tension and urgency of the moment increased. The tanker grew larger in the windshield as he closed to within fifty yards of its tail, and he expected to hear that sudden silence from the engine room at any second.

# Chapter 12

"MONGOOSE One, this is your boomer. You're cleared to the pre-contact position!"

"Negative, Boomer. I'm indicating zero fuel—unable to hold at precontact position. I'm coming right in for a hookup!"

"Roger, One—cleared. I'm setting up the system for the maximum transfer rate. Keep coming forward, come up forty."

The boomer quickly called the cockpit to warn them of the possible flameout condition, which they rogered with a "Standing by." Gates saw the winged boom drop downward from the in-trail position, and point directly at him as he brought the bird up a little and continued closing.

"Up twenty, forward twenty!" called the boomer, as he started to extend the inner segment of the boom from its retracted position and began to reach for the incoming fighter.

The boomer continued his calls with, "Up five, forward ten," and Gates followed his directions with barely perceptible control movements. The approaching brass nozzle of the boom looked like it would surely punch through the windscreen and impale him to the seat back, when at the last second, the boomer lifted it slowly over the canopy toward the open receptacle just to the rear on the turtledeck.

Gates heard the nozzle bump once and then came the familiar *thunk*, as it seated in the receptacle and the hydraulic latches locked it in place. When the green light on the windshield bow illuminated, indicating a contact, he shifted his gaze to the twin rows of director lights on the forward belly of the tanker. These were activated by the position of the boom, and automatically gave him steering directions to maintain the ideal refueling position.

He was just starting to make a minor correction to get the lights "in the green," when his luck ran out. Double flameout! Frantically he called, "Flameout" to the boomer, while reaching back with his left hand to locate the handle for the Ram Air Turbine. With a hiss of compressed air, the multibladed fan extended from the side of the fuselage, as he struggled to stay hooked on the boom and prevent a brute-force disconnect.

The tanker crew responded instantly to his call and backed off the throttles while easing the aircraft over in a gentle dive. The sudden loss of thrust caused the F-24 to drop back, extending the fragile inner boom to its maximum length.

Gates's heart was pounding like a jack hammer, and he was sweating profusely as he slowly lowered the nose to hold the best glide speed. He had to fly perfect formation with the tanker, but even more critical was the need to stay within the operational limits of the boom. Too far forward, and it would bend against the stop and the nozzle would jam in the receptacle. Too far back would tear the nozzle out of the receptacle, most likely damaging it to the point where refueling would be impossible. Swinging out to either side would also result in a jammed nozzle, but with a greater likelihood of structural damage.

The boomer was a real pro, giving a steady stream of corrections to the cockpit concerning airspeed and dive angle. He had to get the two airplanes synchronized in speed so the tanker could gradually start adding power and actually tow the fighter behind it. The coordination between everyone involved was extremely delicate, as the boomer let the inner boom extend to its limit very slowly. All they needed were a few minutes in the towing mode to allow enough fuel to be transferred, so that Gates could then drop off and try an airstart.

Each second was an eternity as Gates battled the controls to stay in position. The hydraulic pump on the RAT was smaller than the engine-driven pump that normally powered the flight control system. This resulted in a sluggish control response and necessitated overcontrolling for every correction required. As soon as the slower moving control surfaces took effect, an opposite overcontrol was necessary to keep the bird where he wanted it.

The boomer called in a confident voice that left no doubt about his having complete control of the situation. "We're pushing up the power now, One, and we'll try towing you for another minute or so. By then you should have enough fuel to drop off and try an airstart."

Gates could feel an almost imperceptible tug at his plane as the tanker pushed up the throttles, and he croaked out a "Roger" from a mouth and throat that had turned to cotton.

Slowly the tanker leveled off, while he worked furiously to keep from exceeding the limits of the boom. In the tow situation, his main concern was pitch control as the tanker came out of its dive. Since he was reacting to the rotation of the tanker, his control inputs were just a fraction of a second late. This, coupled with the lack of a crisp response from the control surfaces, almost caused him to lose it once or twice during the leveloff.

His up and down oscillations on the end of the boom would have been embarrassing in a normal situation, looking like someone trying air-to-air refueling for the first time. However, Gates was beyond embarrassment as he forced himself to settle down through intense concentration on the problem at hand. His very life depended on hanging on the boom for just a little while longer, even though each tick of the clock seemed like an eon. He needed two or three thousand pounds of fuel before he could risk a disconnect and try an airstart. Gates was also aware that this towing setup was strictly an emergency procedure and could not be used all the way to Alaska.

"One," the boomer called, "you've got three thousand pounds. If you're all set, we'll disconnect and be standing by to fill you up after your airstart."

"Roger. Ready any time," Gates replied.

"OK," the boomer came back, "disconnecting now!" Gates heard the metallic *clunk* of the latches disengaging, and in his peripheral vision saw the boom swing up and away from his bird.

The airstart procedure sprang into sharp focus in his mind, as he went through the steps practiced so many times in the simulator: Stopcock throttles while adjusting the dive angle to get on the recommended airspeed, check both engines windmilling at the proper RPM, all boost pumps on.

He was passing twenty eight thousand feet when he made his first attempt—ignition button depressed and held, throttle for the right engine around the detent to the idle position. His eyes were glued to the fuel-flow indicator and the exhaust gas temperature gauge, waiting for some signs of life. The fuel-flow needle rose slowly off the peg, but the temperature gauge didn't budge. No lightoff! Gates pressed the ignition button even harder, hoping it would help, but still no dice.

After he dropped off the boom, the silence in the cockpit became intense, adding an eerie dimension to his worsening predicament. The slipstream was hardly discernible at this slower, best glide speed, and the familiar airframe vibration from the engines, generators, and other equipment was totally absent.

Gates forced this distraction from his mind by concentrating even harder on each and every step of airstart procedure. The boomer's call helped to get his mind back on track.

"White vapor coming out your tailpipe, One. Any luck with the airstart?"

"Negative!" was Gates's clipped reply, not wishing to make prolonged transmissions on the radio to conserve battery power for the ignition system. He knew what the boomer saw coming from his tailpipe was vaporized fuel, blowing through the still-dead combustion chambers.

"I'll give the other side a try," he thought as he stopcocked the right throttle and repeated the procedure on the left engine. Still no response, as the EGT needle seemed frozen on zero. Airspeed remained good passing twenty-one thousand feet.

He was using the correct procedure, which was nothing more than a series of mechanical steps. No special technique or touch was required. The only reason he could think of as to why he couldn't get a lightoff was that maybe this exotic fuel needed denser air before the proper mixture was reached. The rate of descent held at forty-five hundred feet per minute as he glided through eighteen thousand feet and tried another airstart. Again no results, even though he was overly deliberate in each step of the process.

The first tentacles of fear started to wrap themselves around his stomach, as the details of the jagged, windswept surface of the Arctic ice pact became clearer each second. Ten thousand feet, and he decided he would make one more try on each engine, and if it didn't work, it would be time to punch out.

He again moved the right throttle to idle while he pressed the ignition button on the grip. The fuel flow showed an indication once more, and as the altimeter passed eight thousand feet, he heard and felt a low rumble from the aft section. Gates let out a yell as the EGT rose, peaked out, and settled in the starting range. R.P.M. began to increase, and as soon as it had passed the normal idle speed, he gingerly opened the throttle in small increments.

The urge to firewall the go-handle and get back up on the tanker was almost overwhelming, but Gates kept adding power slowly. He wanted to avoid any sudden changes in the delicate balance of conditions that resulted in the airstart, which might cause another flameout. The engine responded smoothly and was soon operating in the normal range, which meant that he could hold altitude while getting the other mill fired up.

"Boomer, this is One. I've got one started—working on the other now!"

As the tanker rogered his call, Gates decided to stay at eight thousand feet for the relight of the left engine, since the new fuel and engine combination seemed to like that altitude best. The second engine torched off with no problems, but he still moved the throttle slowly until it matched the setting on the right engine. Then, he moved both throttles to the firewall as he established a climbing turn to relocate the tanker, while reaching back to retract the RAT.

"Got both of them running now, Boomer. I'm on my way back up!"

"Roger, One. You're cleared into position. Do you have a tally?"

"Negative, I'm passing angels twenty. Control, could you give me a steer?"

The AWACS controller was right on top of the situation, and came back instantly. "Roger, One. Tanker is thirty starboard at twenty, level at angels thirty-five."

Gates cranked his radar antenna up to get a good paint on his target. "Roger, taking a Judy now," he replied, locking the radar on the tanker. With only a little more than two thousand pounds of fuel on board, he pegged the F-24's rate-of-climb indicator until he leveled off behind and slightly below the tanker.

Although his fuel situation was not as critical as the first time, he was not out of the woods yet. He hoped that all the strain on the receptacle and boom during the towing operation had not deformed the seals or the locking mechanism to where he couldn't take on any fuel. Just in case there would be some problems, he barely paused at the precontact position before continuing to follow the flashing director lights. As he inched forward and upward while nearing the contact position, he saw the inner section of the boom start extending.

The boomer was also aware of the potential for problems during the hookup, and realized that every second was precious. Just before he stopped flashing the Up and Forward lights to get Gates into position, he extended the boom to its maximum, and guided it smoothly over the canopy to the receptacle.

The *thunk* of the locking mechanism was reassuring, but not half as much as seeing the green Contact light illuminate. This meant that the nozzle was seated properly, and he should be able to take on fuel. The boomer confirmed this by resorting to the old refueler's cliché of calling that they were now "passing gas!"

Even though Gates always considered air-to-air refueling as one of the most difficult and precise areas of flying, this hookup was a picnic after all the problems associated with the last one. The tanker was level and riding smoothly on its autopilot as they raced eastward toward Alaska, and he had no difficulty in keeping the director lights "in the green." The boomer called each five thousand pounds off-loaded, and as the tanks filled, Gates added a bit of power and nose-up trim to compensate for the increasing gross weight.

From the pilot's point of view, every refueling seems to take forever when you're working up a sweat hanging on the end of the boom. In reality, this one took only a relatively short time because, without drop tanks, the internal fuel cells filled up rather quickly.

"O.k., One," the boomer called. "The transfer rate is almost zero, so you're close to a full load. Disconnecting—Now!"

Gates came back just a hair on the power as the boom snaked up and away. When definitely clear, he slid out to a hundred yards off the tanker's wing and engaged the autopilot. The big numbers on the fuel counter certainly made him feel better, as did the thought that just a short distance away there was more where that came from.

He loosened his seat belt and harness, and stretched as best he could to relieve the aches that had accrued from too many hours in the cramped cockpit. Every moment brought to light another set of muscles that rebelled when disturbed from their stiffness.

Once his circulation got going, he realized he was terribly thirsty, and he downed the eight-ounce bottle of water in his G suit pocket in a gulp and a half. It tasted wonderful, and he could have polished off two or three more, but that finished his entire supply.

"Control, this is One. How did BLUE Flight do against those guys that were chasing me?"

"Real good, MONGOOSE," answered the controller. "Got two with AMRAAMS. A third tried to mix it up but got sandwiched and was taken care of with a Sidewinder, and the last guy panicked and turned tail for home. Our troops didn't get a scratch, but we don't think the show is over just yet. Been picking up a lot of activity on their tactical frequencies. They've got quite a few bases along their northern coast, so I guess they're going to give it the old college try. The task force commander is moving all of us more to the north. It won't add much to our trip, but will put them a lot farther from land and give their fighter jocks one more thing to think about. RED and BLUE flights will parallel us about seventy-five miles to the south. This should give them plenty of engagement time to keep the bad guys off our back, should their interceptors get this far."

"Will they be able to find us way out here? We're beyond the range of any GCI sites, even those on the New Siberian Islands."

"That's true, but we've got some spook gear on board that's picking up a signal coming from an AWACS."

Gates's new-found sense of well-being sank with that bit of news. The Soviets wouldn't put an AWACS into the game unless they planned to have interceptors for it to control. He knew the MiGs barely had the range to operate this far from home, so it might mean they were considering suicide missions. If this were the case, they would certainly have enough fuel to mix it up with RED and BLUE flights for as long as they wanted. And if the opportunity presented itself, they would still have enough fuel to break through the F-24s and make a kamikaze run against the tankers and AWACS. Even though he was driving the most advanced fighter in the world, Gates was as helpless as the airplanes he was traveling with, since he had no armament aboard.

As they were turning thirty degrees left, the task force commander ordered RED and BLUE flights to cycle through their tankers for one last topoff before moving southward. None required very much, since they all tapped the tanker just before the rendezvous, in anticipation of a major engagement during the joinup. RED Flight finished first and formed up in spread formation as they climbed southeastward to angels four five. BLUE Flight needed more time, having burned off a fair amount of fuel during the hassle with the interceptors that had followed Gates. In less than ten minutes they were moving off in the same direction as RED Flight, but staying level at thirty-five thousand feet.

*Kremlin War Room*

Kulikov was feeling more optimistic than he had for the past several hours. He had been very close in his estimate of where the American fighters would rendezvous with the refueling force. The loss of

three interceptors within a few minutes was regrettable, but it confirmed the existence of the tanker force and their escorts.

The AWACS from Srednekolymsk just reported in position east of
De Long Island, and a dozen fighters were outbound from Chokurdakh to join it. A tanker had also been launched and was heading
toward that area, but Kulikov knew that it would be touch and go as to
whether it would arrive in time to do any good. The second AWACS
was airborne as well, and would be at its orbit point in plenty of time.
Interceptor crews at Ambarchik and Pavek were in their cockpits
awaiting launch orders. On the extreme northeastern coastline, the
third AWACS and another group of fighters were standing by in case
they were needed.

Even though Kulikov felt moderately satisfied at the actions he
had taken, he dared not share this with anyone on the dais, since well-
laid plans had gone awry more than once this past night.

The AWACS reported they were starting to pick up the interceptors to the south of their position, but still had no contact with the
enemy. Kulikov had anticipated this, and told Gulayev to head them
north-northeast and vector the fighters accordingly to remain in radar
contact. The change of course was acknowledged as Kulikov stared at
the Situation Board, watching the white arrows representing their aircraft converge with those in red that estimated the position of the
American task force.

His guess was that the latter would be roughly following the 80th
parallel, so the AWACS should have them on their radar by now. It had
been five minutes since they called steady on the new course, yet
there was still no contact. He noticed that Marshal Volzhin and the
General Secretary were also watching the board with more than casual
interest, which did little for his confidence level. Did the Americans
plan to return to Alaska, or after nearly being intercepted at the rendezvous, had they changed their minds and headed across the pole for
Thule?

The specter of doubt loomed before him once more, with the
AWACS now a hundred fifty miles north-northeast of De Long Island
and still finding nothing. Another two minutes went by before they
reported a contact two hundred miles farther north. Relief flooded
through Kulikov as the proof of his theory was replotted on the Situation Board. The Americans had not altered their plans and were still
heading for Alaska, but the task force commander had moved them
farther north than expected.

This latest wrinkle in the enemy's tactics was easily countered, but at what an expense! Kulikov could see that the impending battle would be fought more than four hundred miles northeast of the closest land. Given the high power settings needed in combat, he knew there would not be enough fuel for the MiGs to make the airfield at Zemlya Bunge. He shuddered at the thought of the pilots bailing out over the easternmost New Siberian Islands, which were mere specks of land, and hoping that they didn't drift beyond them into the ice field. The lucky ones in this contest might be those who died in the air.

Pushing these morbid thoughts from his mind, he turned to Gulayev with the new orders. "Have the AWACS position itself to maintain constant surveillance of the enemy force, and commit the fighters to an attack as soon as possible. Also contact the tanker that's en route, and update them on the new situation. We'll have to move the orbit of the other AWACS closer to the 80th parallel. Call the interceptor squadrons at Ambarchik and Pavek, and have them scramble their aircraft immediately."

Trying to visualize the probable course of events, Kulikov's attention was drawn to his last line of defense: the aircraft based on the Chukotskiy Peninsula. He had an AWACS at Uelen and fighters at Provid]eniya and Lavrentiya. Obviously it was much too early to launch the interceptors, but the AWACS was another matter. If the Americans maintained their course north of the 80th parallel, the radar plane would have to fly almost a thousand miles before it would be in position to pick up the enemy.

Further surmising on how things might take place was ended quickly when Gulayev told him that their interceptors were about to engage the American task force. After making first contact with the enemy, the AWACS had pressed on farther north while bringing the MiGs into position. The AWACS commander was suspicious of painting a relatively small number of blips when he made initial contact with the Americans. He reasoned correctly that these were merely the escort force and the real targets lay behind them farther to the north.

The AWACS commander radioed that he was committing the interceptors, but was also moving another hundred miles north to see if he could make contact with the main objective of their mission. Gulayev seemed disturbed at such unauthorized action by the AWACS commander, but Kulikov silenced his concerned look with a wave of the hand.

As the opposing fighters approached each other, the American escort birds suddenly turned south to confront the onrushing MiG formations. Kulikov instructed the battle commander to give him a blow-by-blow description of the action, in order to keep General Secretary Petrov and Marshal Volzhin advised of all developments. This he did, and his graphic descriptions were put through the speaker system on the dais, so that Petrov and Volzhin would hear things first hand.

The chief controller's description of the fight brought out another point that bothered Kulikov no small amount. From the fragmented details radioed by the AWACS, it appeared that the Americans were outnumbered. Yet, the controller's narrative indicated that they had prevented any of the MiGs from breaking through their line of defense to attack the task force beyond. The enemy pilots obviously worked better as a team, and were able to counter each thrust by the now-disorganized Soviet fighters.

Kulikov pondered the surprising effectiveness of the American defense, knowing that in any engagement of so many jet aircraft, the battle would encompass a sizable area. Even given the superior avionics in the F-24, they could not watch the entire area and still maneuver against the MiGs. The only answer was that the task force included an AWACS to maximize the employment of a relatively small force of fighters. This made sense to Kulikov since he would have planned it that way if the shoe were on the other foot, and although this was an additional piece of information, it didn't necessitate any changes in his basic plan.

Soviet losses continued to mount, and despite the downing of another F-24, the MONGOOSE defensive shield held, even foiling one last heroic attempt by the only MiG that had any radar missiles left.

It was painfully obvious to the Air Defense Commander that they had lost this round, and the prudent move would be to withdraw. At least he owed the pilots the chance to make it back to land, even though their odds were very slim at best. He didn't bother clearing his decision with Volzhin, and was about to call the AWACS, when the battle commander came on the speaker.

"I have turned the fighters with no armament to the southwest in hopes they can make landfall. The other two have so little offensive capability that I suggest we turn them homeward also."

"I concur," Kulikov answered quickly. "There is a tanker en route to your area, and you will be needed to expedite the joinup. However, we cannot lose contact with the enemy. There is another AWACS two hundred and fifty miles east of your location. You will continue tracking the American task force until the other AWACS has them on radar. You will not, repeat *not*, turn back until control is definitely assumed by the other aircraft. Do you understand?''

"Message understood! Do you have frequencies and coordinates for the tanker and the other AWACS?''

"Stand by for a moment,'' was Kulikov's quick reply as he handed the phone to Gulayev, telling him to provide the requested information. He then grabbed another phone to call the third AWACS waiting at Uelen, and order it into the air. They should proceed due north at maximum speed and set up an orbit at seventy-five degrees north and one hundred seventy degrees west. He then called Uelen Fighter Operations and told the commander to have his interceptors take off twenty minutes after the AWACS and follow it to the orbit point. The tankers were next, and soon they too were cranking engines to head for the rendezvous with the AWACS.

*MONGOOSE Task Force*

Now that the task force was diverting to the north, Gates figured it would be another two and a half hours before they landed at Eielson. This meant at least one more hookup with the tanker to be on the safe side before he could leave the task force and make a dash for the base.

General Mike Clancy, the battle commander in the AWACS, saw more problems developing on the plotting board. Their detection system had been picking up the radar of the second Russian AWACS for the last five minutes, and they were now getting some faint skin paints on the edge of the scope. If the latest intelligence on enemy radars was correct, he knew the task force would be picked up by the Soviets in another couple of minutes.

As the approaching enemy began to show up a little clearer, the controller estimated there were at least a dozen aircraft, possibly more, heading north on an interception course. The Status Board grimly reminded him of the meager resources he had available to counter such a large number of MiGs—only four F-24s left, and although they had been refueled, the number of weapons available represented a major shortcoming. The first battle had cost a lot of missiles, and the total armament at his disposal had dwindled to eight AMRAAMS and four Sidewinders.

He knew that the odds were against all of his planes surviving long enough to fire every weapon they carried, to say nothing of rounds missing because of enemy jamming or maneuvering. If the Soviets mounted an attack similar to the last one—and all indications pointed that way—the chances of the task force surviving were pretty slim. The fact that they were bringing fighters this far from land, when midair refueling was not widespread in the Soviet Air Force, showed the resolve behind their effort. The use of an AWACS also worried the battle commander, since the enemy could now make even more effective use of their superior numbers.

Realizing that the AWACS was the key to their opponent's success and that every minute of delay worsened the task force's chances, Clancy decided on a bold gamble. He rang the chief controller and gave him the particulars of the new game plan.

"Captain, vector two of our birds toward that Soviet AWACS, and when they get close enough to pick it out from any fighters hanging around, I want it shot down. They must complete this intercept in minimum time, so fly them down there at 'gate' power. If possible, they should avoid tangling with the MiGs and save their weapons for a definite kill on the AWACS. Check that both airplanes have their anti-missile jammers on. Once the AWACS is down, they are cleared to engage any targets they may encounter. Position the two remaining F-24s seventy-five miles south of us, to act as a blocking flight."

The controller answered with a quick, "Roger," and gave the fighters their instructions. As they were moving off, he assigned each pair to separate weapons controllers, who would vector them to their respective targets.

The thought of sending two lone aircraft directly into a hornet's nest of MiGs was particularly distasteful to the battle commander, yet such a brash and unconventional move offered the best chances of getting the task force home safely. He knew the Soviet pilots were operating well beyond their normal radius of action, and were probably getting more nervous about this fact with every mile they continued north. Since the regimentation in the Soviet Air Force allowed no room for nonprescribed actions, he was betting that doing something unusual might help even the odds. The loss of the AWACS would just about kill any possibility of the MiGs quickly rendezvousing with a tanker, and this thought, too, would be preying on their minds. Also, now the interceptors would be operating almost blind, while the U.S. AWACS could vector the F-24s to where they could deliver the most telling blows.

Those two planes heading toward the AWACS still bothered him, and looking at their position with respect to the target, he estimated that the Soviet controllers would be painting them shortly. He needed something to occupy the Soviets while BLUE Three and Four were scorching down from the north at Mach 1.5. Even at this speed, the MiGs could head them off before they were in position for a shot at the AWACS. RED One and Three were on station, and as he eyeballed the geometry of all the participants, he suddenly had an idea.

Rushing to the scope controlling RED Flight, he told the lieutenant, "Move your fighters ahead of our beam by fifteen miles or so, and have them activate their barrage jammers on a random, intermittent basis. Those MiGs around the AWACS should take the bait and start northward, which just might give BLUE Flight a chance for a shot. Tell RED Flight to cut the jammers once the MiGs get within seventy-five miles of their position."

A few seconds later, each scope lit up with pie-shaped wedges of bright, flashing light. This same type of interference also registered on the enemy radar screens some two hundred miles to the south, and they reacted instantly. It only took three or four sweeps of the radar to determine that blips near the AWACS were picking up speed and heading toward the jamming. Once the MiGs were fifty miles north of their AWACS, they spread out in a line-abreast arrangement of flights.

Clancy could see that BLUE Flight would pass west of this line in another minute or so. Chances were that the AWACS hadn't picked them up yet, since all the MiGs continued heading north-northeast, but he knew they would be detected any second now.

At that moment, the line from the communications console lit up, and the new crewman assigned for just this mission had some interesting news. He had been searching the part of the UHF spectrum normally used by Soviet Air Force fighters, and discovered the frequency the AWACS was using to control its interceptors. The tech sergeant also told him that he was fluent in Russian, and could keep the battle commander informed about what the enemy was doing. The phrase *fluent in Russian* finally turned on the light in Clancy's mind as to why his regular communications man was suddenly replaced for this mission. "Great!" he replied. "Let me know if they plan to try something unusual, as well as anything else you pick up that you think is important."

"Nothing out of the ordinary as yet, sir. They've committed everybody to attack the source of the jamming. All fighters have been ordered—wait a minute! Something's got the controller all excited! Apparently they've just picked up BLUE Flight, and are diverting half the MiGs back to protect the AWACS!"

"That's great, Sarge," Clancy replied. "Keep tabs on them while

I get the word to BLUE Flight.'' With that, he told the controller to pass
the word that part of the MiGs had been diverted back to the AWACS.

"Roger, General. I've just finished telling them. We noticed that
some of the MiGs had started a turn and called this to the fighters right
away. But, based on the speeds and relative positions, I don't think
they'll be a factor before BLUE Flight reaches the AWACS. Gotta go—
they're calling for target information."

Looking at the plotting board, Clancy saw that if BLUE Flight kept
up their Mach, they should be on and off the target before the MiGs
could get within firing range. He dared not interrupt the controller
now that the final phase of the intercept had begun, but his curiosity
about their progress was too much to bear. He flipped the key on his
console to monitor the transmissions to and from BLUE Flight.

"Steady one six five, BLUE. You hold the target twenty starboard
at ninety. Repeat, target heading zero nine zero at angels three five.
Target speed point eight Mach!''

"Roger. No joy!''

"Roger. Continue one six five. Bandits in your eight o'clock position at fifty, and closing. Target now twenty starboard at seventy. Your
breakaway will be port to zero four five—target range sixty!''

"Contact there. BLUE Three Judy!''

"Four has Judy!''

"Roger, BLUE. You are cleared to fire. Check switches hot!''

"Three armed hot!''

"Four armed hot!''

"Roger, BLUE. Repeat you're cleared to fire!''

BLUE Three and Four called, "Fox One!'' almost simultaneously,
as an AMRAAM streaked off a pylon under the wing of each airplane.
The twin smoke trails lanced toward the AWACS, while the F-24s broke
hard left to put the approaching MiGs at a higher angle off. Just before
the MiGs flashed by overhead, BLUE Flight reversed their turn to start
working their way northeast to support RED One and Three. Rolling
out, they saw the blackish remnants of an explosion capping a pillar of
burning fuel and fiery wreckage plunging to the ice fields below.

During the wild, twisting and turning melee that ensued, General
Clancy was hanging on every word as Sergeant Novak relayed the calls
between the remaining elements of the Soviet formation: the frantic
requests for target information, the even more prevalent complaints of
low fuel, and the requests for vectors to the tanker.

One of the pilots who had seen the final agony of the AWACS
passed the word that there was no control available, and each flight

was on its own. There was a profound silence on the radio as the implications of their predicament loomed in each man's thoughts. Some discussions followed between flight commanders as to the whereabouts of the tanker and the backup AWACS. The few requests from nervous wingmen as to what they should do were quickly silenced by the older heads who were trying to sort out their next move.

The battle had spread out to where it would be nearly impossible to locate the American task force and carry out a concentrated attack. Some aircraft reported having a contact on the enemy and felt that even a limited assault was better than none. However, everyone's concern was fuel, and if the promised tanker could be located, they could catch up with the Americans after refueling and finish them off. The main problem was a quick rendezvous with the tanker, and this required the radar assistance that only the backup AWACS could provide. One flight commander finally took control of the situation, and told everyone to stay off the air while he tried to raise the AWACS.

Listening to the Soviets' arguments, Mike Clancy knew that if the MiGs did get refueled and found the task force again, it would all be over. The two remaining F-24s had only a few missiles between them, and when reduced to gun attacks, both fighters could be tied up by a few MiGs, while the others attacked the tankers and AWACS. He knew the Soviets could pull it off, even if a few of their birds tapped the tanker and were recommitted.

Then a thought occurred to him that might work, even though it was an extremely long shot. Hustling down the aisle to Sergeant Novak's position, he beckoned to the controller who had been working BLUE Flight. The lieutenant quickly turned BLUE Three over to his partner and joined the general and Sergeant Novak.

"I know this might sound farfetched, but if those MiGs get refueled, we've had the schnitzel. Lieutenant, I want you to give Sergeant Novak the proper jargon for joining up those MiGs with a tanker. Sergeant, you translate everything into Russian, and give the instructions to that flight commander trying to raise their AWACS."

The young controller looked a little puzzled, so Clancy had to explain things a bit further.

"If we can move those interceptors just a little west of their position, they could never catch us and would be out of the fight even if our plan works for only a short while. It's my guess that those jocks are so desperate for fuel, that they're ready to believe anyone that even mentions the word *tanker*. But, we've got to make it believable so that they're convinced it's business as usual. Stay calm and matter of fact if they spring any oddball questions on you. We'll work out some answers to keep them believing that everything is on the up and up."

Clancy went to the plotting board and yelled back to the controller, "Turn the MiGs southwest, and head them for the *tanker*, which we'll say is located here," as his finger indicated a spot northeast of the New Siberian Islands. The smiles on the faces of the noncom and lieutenant showed how they relished the game of deception they were about to play. If only they could pull if off!

Sergeant Novak followed the lieutenant to the control scope, and the first morsel of bait was cast. "Aircraft calling Control Ten, say again your callsign. Your transmissions are very weak and broken."

The Russian flight commander responded instantly, eager to grasp the slightest straw in the wind. "This is POLAR Two Six with eight other aircraft. We are very low on fuel and need vectors to the tanker! Do you have us on your radar?"

"I believe so, POLAR Two Six. We have a weak contact on the edge of our scope, but there is an American task force in your vicinity, and we're not sure whether we're picking up your formation or theirs."

The flight commander was obviously irritated at these procedural delays when he needed information on the tanker so badly, and his voice was showing the strain. "The Americans are north of our position, and I am activating my transponder now. Are you picking it up?"

"We have positive confirmation on your position, POLAR Two Six. Turn to a heading of two four zero. The tanker will be directly ahead at two hundred miles. Tanker is heading—"

"Wait a minute, Control Ten. Why are you turning us southwest? Our tanker was coming from Pevak, and should be south and east of our position!"

The flight commander had apparently smelled a rat since things were not going as he was briefed. Maybe Sergeant Novak's accent wasn't quite right. Whatever it was, they had to give him a plausible reason for the new heading.

Being used to such last-minute changes that are common to all military organizations, Novak was equal to the task. He replied in a bored, haughty tone, "We are well aware of your original briefing, POLAR Two Six; however, that aircraft developed engine problems and was forced to return to base. When we became aware of this change of plans, we diverted another tanker into your area. This new tanker is currently refueling other interceptors, and has set up an orbit about one hundred fifty miles from your position. We are in contact with the tanker, and have ordered them to offload only the minimum amount of fuel to get those fighters to the nearest base. The remaining fuel is allocated to your flight. Confirm that you are heading two four zero. Tanker is directly ahead at one hundred forty miles.''

A couple of the other flight leaders quickly answered that they were steady on two four zero, but POLAR Two Six was still skeptical.

"Control Ten, this is all highly unusual! Before he was shot down, Control Thirteen made no mention of our tanker aborting his mission. I am not satisfied with this entire situation. I request that you authenticate the following code group: twenty-seven, eighteen. Repeat, twenty-seven, eighteen.''

Clancy's heart nearly stopped at hearing this, since a wrong answer here would blow the whole scheme. He could see from the plotting board that some of the MiGs were already heading southwest, while Two Six Flight was still orbiting ninety miles south. The lieutenant had an idea that gave them more time to think, and hurriedly briefed Sergeant Novak.

"Understand, POLAR Two Six, you wish us to authenticate code group twenty-seven, fifteen. Is that correct?''

"No! No! Ten. That is not correct!'' came the flight leader's exasperated reply. "The code group was twenty-seven, eighteen! Repeat eighteen! Do you understand?''

Clancy could sympathize with the frustration of the flight leader, who was torn between the urgent need for fuel and following standard procedures in a situation he was not quite comfortable with. He leaned over and gave Sergeant Novak the answer to the authentication problem.

"Control Ten understands, POLAR Two Six. You request authentication for code group twenty-seven, eighteen. Stand by momentarily while I have General Petrovich approve the code response.''

Sergeant Novak paused for at least a minute, while they figured out an answer that would be, in essence, their trump card. By now, most of the MiGs were far enough away that their return to attack the task force would be problematical, even if their ploy was discovered. Wherefore, Clancy decided to bluff it.

"POLAR Two Six, this is Control Ten. The special commander for this mission, General Petrovich, wishes to inform you that we do not have enough time for this authentication nonsense. The Americans are getting farther away every minute that you tie us up with procedural delays. We need every available interceptor refueled and committed to the primary mission of shooting down the enemy.''

Novak hesitated momentarily to let that sink in, and then continued in the severest tone he could muster. "POLAR Two Six, you are
ordered to take up a heading of two four zero to rendezvous with the
tanker. If you do not turn immediately, you will be dropped from our
control and directed to clear this frequency. Do you understand?"

There was a pregnant silence for a moment or so, and you could
almost hear the wheels turning as POLAR Two Six wrestled with his
decision. Before he could answer, Novak continued. "Interceptors
heading for the tanker, this is Control Ten. Who is the flight leader of
your group?"

"Control Ten, this is POLAR One Nine. I am leading these aircraft."

"Understand, POLAR One Nine. The tanker is ten degrees right at
one hundred miles. The last interceptor has just hooked up, and
should be off by the time you arrive. POLAR Two Six, are you steady
two four zero?"

The flight leader's clipped response of "Steady on course!" fairly
dripped with the chagrin of someone who knew he was right but was
forced to comply unquestioningly to orders.

Mike Clancy watched the plots of the MiG formation get farther
astern of the AWACS with every sweep of the radar. Even with a separation rate of almost seventeen miles per minute, he was still uneasy. The
first group of MiGs would expect to see the tanker on radar at no less
than fifty miles range, and they were close to that distance now. It had
been five minutes since the first group turned southwest, and if they
could string them along for another minute or so, they would be too
far behind and too low on fuel to be a threat.

Sergeant Novak kept up the patter by giving them range and bearing to the tanker, while mentioning that the last interceptor had just
finished refueling and the tanker was ready for their arrival. The
replies from the flight leader gave no indication that he was suspicious—perhaps his dire need for fuel made him ready to believe anything plausible. Two Six was about three to four minutes behind One
Nine Flight, and could be a problem if he realized they had been
duped. Finally, when the MiGs passed the hundred-mile arc on the
plotting board, Clancy knew the game was just about over.

"Control Ten, this is POLAR One Nine, we have no contact on the
tanker. Repeat the range and bearing!"

Clancy could only tell the lieutenant to stall as much as possible to
gain even another minute, so the controller-translator team fell back
on the standard jargon.

"POLAR One Nine, we have the tanker twenty degrees right of your position at fifty miles! You should have a contact there! Turn right to a heading of two six zero!"

"We see nothing there, Control Ten. What is the tanker's altitude?"

"Our last report showed they were at thirty five thousand feet. Stand by while we confirm that with the tanker."

Clancy was determined to wait at least fifteen seconds before answering, and during that time, Novak reported other members of One Nine's flight stating that they were very low on fuel. One pilot suggested trying to make the New Siberian Islands. At the next lull in the chatter, Clancy had them play their last card.

"POLAR One Nine, we have you merging with the tanker. Orbit your present position. We have a report from the tanker that they have a slight pressurization problem, and now are level at twenty-five thousand feet. Have all interceptors search low."

The MiGs, including Two Six Flight, were approaching the one-hundred-fifty mile mark from the AWACS, including Two Six Flight, so Clancy gave his team the "cut" signal.

Sergeant Novak continued to monitor the frequency, but made no more transmissions to the now frantic interceptors. He reported they were in mass confusion, with recriminations between the flight leaders and desperate calls for information from the wingmen. Several attempts were made to contact the tanker on their universal emergency frequency, but the lack of an answer coupled with the absence of any radar contact crystallized the worst of their fears. They had been tricked! There was no tanker, and they were close to three hundred miles from the easternmost of the New Siberian Islands. POLAR Two Six had been right all along.

Most of them had between fifteen hundred and two thousand pounds of fuel remaining, and this meant, at best, a bailout over a very sparsely inhabited island. In addition, they all knew there would be no help from the wind while heading in that direction. If it was blowing at all, it would undoubtedly be a quartering headwind, which would complicate things even more. Those lucky enough to have a little more fuel might reach the airfield at Zemlya Bunge on the main island. However, getting that far would be stretching things to the absolute limit, and would most certainly mean landing from a flameout approach. The MiG plots on the board were all heading southwest, and their fading transmissions indicated that each had dropped external tanks, jettisoned all armament, and fired out any remaining ammunition, and were cruise-climbing as high as they could. If they were to get even close to the New Siberian Islands, they had to reduce drag and gross weight as much as possible, and take advantage of the reduced fuel consumption at the higher altitudes.

Clancy and his task force could now breathe a little easier, at least for the moment. They were still a long way from Eielson, but with only a pair of fighters armed with just a few missiles, they were virtually defenseless. And, given the Soviet response to MONGOOSE thus far, he felt sure that they were not about to give up.

# Chapter 13

Clancy was almost positive that the Soviet Air Force would take another crack at downing the task force and the fighters would come from the bases on the Chukotskiy Peninsula. About 1,200 miles northwest of Point Barrow, his suspicions were confirmed as the AWACS ultrasensitive detection gear picked up the search radar of an enemy AWACS. MONGOOSE One was immediately ordered to hit the tanker for a topoff, and when he had a full load of fuel, to make a supersonic dash for Eielson. While Gates was on the boom, MONGOOSE Control received a call that a large group of F-24s was en route from Alaskan bases to engage the Soviet force. Just before the battle was joined, Gates called.

"Control, this is MONGOOSE One, off tanker, turning starboard to one six five for Eielson."

"Roger One, you're cleared. Contact BIG EYE on discreet Bravo in three minutes for flight following."

Gates acknowledged the instructions as he rocked the throttles outboard around the afterburner detent and felt the nudge of power as both engines lit off simultaneously. The Machmeter stirred to life as the needle started climbing, paused momentarily at point nine eight, and then flicked over to one point zero two. Still accelerating, he took the bird to forty-five thousand feet, leveled off, and let the speed build to the best cruise Mach.

After checking in with the AWACS monitoring the slugfest between the F-24 reinforcements and the MiGs, Gates's controller kept him advised of any Soviets straying from the battle in his direction.

According to BIG EYE, the main concentration of fighters was now in his two o'clock position, and Gates would occasionally catch a sun flash off one of the contestants as they dueled with each other through miles of sky.

"MONGOOSE One, this is BIG EYE. You've got another bandit forty-five degrees starboard at twenty miles." Up 'til now, the controller's voice had been quite calm and almost matter of fact, but with his next transmission, there was a definite tone of anxiety.

"MONGOOSE One, that guy isn't turning back. It looks like he's set up for an attack against you. I can't understand it. We're not skin painting you at all, and yet he seems to have a lockon. At that range, he can't have a visual, but he's been turning starboard to keep you at the right angle off. Check Snowflake!"

Gates assumed that the MiG was low on fuel and was making a run for the coastline to bail out. The fact that he was on an interception course was purely coincidental, since there was no way he could be tracking him with radar. The HUD sensors were giving no indication of a lockon, and even if the pilot had exceptional eyesight, the Chameleon lights would have prevented visual acquisition until he was much closer. But the word *Snowflake* stunned him like a blow to the solar plexus. How could he have been so stupid not to think of it?

He rolled into a gentle right turn and tilted the rearview mirror to look directly behind his plane. There, stretching out for at least twenty miles behind him, was a thick white contrail. Even as he reacted, his racing thoughts flayed his conscience for this grievous sin of omission. "Here I am, flying the most sophisticated fighter in the world, all but invisible to enemy radar, and I give myself away by failing to observe one of the basic rules of jet combat: Stay out of the contrail layer!"

"Bandit forty starboard at twelve miles, MONGOOSE!"

Realizing that the MiG was indeed stalking him with the help of a huge arrow pointing directly at his aircraft, Gates knew that his only defense was speed, and perhaps some maneuvering. He slammed both throttles to the full afterburner range, and pushed forward on the stick to put the bird into a zero-G condition. The resulting dive would serve two purposes: accelerate the F-24 out to its limiting Mach and maybe outrun the pursuing MiG, and hopefully put him in a different layer of air, where conditions would not be so favorable for producing contrails. No luck! The con stayed with him as he arched down through forty thousand feet, and BIG EYE's next call made it look like the MiG's position would negate any try at outrunning.

"Bandit sixty starboard at seven. Looks like he's going to roll in behind you! We've committed two birds from CARIBOU Flight on the MiG, and they're getting close to firing range now. I doubt they'll be able to launch a missile before he's close enough for a shot. He's four o'clock at five now. Do you have a visual?"

From this last call, Gates knew it was time to take some defensive action, and fast, so he rolled over in a hard right turn and reefed the stick back into his gut. The airplane was indicating one point nine five Mach when the turn was started, and the controls felt like they were moving in thick mud. The artificial feel system was programming very heavy stick forces, to simulate the air loads on the control surfaces at the higher Mach numbers. As a result, the response wasn't as snappy as Gates needed to counter the threat behind him, and because of the head of steam he had built up, there was no way he could outturn a missile once the MiG got inside launch range.

His speed began to bleed off as soon as the turn was started, but the computer-regulated flight control system would not allow the elevators to deflect beyond the point where the aircraft's G limits would be exceeded. Even with the stick against the rear stop, the G loading was not increasing fast enough to rotate his tail away from the MiG.

Straining to look over his right shoulder, Gates saw that the Soviet's cutoff turn had moved him in a little closer. He knew the MiG couldn't turn any tighter than the F-24 at this speed, but it didn't really have to. The pilot only had to keep his IR missile looking at Gates's tailpipe, close to firing range, and let the missile pull the higher G's necessary to make the kill.

It was possible to outturn the Soviet's Acrid, but you had to have a full nine G's available, and most importantly, the turn had to be made at precisely the right time. There would be no help from decoying flares this time, since he had dispensed his last one during the battle near Tiksi. It would be the turn or nothing.

The stick was still in his lap, but the G meter was only reading five, and the Machmeter had decreased to one point three. Staying supersonic wasn't going to hack it!

"Bandit holding four o'clock at three, MONGOOSE!"

Hearing the "three-mile" call, Gates knew he was a dead duck if he didn't do something fast. Twisting around in the seat as far as he could to keep an eye on the MiG, he gave the speed brake switch a fast jab to open the boards just a bit. His plan was to slow down only enough to get barely subsonic, where a lot more G would be available to tighten his turn. The sudden deceleration slammed him against the shoulder harness, and at the same instant he saw a thin trail of smoke stab out from under the MiG's wing.

A chill went completely through him as he stared wide-eyed at the missile rushing toward his tailpipe in an ever-tightening curve. Despite tugging desperately at the stick and twisting the throttle grip for maximum translation from the Decoupled Mode, Gates knew the plane was responding too slowly. He saw the Acrid making small corrections to center the heat source, as his tightening turn moved the hot section of his engine farther from the missile's field of view.

Suddenly, the Machmeter jerked back through one point zero, and with the accompanying shift of the aerodynamic center of pressure, the elevators bit in with savage effectiveness. The tail seemed to dig in and pitch the nose around as the instant onset of G's pinned Gates to the seat with a numbing force. Instinctively, he fought the G load with the M-1 maneuver and was just able to keep the grayout from progressing to a full blackout. He kept his narrowing vision focused as best he could on the missile, but it still looked like it was going to hit.

The blinding flash of the exploding Acrid filled his entire world, and the plane flipped over to an inverted position before he could stabilize it. His immediate reaction was that he had taken a bad hit and had to get out before the whole thing exploded or started tumbling uncontrollably. Yet, he was still flying, and a quick scan of the instruments showed that the engines were running and the other systems were normal. Best of all, he saw no Fire Warning lights.

A couple of other lights were on, but there was no time for Gates to analyze the trouble right now. Uppermost in his mind was a follow-on shot by the MiG, once he saw that his first missile didn't do the job completely. Gates rolled the fighter up on one wing and then quickly over on the other, frantically searching the sky where he thought the MiG would be. There was nothing on either side, which meant that the MiG was in his deep six. Full back stick and hard left rudder made it feel like the bird was swapping ends. After thirty degrees of turn, he spotted his opponent.

But the hunter had become the prey and had just started his long death dive, trailing heavy black smoke and huge gouts of flame. From the looks of things, the F-24 from CARIBOU Flight tagged the MiG right after he had fired the Acrid that nearly hit Gates's aircraft.

"MONGOOSE One, this is BIG EYE. Do you read? Over!"

"One here, BIG EYE. Go!"

"Roger, One. CARIBOU One Two reports a kill on the MiG in your six, but thought you had taken a hit before he lost sight of your airplane while maneuvering against the MiG. Are you o.k.?"

"I'm not sure just yet, BIG EYE. Everything looks all right, but the bird feels a little funny. Haven't had time to check out everything. I'm back on course for Eielson, and will give you a call in a few minutes."

Gates leveled at forty thousand feet, but stayed subsonic until he could determine what was damaged and why the flight controls did not feel just right. The Master Warning light was on, calling his attention to the idiot panel, where he found the Flight Controls Damaged light illuminated. Even though they felt normal, the aircraft had a different sound to it, and control response was not as positive as before. The wingtips were too far back to be seen, so he tilted the left rearview mirror to check out that side.

A bolt of apprehension shot through him when he saw that the rear portion of the outer wing panel had been blown away by the missile's warhead. Apparently, his hard turn at the last second had broken the weapon's lockon and averted a direct hit. But the Acrid's proximity fuse had fired, and the fragments from the blast tore up the aft section of the wing. Twisted structure, ripped skin, and torn lines and electrical wiring extended a good ten feet in from the tip. Fortunately he saw no trailing vapor, indicating that the fuel and hydraulic lines were still intact, or at least protected by check valves. The gauges for these systems were still in the green, and as far as he could determine, there were no large pieces ready to tear off. A look with the right mirror showed no damage to that side.

Knowing he had serious problems to contend with, Gates hit the Damage Report button beneath the Auxiliary Data screen. The information flashed on the CRT was both encouraging and worrisome. The good news was that the aircraft was flyable under the prevailing conditions of speed and altitude, which meant that he shouldn't have any trouble getting to Eielson. The bad news was that he had lost his left aileron, with an even more dangerous condition indicated. The explosion had jammed the variable camber wing in the shape designed for high-speed flight. The on-board computer analyzed the effect of all these problems, and was displaying a red-bordered message on the screen: WARNING! UNDER THESE CONDITIONS, AIRCRAFT MAY NOT BE CONTROLLABLE IN THE LANDING CONFIGURATION!

Reflecting on this report, Gates grimaced at the irony of his situation. He had flown across China and the Soviet Union at night on the deck, fought his way over the last thousand miles, only to be betrayed by a lousy contrail, and get tagged by some Russian jock who was looking in the right place at the right time. Nine hours of the toughest and most dangerous flying he had ever done, and he had to punch out over home plate.

Even though it seemed to be pouring salt in an open wound, he called up the graphic showing how the various control surfaces had been programmed to counteract the damaged wing. The picture showed an astonishing mishmash of crossed controls, involving the canards, differential elevators, and the rudder in combinations only a computer could devise. The deflection on some surfaces was close to their limits, meaning the additional movement needed for slow-speed flight would most likely not be available.

The coast of Alaska was fifty miles behind when BIG EYE called again. "MONGOOSE One, do you have a damage report as yet?"

"Roger, BIG EYE. I've lost the rear outer portion of my left wing. The plane is flying o.k. now, but the computer says it may be uncontrollable for landing. I'll check it out in the landing configuration when I get over Eielson."

"Understand, MONGOOSE! We will alert Eielson on your problems and have crash crews and the rescue chopper standing by. You're getting out of our range now, so contact Fairbanks Center on this frequency. They're waiting for your call."

Gates checked in with the center, and they provided a radar vector direct to Eielson. After a few minutes, they confirmed that all emergency equipment was in place, ready for his arrival. The destination weather was clear and expected to stay that way, with light and variable surface winds.

He rogered the call, and then realized that the excitement of the last half hour had exhausted whatever lift he had gotten from the last GO pill. He was dog tired, and every movement and thought process seemed to be an enormous task, with even the simplest switch action requiring conscious effort. Under normal circumstances, Gates knew he could get the bird on the ground, but the problems with the airplane made this landing anything but normal.

He dug a GO pill out of his sleeve pocket and was reaching for the water bottle, but remembered that he had polished off the last drop quite some time ago. There was nothing left to do but chew it up and try to get it down a throat parched from an overlong exposure to the drying effects of pure oxygen. He almost gagged as the bitter taste welled in his mouth, and it took quite a few dry swallows to work it

down. A couple of minutes passed before he could feel some sem-
blance of normalcy returning.

Gates started down from forty thousand feet, but told the controller he would level at twenty to check out the airplane's low-speed
handling characteristics, just west of the runway. During the letdown,
he tightened the seat belt and harness in case he got into some unexpected gyrations. Over the nose, the huge runway at Eielson was easily discernible as a white slash in the surrounding greenness. Leveling
at twenty, he let the airspeed bleed off to three hundred knots, where
he would commence the stability checks.

Things felt pretty solid at three hundred, but he noticed he was
trimming in a lot of right stick. This was expected, since the variable
camber mechanism had changed the airfoil on the right wing to the
high-lift configuration needed for the slower airspeeds. With the left
wing's airfoil still set for high-speed flight, the F-24 had a pronounced
tendency to roll left. At two hundred and seventy-five knots the controls were still o.k., but now he had in maximum trim to the right, and
still had to hold additional stick in that direction.

As the airspeed needle went through two hundred and fifty
knots, Gates hit the gear switch to the down position. When all the
gears indicated down and locked, his speed was dropping through
two hundred and thirty. Suddenly, the plane rolled violently to the
left, completely uncontrollable, and even a combination of full right
stick and full right rudder would not hold it. Gates firewalled both
throttles, and as the roll continued through the inverted position, the
nose dropped toward the ground and the airspeed started building. He
finally got it under control after completing three-quarters of a full
roll, and then gingerly eased out of the dive and back to level flight.

He yanked back the power to keep the airspeed below two hundred and fifty knots, which was the limiting speed for the landing-gear
doors. Gates didn't want them tearing loose and adding to his problems.

It looked like two hundred and thirty knots was the magic number, and if he was going to get this beast on the ground, he had to stay
well above that mark. Although it required considerable right stick to
hold the bird's wings level at two hundred and fifty knots, he decided
this was as slow as he could safely get until the gear was on the runway.

Flying an approach at this speed would be a little tricky, since the
F-24 normally came down final at about one hundred and eighty
knots with the amount of fuel he had remaining. Even though it

wouldn't be easy, Gates never seriously considered taking the airplane up to altitude and ejecting. He had made heavy-weight, no-flap landings before that required high speeds on final, although two hundred and fifty would be a new experience.

Because his dash from the task force to Alaska had been mainly subsonic, he had plenty of fuel remaining. To burn some of this off, he left the gear down while circling back to the north of Eielson to set up for the landing. "Better let them know what I'm doing," he thought, and called Approach Control to tell them he must make a straight-in approach from the north, and requested clearance to tower frequency. Approach o.k.'d this, and instructed him to contact the tower on two five five point six.

While making his wide sweep to the north, Gates descended to fifteen hundred feet above the ground and started a gentle left bank to line up with the runway centerline.

"Eielson Tower, this is MONGOOSE One making a straight in from twenty miles north. My aircraft has been damaged, and I must make the approach at two hundred and fifty knots to maintain control."

"Roger, MONGOOSE One, understand! You're cleared to land. Winds two six zero at two. Crash crews are in position along the active. Altimeter two niner eight seven. Call three miles on final."

Gates acknowledged the call, then concentrated on keeping the plane at exactly two hundred and fifty knots while aiming for the numbers on runway One Three. The high speed made the angle-of-attack indicator useless, and the entire approach became a judgment call on how well he could hit the end of the runway from five miles out. It would really be unorthodox—steaming in on a long, low final seventy knots above normal and still trying to plunk it on the concrete just beyond the threshold lights. He wouldn't be able to cut the power until all three gear were planted firmly on the runway, and he knew he would use up a big chunk of Eielson's fifteen thousand feet just getting the nose wheel on the deck.

Another mental note he filed while passing the ten-mile mark was that he had to keep the stick in the right forward corner after touchdown. At two hundred and fifty knots, the bird definitely had enough speed to fly, and any back pressure would cause him to leap back into the air. And he would hit the all important two hundred and thirty knots before he could get the engines up to speed and the airplane under control.

Gates's arm was beginning to tire from holding constant right stick pressure against the artificial feel system. With the airspeed pegged at two hundred and fifty and the gear down, the aircraft had a slight nose-high attitude. Passing the five-mile mark, he only had to pull the throttles back a couple of percent to start a slow, controlled descent.

"Flaps would sure help," he thought, but not knowing the extent of the damage to the left wing, he couldn't risk it. If the right flap extended, and the left one was still jammed in the up position, there would be no way he could control the airplane. It took a couple of power adjustments to find the R.P.M. that kept him pointed at the runway numbers, and still maintain a somewhat constant rate of descent.

"MONGOOSE One—three miles. Gear down and locked!"

"Roger, MONGOOSE One, we have you in sight. You're cleared to land."

Gates wanted to use his left knee to add a little side pressure on the stick and ease the strain on his arm, but he was using the rudders exclusively for maintaining directional control. Since the plane was behaving itself, he didn't want to disturb things by introducing too much of a bank, and possibly changing the airflow over the wings and losing some of his controllability margin. The antiskid system would be critical during his after-landing roll, so Gates stole a quick glance at the left console to make sure the switch was in the On position.

Just over a mile from the threshold, he gently ruddered the aircraft to the left of centerline to line up in the middle of that half of the runway. The drag created by the fully deflected right aileron would result in the bird wanting to turn right once the wheels were on the ground. He would be going too fast to engage nose-wheel steering, and differential braking would be a little tricky at that speed, so he needed a small cushion to let the airplane have its head until he got the speed under control.

"Thank God for a three-hundred-foot-wide runway," he said half aloud. "I might need every inch of it." Roaring over the flat terrain for the last half mile to the overrun, everything seemed pretty good. He was almost fifty feet in the air, the rate of descent was holding around three hundred feet per minute, and it appeared that the touchdown point would be nearly five hundred feet down from the threshold. With all the flashing red lights at each taxiway along the active, he thought they must have scrambled every piece of crash equipment on the base. As he dropped down a little farther, the F-24 bobbled slightly when it hit the ground-effect region, but Gates corrected for this quickly without getting into any hairy attitudes.

The lip of the runway flashed beneath the aircraft, and the concrete was coming up awfully fast. He had to fight an instinctive and almost overwhelming urge to break the glide and touch 'er down nice and easy. Only conscious determination kept the stick where it was, as he braced himself for a full-scale carrier landing.

A split second later, the main gear slammed onto the runway with a jolt that made him feel that the top of the struts must be sticking up through the wings. But everything was still glued together since the bird was rolling straight as he moved the stick briskly forward to get the nose wheel down. Another hard thump when it hit, then full forward stick to keep it on the ground. The first thousand foot marker went by in a blur, and the airplane was tracking fairly well, with only a slight drift-right tendency that was controllable with rudder at this speed.

Gates yanked the throttles back to idle while abreast of the second distance marker, lifted the detent, and threw them into full reverse thrust. As the airspeed dropped through two hundred and thirty, the plane definitely wanted to roll left, but full right aileron, combined with all the right rudder he could get in, plus a touch of brakes, kept it going almost straight. Gates didn't dare use too much braking just yet because the aircraft was still light on the gear and any hard application might square off a tire.

The engines howling through the thrust deflectors finally started to have some effect as the midpoint of the runway whipped past the cockpit. The needle trickled through one seventy-five and Gates decided he couldn't wait any longer to start some serious braking. "No time for niceties," he thought and began with a moderately heavy push on the pedals. The results were not dramatic as the antiskid started cycling immediately, but the aircraft was slowing down some. Since the antiskid was working, he decided to go for broke and stood on both brakes for a maximum application. He engaged nosewheel steering to keep the bird running down the centerline, even though the high speed made it a little sensitive.

Finally, and almost begrudgingly, the F-24 yielded to all the forces trying to slow it down, and with just over fifteen hundred feet of runway remaining, Gates shoved the throttles back to idle and released the brake pressure. The airplane was now moving at a slow walk, and was easily controllable with the steering. His legs were still shaking from the exertion of braking as he turned off the active and opened the canopy for his first breath of fresh air in what seemed like ten years. The crisp fall air of central Alaska tasted like vintage wine, as he repeatedly filled his lungs to almost bursting.

A crew chief ran out from the surrounding cluster of emergency vehicles, and Gates gave him the "thumbs up" sign to say everything was o.k. Apparently, they wanted him to shut down here on the taxiway, since the crew chief was motioning him forward with two orange wands. After going about thirty feet, he crossed the wands for the stop signal, and then gave the "cut" sign.

The throttles had barely hit the idle cutoff when technicians dashed from a van with a ladder and scrambled up on the left wing to remove the radiation detection package. The realization that it was finally over hit Gates like a ton of bricks, and after unstrapping from the seat, all he could do was sit there, as relief and total fatigue swept over his entire body.

Jack Dumont ran over from his staff car and climbed up the cockpit ladder wearing a mile-wide grin. Gates was too washed out from his ordeal to do much more than sit there and submit to the enthusiastic back slapping and hand pumping. About all he could manage along with a weak smile was, "Hi ya, Colonel. A Sierra Hotel mission!"

# Glossary

**ACRID**  NATO code name for the Soviet IR or radar-guided air-to-air missile, whose official designation is AA-6.

**AI**  Abbreviation for Airborne Intercept, radar carried by fighters that enables them to detect, track, and attack airborne targets.

**AMRAAM**  Abbreviation for Advanced Medium Range Air-to-Air Missile, a radar-guided, fire-and-forget missile, designated AIM-120A.

**Andrews**  Andrews Air Force base, located southeast of Washington, D.C.

**angle deceiver**  An electronic device used to combat opposing interceptors by providing false position information to the interceptor's radar, causing them to steer to an empty point in space.

**Angstrom**  A unit of measurement of the wavelength of light, equal to one ten-billionth of a meter.

**AWACS**  Acronym for Airborne Weapons and Control System, an airborne GCI site.

**bingo fuel**  The amount of fuel that will allow you to make a normal recovery at your home base, plus the amount necessary to divert to an alternate base, if required.

**BIT**  Acronym for Built-In Test, a procedure that allows a pilot to check the operation of a variety of subsystems in an airborne radar set by inputting certain values that generate various readouts.

**blood chit**  A document printed in the indigenous languages of the area, offering a reward to anyone helping a downed aircrew escape to friendly lines.

**BMEWS**  Abbreviation for Ballistic Missile Early Warning System.

**boomer**  Operator of the refueling boom on the rear underside of a tanker.

**bought the farm**   A term denoting that someone was killed.

**canards**   Small, winglike surfaces on the forward fuselage of an aircraft to provide increased stability. In some cases, these surfaces are movable, and are integral parts of the flight control system.

**CG**   Abbreviation for Center of Gravity.

**chaff**   Small, thin strips of aluminum foil cut to exact lengths determined by the wavelength of the radar to be jammed. When dropped from an aircraft, the packages are blown open by the airstream, and the chaff disperses to form a "cloud" of the material, which then falls at a very slow rate of descent. This "cloud" is an extremely good reflector of radar energy, thus masking any real targets above or below the chaff drop.

**charge-coupled device**   An extremely sensitive radiation collector, usually smaller than a postage stamp, that captures energy emissions across the visible and invisible band of the spectrum, which are then amplified and turned into real-time pictures.

**CINCPAC**   Acronym for Commander In Chief-Pacific, the commander of all military forces assigned to the Pacific Theater.

**clock code**   A code used to locate traffic in the vicinity of a given aircraft, with the nose of the airplane being twelve o'clock. "High" and "low" are also used with clock code directions to further pinpoint a position. For example, "Bogey at two o'clock high" would mean that an aircraft is approximately 60 degrees to the right of the nose of your aircraft, and above your present altitude.

**Cockpit Alert**   An alert condition in which crews are sitting in the aircraft and can be airborne within two minutes.

**combining glass**   A flat glass plate on the top of the HUD, on which is projected flight and target information.

**DF'ing**   Abbreviation for Direction Finding, determining the position or bearing of another aircraft by homing in on a signal transmitted by that aircraft.

**DME**   Abbreviation for Distance Measuring Equipment, a system that shows the mileage from the aircraft's present position to or from a navigational aid or GEOREF fix.

**ECCM**   Abbreviation for Electronic Counter Counter Measures, electronic devices used to work through or thwart enemy jamming/decoying efforts.

**ECM**   Abbreviation for Electronic Counter Measures, an electronic system designed to jam or deceive enemy radars.

**E & E map**   Abbreviation for Escape and Evasion Map, a map detailing ground features, usually printed on silk or water-resistant material and used by downed aircrews for finding their way back to friendly lines.

**EFT**   Abbreviation for Emergency Flash Transmitter.

**EGT**   Abbreviation for Exhaust Gas Temperature.

**ELINT**   Acronym for Electronic Intelligence, specially equipped aircraft used to sample enemy radio and radar transmissions as part of the routine intelligence-gathering mission.

**El Scan**   A knob that controls the angle at which an airborne radar antenna searches above or below the longitudinal axis of the airplane.

**ETA**   Abbreviation for Estimated Time of Arrival.

**ETD**   Abbreviation for Estimated Time of Departure.

**ETE**   Abbreviation for Estimated Time En route.

**exhaust pressure ratio**   An instrument that shows optimum engine performance by comparing turbine discharge pressure with pitot pressure.

**flameout**   Stoppage of a jet engine due to fuel starvation.

**Form 1**   A form accompanying each Air Force aircraft in which is logged flying time, as well as discrepancies, malfunctions, and the actions taken to correct them.

**Form 175**   A military flight clearance.

**Fox One**   Brevity code word for, "I have fired a radar-guided missile."

**G**   A unit used to express the force of gravity; e.g., a force of two G's will cause an object to double its weight while the force is being applied, due to the doubled gravitational pull on the object.

**Gate**   Brevity code word for, "Fly at maximum power;" i.e., full afterburner range.

**gate stealer**   An electronic device used to combat opposing interceptors by providing false range information to the interceptor's radar.

**Gatling gun**   A six-barreled 20mm canon capable of firing 6,000 rounds per minute.

**GCA**   Abbreviation for Ground Controlled Approach, a precision approach to a landing using a ground-based radar system and requiring no special equipment in the aircraft other than a radio.

**GCI**   Abbreviation for Ground Controlled Intercept, a radar site used for surveillance and control of fighters against hostile targets.

**Geneva Convention Card**   A card carried on combat missions that identifies the aircrew as a member of the United States Armed Forces.

**GEODSS**   Acronym for Ground-Based Electro Optical Deep Space Surveillance system, a computer-linked telescope system utilizing charge-coupled devices to get real-time images of objects as small as a basketball that are in geosynchronous orbit.

**GEOREF**   Acronym for Geographical Reference, designation of positions on the surface of the earth by means of longitude and latitude.

**geosynchronous orbit**   The orbit of a satellite that travels above the equator at the same speed as the earth rotates so that the satellite seems to remain in the same place. Approximately 22,300 miles high.

**Global Positioning System**   A navigational system enabling the user to determine his position within 16 yards and his velocity within a few centimeters per second, by receipt of oscillating radio signals transmitted by Navstar satellites.

**go fast pants**   Pilot's nickname for a G suit.

**Go pill**   A stimulant, usually Dexedrine, used to keep aircrews awake on long missions.

**guard channel**   An emergency UHF frequency (243.0 MHz) that can be received by any aircraft operating on other frequencies, providing they have guard channel monitoring selected.

**Heads Up Display**   Abbreviated HUD, a device located just behind the windscreen that displays both target and flight information to the pilot in such a way that his eyes never have to be refocused into the cockpit. Information displayed on the HUD includes, but is not limited to, aiming and target data, weapons impact point, projected flight path of the airplane, time to target, missile status, G loading, heading, airspeed, altitude, and artificial horizon.

**Horizontal Situation Indicator**   Abbreviated HSI, an instrument in the cockpit that displays information relating to heading, course, bearing, and distance.

**HSI**   Abbreviation for HORIZONTAL SITUATION INDICATOR.

**Hubble Space Telescope**   An unmanned telescope, designed to be carried into its 373-mile-high orbit by the space shuttle and send back images of deep-space objects 50 times dimmer than anything seen to date.

**HUD**   Abbreviation for HEADS UP DISPLAY.

**idiot panel**   A grouping of 25 to 30 small light panels that illuminate individually when various systems fail. Since these are located on a sub-panel, a Master Warning Light on the instrument panel comes on when any failure occurs, calling the pilot's attention to the panel to determine which system has the problem.

**IFF** Abbreviation for Identification Friend from Foe, a transponder that transmits a signal when triggered by a radar beam, permitting the airplane to be identified and tracked by ground radar through coded signals.

**IFR** Abbreviation for Instrument Flight Rules, a method of flying in the weather with the aircraft's instruments as the primary reference.

**Inertial Navigation System** A self-contained fully automatic unit that provides navigation and attitude information to various aircraft systems. It uses a gyro-stabilized inertial platform mounted on three sensitive accelerometers. The platform is stabilized in pitch and roll by gyros and is oriented to true north, and the accelerometers sense movement in any direction.

**inertial platform** *See* INERTIAL NAVIGATION SYSTEM.

**IP** Abbreviation for Initial Point, an imaginary point at a fixed distance from the target at which timing begins for the bomb release and/or pop-up maneuver.

**IR** Abbreviation for InfraRed.

**isotope** A variety of a basic element that is identical to the element in general chemical properties but differs essentially in mass. For example, deuterium and tritium are isotopes of hydrogen that are two and three times heavier than hydrogen, respectively.

**JCS** Abbreviation for Joint Chiefs of Staff.

**jizzle band** A vertical band of light presented on airborne-intercept radar scopes that moves with the antenna and shows the azimuth it is sweeping.

**Judy** Brevity code word for, "I am taking over the intercept."

**LANTIRN** Acronym for Low Altitude Navigation and Targeting, Infra Red at Night, a device that allows navigation, target acquisition, and attack on low-level missions at night.

**laser** Acronym for Light Amplification by Stimulated Emission of Radiation, a device that uses the natural oscillations of atoms or molecules between energy levels to generate coherent electromagnetic radiation.

**LOX** Acronym for Liquid Oxygen.

**Mach 3** Three times the speed of sound.

**Mach diamonds** Diamond-shaped patterns of light that form in the exhaust plume of a jet engine operating in the afterburner range.

**No Joy**   Brevity code word for, "I do not have a contact in that location."
**NORAD**   Acronym for North American Air Defense Command, headquartered in Cheyenne Mountain near Colorado Springs, Colorado.
**nylon letdown**   A descent by parachute.

**Parrot**   Brevity code word for an aircraft's transponder or IFF.
**pickle**   The act of dropping a bomb, or if used with an altitude, the height above the ground the bomb is released.
**pipper**   A dot of light at the center of the image projected on the combining glass of the HUD. Used as the primary aiming reference for air-to-air or air-to-ground weapons delivery.
**pop-up attack**   An attack initiated by a low-level approach to a ground target, where the aircraft enters a 30- to 45-degree climb close to the target to acquire it visually, and then commences a normal visual weapons delivery. This maneuver can be used for loft bombing, over-the-shoulder attacks, or radar bombing.
**PRF**   Abbreviation for Pulse Repetition Frequency, the transmitting frequency of a radar set.
**punch out**   To eject or bail out of an airplane.

**range gate**   A bright line of light in the jizzle band of an airborne radar set that can be moved by the pilot to supply range information to the radar tracking system. By placing the range gate marker over the return of an airborne target, the radar system can be locked onto the target and follow its movements automatically.
**Red Flag**   A training and evaluation exercise conducted at Nellis AFB, Nevada, under wartime conditions, involving realistic targets and enemy air defenses.
**RHAW**   Abbreviation for Radar Homing And Warning, a sensing device that picks up radar energy hitting the aircraft, determines its PRF, and displays the appropriate warnings in the cockpit as to the type of radar and the direction of the source.

**Sidewinder**   An infrared-guided air-to-air missile whose official designation is AIM-9.
**Six**   A CLOCK CODE term that refers to the area directly behind the aircraft.
**Snakeye**   Nickname for a 500-pound, high-drag bomb.
**SOPs**   Abbreviation for Standard Operating Procedures, written rules and guidelines for performing routine functions.

**spotlighting** A technique used by the pilot in which he moves the radar antenna by very small amounts in an attempt to focus the maximum energy on the target, and thus generate a brighter image on the scope.

**STOL** Acronym for Short Take Off and Landing.

**Stop pill** A sleeping pill, usually Seconal.

**TFR** Abbreviation for Terrain Following Radar.

**TWX** Abbreviation for TeletypeWriter Exchange, a military telegram.

**UHF** Abbreviation for UltraHigh Frequency, a communications band used for air-to-air and air-to-ground transmissions.

**variable camber wing** A wing that can alter its shape in flight for better range or maneuverability as the situation demands, by changing the camber from the wing root to the tip, and varying it from the leading edge to the trailing edge.

**VFR** Abbreviation for Visual Flight Rules, a method of flying in the clear or in partially cloudy weather when the ground or a lower cloud deck can be used as a reference.

**VORTAC** A ground-based navigational aid that combines a Visual Omni Range, and Tactical Air Navigation system.

**Zulu** Military designation for Greenwich Mean Time.